Pepe
Reina

PEPE
MY AUTOBIOGRAPHY

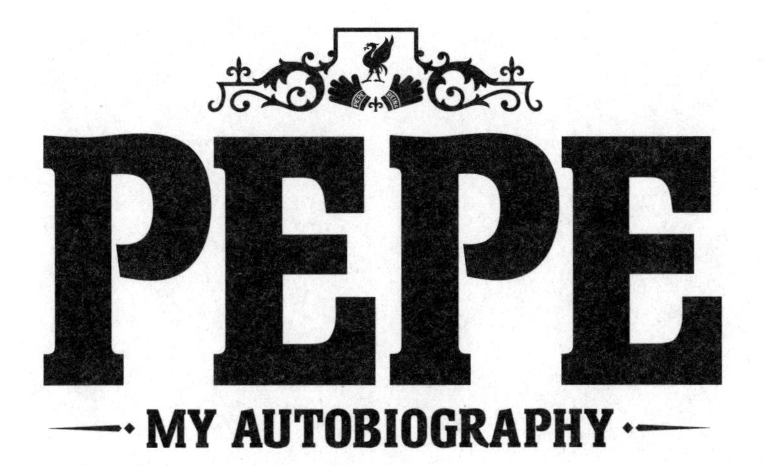
PEPE
MY AUTOBIOGRAPHY

Sport Media

In memory of Miguel Reina (1921-2008):
grandfather, mentor and inspiration.

A CIP catalogue record for this book
is available from the British Library.

Published in Great Britain in hardback form in 2011.
Published and produced by: Trinity Mirror Sport Media,
PO Box 48, Old Hall Street, Liverpool L69 3EB.

ISBN: 9781906802790

Photographs/images: Trinity Mirror/Liverpool Daily Post & Echo,
Press Association Images, Pepe Reina collection.
Every effort has been made to obtain the necessary permissions with
reference to illustrative copyright material.
Any oversight will be rectified at the earliest available opportunity.

With thanks to Medialive and Susanne Theune & Asociados

Printed and bound by CPI Group (UK) Ltd, Croydon, CR0 4YY

Contents

Acknowledgements

For everything that a wonderful career in football has given to me, I must first thank my family for putting me on the path that has brought me to Liverpool.

My gratitude goes to Manolo Garcia Quilon, my agent, and VOS Marketing for everything that they have done for me.

This book wouldn't have been the same without my friend Tony Barrett doing a top job of writing it with me. We had some laughs along the way – usually at his expense. Thanks also to my publishers Trinity Mirror Sport Media.

To my managers and team-mates past and present, for club and country, and my friends in Madrid, Cordoba, Liverpool and beyond I thank you for being part of my journey.

For being there for me in the bad times as well as the good, for making me laugh and cry and for giving me everything that a husband and father could ever wish for I thank Yolanda, my beautiful Cordoban wife, and Grecia, Alma and Luca, our wonderful children.

Pepe Reina,
September 2011

There are lines you can come back from and lines that you just have to take on the chin because there really is no comeback. "Hey Barrett – why are your shins the colour of Serrano Ham?" undoubtedly falls into the latter category. Sat in the swanky Nassau Beach Bar on Ibiza's Playa Den Bossa, Pepe Reina had just realised that the combination of the midday sun and a particularly pasty Englishman without an obligatory bottle of Factor 50 is made for comedy and the lower half of my legs quickly became the object of his incessant wisecracks.

In the absence of a witty retort, the only option was to change the subject. "Do you think goalkeeping is in your blood?" I asked, highlighting the likely influence of his father, Miguel, a fabled custodian for Barcelona and Atletico Madrid, on his own career.

And so began a fascinating journey into the past, present and future of Spanish football as seen through the eyes of arguably the greatest goalkeeper in Liverpool's history, a player whose record stands comparison with that of any of his predecessors – even if he is still waiting for the medal haul to match his talent.

At the heart of Pepe Reina's story is an age-old tale of gifts being passed on from father to son, with a sub-plot featuring a shared love for football that links the generations and inspires achievements that will stand the test of time. Hearing Reina tell that story was a privilege. At times it was deeply humbling.

Every footballer has a career to chronicle, but few will do so with as much candour and integrity as the subject of this autobiography. At times there were tears, none more so than when Pepe told of how much his grandfather, who sadly passed away in 2008, still means to him. This is someone who has shared a dressing room with some of the best players in the world and who has won some of the game's biggest honours. Yet he retains the same keen sense of humility that his family instilled in him as a child, growing up in the suburbs of Madrid.

For choosing to share the events of his life so far with me, when he could have opted for a renowned author who would have bugged him far less, I can only be enormously grateful. I hope I have done justice to his decision and his story.

There are countless others without whom this book would not have been possible, or at least it would not have been turned into something that people will hopefully read with the same kind of enjoyment that I got from writing it. I would like to thank our publishers, Trinity Mirror Sport Media, in particular Steve Hanrahan, Paul Dove and Ken Rogers, who carried me when the going got tough towards the end of the project. Thanks also to Andy Hunter, Paul Joyce, Dominic King and Rory Smith for giving me support whenever I needed it. Without their expertise, I would have been lost in a fog of my own making.

As ever, Brian Reade was an inspiration, a role he has fulfilled for me ever since I was a kid reading the Liverpool Echo and dreaming of one day being able to write half as well as he does. I'm still dreaming that same dream today. My boss, Tony Evans, won't want gratitude, but he's getting it anyway as none of this would have been possible without the backing and support he continues to give me.

To those I have plundered ideas from and looked to for advice – especially Peter Furmedge, Peter Hooton, Oliver Kay, Andy Kelly, Sid Lowe and Philip Smart – I hope to be able to repay at least some of your generosity with a pint or two.

But the majority of my gratitude must go to my family for everything they have ever done for me. In particular my wife, Sharon, for putting up with me while I was working on this book and my son, Sean Patrick, for constantly making me laugh and reminding me that there are some things that really are more important than football.

Last, but by no means least, my dad for being the greatest father a son could ever wish for and for passing on a love for Liverpool that will always bind us.

Tony Barrett, September 2011

Foreword by David Villa

After scoring Barcelona's third goal in our 3-1 win over Manchester United in the 2011 Champions League Final, I was preparing to parade the trophy around Wembley with the rest of my team-mates when a TV interviewer asked me for my thoughts on our success.

"I couldn't be happier," I said. "It's a fantastic result for us in what is such an important stadium in our club's history. I dedicate it to all my family and my daughters. I dedicate it also to Pepe Reina and to his baby son and my niece, who were born on the same day."

It was not rehearsed because I had not given any thought to a victory speech. I was just so happy to have won and I said the first things that came into my head about people who mean so much to me, and who had helped me to produce one of the greatest moments in my career.

Pepe is not just a team-mate, he is like a brother. I first met him when we were both still teenagers and we had been called up to train with the Spanish Under-21 squad. From the very beginning we got on well with one another, sharing jokes and helping each other in whichever way we could.

More than a decade on, we are still as close as ever. He may be in England with Liverpool and I might be in Spain with Barcelona, but we talk on the telephone all the time. When we meet up for national duty it is always the same – laughing, joking and talking about our families and our careers.

Pepe is a one-off. He is always positive, no matter what is happening; he always looks out for his friends, and he always tries to have fun. It is these qualities that made him such an important part of Spain's success at Euro 2008 and at the World Cup in South Africa two years later. He may not have played as much as he would have liked, but his importance to the squad went beyond minutes on the pitch. He was the glue that stuck us all together and without his enthusiasm and positivity we may not have been as strong a group as we turned out to be.

None of this surprised me because I already knew about Pepe's character and his willingness to help others. When I first got into the Spain team it was not easy for me because I was replacing Raul, a massive legend, and I was even given the number 7 shirt which he had worn. I felt the pressure straight away and after one game – when things had gone really badly for me – I decided to ditch the number 7. I told Pepe about what I was going to do and he stopped me, telling me I was born to play for Spain; that I had to keep going and to stick with the shirt that I had worked so hard to earn.

Everything that I have achieved since that day I have to be grateful to him for because without his advice and support I could have made the problems that I was having even worse. As a true friend and an unbelievable team-mate he helped me through a really difficult moment and I will always appreciate him for doing that for me.

Our friendship has not been totally pain-free though, and I will never forget the moment when he head-butted me after I had scored one of the most important goals of my career! It happened at Euro 2008 when I scored a late winner against Sweden and as usual Pepe, who was on the bench that day, was the first player I saw racing towards me. If there is a celebration going on you can always guarantee he will be there and he jumped on me, catching me with his head before we got mobbed by the rest of our team-mates. It hurt, but it was so funny.

Pepe's qualities as a goalkeeper are there for all to see and in my opinion he is one of the most complete keepers in world football. He is difficult to beat, good in the air, handles the ball well and his distribution is second-to-none. If he played for any country other than Spain he would probably already have 100 caps.

That is how good he is. But it is his qualities as a person that are worthy of the greatest admiration and I am proud to count him as one of my closest friends, and a really special team-mate.

David Villa,
September 2011

Mind Game

Six hours before kick-off at Anfield and before I can even think about the game I have to get to a petrol station. After getting into the car, I turn the engine on and look at the fuel gauge. It is almost full. I still need petrol, though, so I head to the same garage that I always go to when Liverpool are at home, a small filling station on Queens Drive that is almost exactly halfway between my home in South Liverpool and the stadium.

I get there, open the petrol cap and begin to refuel. I am only at the pump for 20 seconds or so and the tank is full so I go in to pay. The cashier gives me a bit of a funny look. To be fair, I cannot blame him.

I have just pulled onto his forecourt, queued up for five minutes behind other motorists and all for £8 worth of petrol, just so that my tank is full to the brim. He does not know it but I do the same thing before every home game. It is one of countless rituals I have to perform to make sure I am in the right frame of mind to play for Liverpool.

My desperation for success makes me superstitious. If I have done something on the day of a game and we have gone on to win the match I try to repeat it the next time we play. I try to pretend that I'm not superstitious – but I know that I am.

My own personal pre-match routine begins the night before a game. I stay at my home and go through the same steps as always, out of a fear that if I do anything even a little bit differently it could stop things from turning out the way I want them to. That might sound strange and there will be plenty of people who say it isn't logical to be like this but the smallest details can make the biggest difference in football. Once I find something that works for me, I stick to it no matter how hard it can sometimes be.

Before I go to bed I have a couple of cheese and ham toasties that Lucia, the nanny to our children, is kind enough to prepare for me. Then I have a glass of wine. Fitness experts and nutritionists would not advise that kind of diet for a sportsman but I never feel able to eat a proper meal the night before we play, and the wine helps me to sleep.

On the morning of the game, I get up and have a shower, put my suit on and then head out to the car to get petrol that I usually don't need. When I get to Anfield I always park in the same space – bay number 39 in the car park in front of the Centenary Stand. I have tried number 41 and 42 and a few others but when I went to 39 we kept clean sheets two weeks in a row and so I have stayed there ever since.

We have to be at Anfield for quarter past 11 when it is a three o'clock kick-off and after we've left our cars there we get the team bus to Melwood. We always have a walk at the training ground and after I've had my pre-match meal of pasta and fish, I have a shower just to make sure I'm fully awake before the manager gives us his pre-match team talk.

Now that Kenny Dalglish is in charge we never get to find out who is in the team until an hour or two before kick-off. That is the way he does things and seeing as he has won four league titles as a manager and is Liverpool's greatest ever legend, his way is good enough for me.

We have a meeting, Kenny names the team and we find out whether we will be playing or sitting on the bench. There are always clues about who will be involved that come from the way we have been training and some of the routines we have been doing in the days leading up to a game. No-one knows for sure until the meeting takes place. No matter how sure any of us might be about what the team will be there can still be surprises, especially with the squad being as big as it is and everyone thinking that they have a right to be in the team.

We got a new team bus in the summer but with players you can always guarantee that it will not be too long before everyone has their own favourite seat. I like to sit on my own for the journey back to Anfield, just thinking about the game and visualising certain situations that I might have to deal with.

Some of the other lads listen to their iPods but I usually just sit there, sometimes talking about the game and sometimes just taking everything in around me. As we get closer to the stadium I always ring my missus just to check everything is okay with her and the kids. It is a habit that I always keep. I look out of the window so I can see the supporters on their way to the ground and it never fails to make me feel proud just to know that they are going there to support us, enjoy the game and hopefully see us win.

This only adds to the sense of responsibility that I have. I know that I owe them for the backing that they give to us. We are their passion, their hope and at times we can give them something positive to enjoy, even when they might have problems in their lives or times are tough. It is special for them to watch Liverpool at Anfield but it is also special and a huge honour to play at Anfield in front of them.

It also takes me back to when I was a kid, going to see Barcelona play with my own father. Those kind of memories are so important because they remind me of what it means to be a supporter. I have been a fan in the stand, shouting and screaming and desperately hoping that the players I love could give me a special moment by winning the game. I know how important that is.

I feel really proud when I see children wearing a Liverpool goalkeeper kit with my name and number on the back. It still surprises me whenever it happens because I just naturally expect them to have Stevie Gerrard's, Andy Carroll's or Luis Suarez's name on the back – not mine. They are the players who score the goals and make the game beautiful. I am just a keeper, the drummer in a band in which almost everyone else is a lead singer. This makes it really special for me when I see a kid with my name on his shirt. It makes me even more determined to do well for them.

Once I get into the dressing room the ritual continues. I always get undressed in the same order – jacket, tie, shirt, shoes, trousers and socks – and then I get onto the massage bed so that Rob, our physio, can work his magic on me.

I lie there reading the match programme while he is bending and stretching my legs. Then I strap myself up and put my kit on. I always sit in the same place, just next to the wall as soon as you walk in, right next to Carra. I go to the toilet to have a pee about three or four times in the hour before kick-off because of my nerves. Then I go out a little bit before the rest of the lads to do my warm-up.

We have the iPod on in the final minutes before we head out for kick-off. Normally the music choice is down to Dirk or me. That helps get rid of the nerves, and puts us all in the mood for what is to come.

When we come back in after the warm-up we always play 'You'll Never Walk Alone', but there have been times when I have had to complain because it is put on too late. It has to be played at least a couple of minutes before we are due to go out. There have been occasions when the referee has been pressing the buzzer telling us to go out into the tunnel and it still hasn't been on. I'm not happy when that happens. It's important for us to listen to that song because it gives us the motivation we need for the game. I then have to make sure that I am the last one out onto the pitch before kick-off, and I always touch the This Is Anfield sign with both hands as I walk down the tunnel.

When I cross the white line I have to do it twice with my right foot. Stepping on, then off and then back on again. For some reason – and probably not a very good one – it helps keep me calm. Then I head towards my goal but before I get there I have to touch fists with my back four – except Carra, who doesn't like doing that so we share a high five instead – and then clap the supporters on the Kop to show my appreciation for their support of me.

As I get to my goal I go straight to the right post, bang my studs against it, then touch the crossbar, then bang my studs against the left post, then go back to the middle. That isn't the end of my routine, though. Next, I take six steps to the edge of the six yard box, another six steps to the penalty spot, another six to the edge of the 18-yard box and then do the same thing in reverse so that I return to where I started on my goal-line.

Then I stretch up on my toes, do some high knees into my chest, jump, sprint to the right, jump, sprint to the left, wave hello to my wife in the stand and then I'm ready to start the game. Anyone watching me must think I'm crazy but it works for me. It keeps me calm, so I always do the same thing.

Even now, six years after I first arrived at Liverpool, I still get excited on the day of the game. It is something that will never change and if anything my pre-match nerves are worse than they have ever been because now I feel a greater responsibility to the team. I am now one of the senior players and this brings a pressure that I did not have in my early days. I know that if I make a mistake it could really cost the team. If we lose I feel like I have let everyone down, even when it is not my fault. This makes me scared of doing badly.

My responsibility at the club is getting bigger all the time and I am always aware of what this means. I don't want to lose and I don't want to make mistakes, I want to help the club do well at all times. I want to come off the pitch at the end of a game knowing that I have done well.

All of these things create a pressure but for me this is good because it means that I have a nervous energy which makes me even more determined to play well.

I know it sounds like a cliché, but I do feel like a warrior when I am out on that pitch, especially with the massed ranks of the Kop on a steep embankment behind me and with 10 soldiers dressed in red in front of me.

Our belief is that Anfield is our fortress and no-one is going to take it from us. It is only football, it isn't life and death, but in Liverpool, as a much greater person than me once said, it can sometimes feel like it is much more important than that.

Everything is at stake. The honour of our club. The pride of our city. Our reputation as one of the world's greatest clubs. I could play for almost any other team and it would not be like this.

Liverpool is special, it is unique and it is where I belong.

I look ahead and see the referee put the whistle to his lips. The fans become absorbed in the game as the action starts.

Little do they know I came so close to leaving this club I love not once, but three times...

Back From The Brink

As I sit with a pen in my hand, preparing to sign the contract that will commit me to Liverpool for the next six years, the worries that have been dogging me for some time begin nagging away at me a little more.

'Am I doing the right thing?'

'Will the ownership situation be sorted out soon?'

'When will the club start making good on the promises that have been made?' 'How soon will we be able to challenge for honours again?' I had been constantly asking myself the same questions for more than a year.

It was April, 2010, and Liverpool's standards had been lowered. We found ourselves drifting aimlessly as the problems in the boardroom caused a malaise that was affecting everyone. If anything, my concerns seemed even more justifiable as I prepared to put pen to paper, but I put them to the back of my mind. 'This is Liverpool,' I said to myself, 'it won't be long before we are back to where we belong.'

The thing was, I really wanted to be a part of the good times at the club. I was so desperate to enjoy the kind of special moments I had imagined when I first signed for Liverpool five years earlier that I was prepared to gamble the rest of my career on it. As I signed the deal I was relieved that my future had been sorted out once and for all. Or at least I thought it had.

I have been through three dark nights of the soul at Liverpool and on all three occasions I have questioned whether I should stay at the club that I have come to love. On each occasion I could have walked away. I had opportunities to continue my career elsewhere, but I never took that final, decisive step that would have severed my ties with Liverpool forever. Thankfully.

For tens of thousands of footballers, Liverpool is a difficult club to join because it is one of the greatest in the world. But I know from my own personal experience that it is an even more difficult club to leave behind.

Perhaps you are not that shocked to hear about the fears I had in 2010, given the turmoil that the Reds were in on and off the pitch. But you will be surprised to hear that the closest I ever came to leaving Liverpool was actually back in 2006.

This was nothing to do with the shortcomings of the club – it was simply down to my own failings as a goalkeeper.

The start of my second season at Anfield – 2006/07 – was a time when things were not going so well for me on the pitch. I had ended the previous campaign as an FA Cup winner but I knew that I had been a long way short of my best in the final against West Ham United and I was desperate to get my form back early in the new season.

That didn't happen. In our very first home league game I allowed West Ham's Bobby Zamora to score an easy goal. He had mishit a cross from out wide and I failed to stop it going in at my near post. It was a really bad goal to concede and even though we went on to win the game with goals from Daniel Agger and Peter Crouch, I felt that I had let myself down, a feeling that would only get worse in the days and weeks that followed.

There were three or four games during that period which really put me to the test and, if I'm honest, there was a stage when I started to wonder if I was really cut out for English football. Everyone – especially the Evertonians – remembers the day we lost the Merseyside derby 3-0 at Goodison Park on September 9, 2006.

The moment that stands out the most for me was when Andy Johnson scored Everton's third. It all started when Lee Carsley had a shot from outside the area in the 94th minute. I parried it away, but as the ball went into the air, it headed back towards the goal. I turned to get it but in a split second opted to try and catch it, realising too late that I would carry it over the line. I tried to push it over the bar but could only direct it into the path of Johnson, who had an easy task to head it into the roof of the net. Needless to say, Goodison exploded with delight as I turned and thrashed the ball back into the empty goal out of frustration.

That was a bad, bad day for the team and a bad, bad day for me personally. When things like that happen you feel like you have let everyone down, especially when it happens against your local rivals in a game that the supporters are desperate to win. But that wasn't even the worst of it for me because that mistake wasn't a one-off. If anything, it summed up my form as I struggled to get out of one of the most testing slumps of my career.

My own situation wasn't helped by the team not doing well. Up to mid-November we really struggled to find our form, winning only once in our first four Premier League games and then losing to Chelsea, Bolton Wanderers, Manchester United and Arsenal. It was a tough time for everyone because after winning the FA Cup in the previous May we had started the season with high hopes. The expectation was, as usual at Liverpool, that we might even challenge for the title. But less than six months after that memorable day at the Millennium Stadium, that already seemed out of the question. We had to rebuild a season that was in danger of becoming a major disappointment.

In order to help the team I first had to deal with the problems of my own and eliminate the mistakes that were blighting my form and damaging my confidence. I would love to be able to claim that I got through it all by myself, but I didn't.

Like every other player when things go wrong you need the help of the people around you and in this case it was the support of Rafa Benitez that made the biggest difference. He gave me such strong backing at the time, and showed he believed in me.

Even back then, there was a club waiting in the wings showing interest in me, willing to take me if I had shown any indication that I needed to pursue my career elsewhere.

Valencia had wanted to sign me in 2005, the summer I moved to Liverpool and their interest had never gone away. They came back for me the following summer when they were still looking for a keeper but I was happy at Liverpool, and did not have any reason to change.

But then the season started really badly and I made two or three mistakes in a row. People were doubting me. I understood that because to be a goalkeeper at a club like Liverpool you have to be reliable – and I wasn't at that time. I knew that Valencia were there and their interest was in the back of my mind.

Rafa changed everything and put all those fears to rest. He made me forget about the possibility of leaving Liverpool before I had even proved myself here. Sometimes when you focus too much on your own problems you stop seeing the bigger picture, but Rafa said to me: "I know that you are tempted to go back to Spain and I understand that but I will tell you right now that if you were having this kind of run in Spain the pressure would be much, much worse. When the football is good in England it is better, but when it is bad it is worse in Spain."

He was totally right. When things are bad in England they are not that bad, especially at Liverpool where the people are so respectful and patient and will always support you even if they have doubts – as long as you are trying your best. Just by telling me this, Rafa triggered something in my mind that allowed me to start the process of emerging from my slump.

I was so worried about my own form but with the help of the boss and Jose Ochotorena, the goalkeeping coach, I came through it. From the middle of January to the beginning of May 2007, we conceded only 12 goals and managed 11 clean sheets – including one against Everton in the return league fixture at Anfield.

I had been strong enough to cope with a difficult situation with their support, and I ended up having a good season.

When I signed my six-year contract in April, 2010, I did so because my belief in the club outweighed my doubts about it. But as early as July – just three months later – I had cause to ask myself if I had really done the right thing.

I had pledged my future to Liverpool because I felt I owed it to the club to stay. Liverpool had brought me to England, improved me as a goalkeeper, taken me to the final of the Champions League and given me an opportunity to enjoy a new country and a different culture with my family. In my eyes, this meant that I was in their debt. No matter what I had done for Liverpool, I felt that they had done more for me and so when the time came for me to show my commitment to them I did so, even though I had my doubts. It was a question of honour as much as anything else and it was also a matter of pride for me, that Liverpool saw me as a key player who they wanted to tie down to such an unusually long deal.

The love and affection that the fans have shown to me from the moment I first wore the famous Liver Bird on my chest was also a key factor. I can remember in the press conference when my contract was signed. A journalist asked me: "Why are you committing yourself to Liverpool for so long at such a crucial moment in your career when the club is in such a mess?"

It was a fair question, but I didn't see it in the same way. Not to that extent, anyway. I told the reporter that it was not a sacrifice, it was a privilege to be given such a long contract by Liverpool and for them to show so much belief in me. We may not have been in the running for trophies, our debts may have been mounting and uncertainty may have taken a hold of the entire club. But it was still Liverpool, and my principles told me that I should be honoured to sign another contract with them. It may not have been the most successful club or the biggest club at the time, but it was still the right club for me.

So when I signed my contract, I hoped that better times were just around the corner, a feeling that was fuelled by the promises of improvement from people at the club. It didn't take me long to feel that their promises were hollow. I felt betrayed.

At that time, you'll remember well, our owners were at war with each other, the club's debts were spiralling out of control and a change in manager had failed to dispel the feeling that we were on the road to nowhere. Instead of getting better, things had only got worse.

The club was walking through a storm and what made it even worse for me personally was it came on the back of the greatest moment of my career. I was ecstatic when Spain lifted the World Cup in South Africa, but I went from elation one minute to depression the next as the realisation dawned that Liverpool were going nowhere fast.

The sparks of doubt were back, ignited by broken promises, and now fanned by new interest from a major Premier League rival. This came from Arsenal – they were ready and willing to offer me an escape route from the turmoil at Liverpool.

I thought again about the situation at the club. I could not help but continue to ask myself how long it would be before we became competitive again. We had lost our way on and off the pitch and there were no easy answers to this question. Like every player, I want to win trophies – that was one of the main reasons why I came to Liverpool, after all – and at that time it seemed we were as far away from being successful as we ever had been.

I knew when I signed the contract in April that we were not even going to qualify for the Champions League because we were having such a bad season. Even though I kept on saying that it did not matter, that was only a half-truth. Qualifying for Europe is the most important target and my hope was that we would only be in the Europa League for one season anyway.

I had been so hopeful that we would rebuild. Looking back, that might seem crazy because of everything that happened during the summer of 2010 when Liverpool hit the headlines for all the wrong reasons. My attitude was that WE ARE LIVERPOOL and at some point we have to start acting again like the big club that we are, no matter how bad the problems off the pitch. We have to be fighting for titles because this is what this club is all about.

The problem was that by the time we got to July I already sensed that a title challenge would not be possible. I knew that it would be extremely difficult for us to get back into the Premier League's top four because our rivals were so far ahead of us.

In fact, you could even say that we went backwards. For the second summer in succession we lost one of our most important players as Javier Mascherano followed Xabi Alonso out of Anfield to Spain, signing for Barcelona. Xabi had left for Real Madrid a year earlier without really being replaced and it goes without saying that all this was not what I signed up for.

So the way I saw it, there were two sides to signing the contract. Firstly, it was because the club wanted me to prove I was one of the key members of the squad by committing so many years to Liverpool, but there was also an understanding on my behalf that the club would start to deliver. That they were not doing so made me even more frustrated because before we had even kicked a ball, it was obvious that we were in for a very long season.

Pre-season should be a time for optimism, and I really wanted to be positive about our chances but everything that was happening made this impossible. The club was up for sale because the banks wanted to force Tom Hicks and George Gillett out, we were in massive debt, Roy Hodgson replaced Rafa Benitez as manager – but it happened too late for him to build a team – and the mood around the club was not the best. It was a very difficult time.

Arsenal had made their determination to sign me clear by offering £20 million – a phenomenal amount for a goalkeeper. A part of me felt that I was well within my rights to consider my future even if I did so with a heavy heart.

I had ended the previous season, 2009/10, knowing that Rafa would go but hoping that the situation could be sorted out quickly enough for the new manager to do something with a team that had finished a distant seventh in the league.

When this did not happen and the other problems worsened then

Arsenal's offer was made to look very attractive to me. They were in the Champions League and were almost certain to qualify for Europe's top competition again. We were a long way short of that kind of standard so it was inevitable that my head would be turned.

But I was going nowhere. When Liverpool received the bid they rejected it. Things never went any further because Liverpool were not willing to do business.

This was not because I had been told that I was too good a keeper to leave or that, as a senior player, the club could not afford to let me go no matter how big the financial offer was. The reason I was given was quite different – and it left me feeling down.

I was told that my continued presence at the club, along with some of my team-mates, was crucial to the sale of the club. I was simply a bargaining chip in the sales process. The same was true for Fernando Torres. They wanted to keep us to sell the club.

People will criticise some footballers and say that they will stay or go for money. I can also assure you that the clubs can operate in this way. When a club is happy with a player everything is fine, but as soon as the club decides to let you go then that's it, you're out of the door. So when a proper offer comes along from a well respected club – like Arsenal – I think we should at least be allowed to think about it. On this occasion, it was taken out of my hands. I had to accept the situation.

This news was broken to me by Christian Purslow. Purslow had been recruited by the club as its managing director in June, 2009. As far as I knew, he had never even been involved in football, but he was the one who told me that I could not leave for these reasons. Purslow said that no big players or star names would be allowed to go. That didn't turn out to be true. As I've said, Liverpool ended up selling Mascherano.

Looking back, I still don't know what to think of Purslow because I understand that he was there to look for new owners and to try to sell the club, but ultimately he was making big football decisions that he was not qualified to make. He may well have been really good at doing his business in the world of finance, but football-wise he probably wasn't the right person to run a football club. I don't know Damien Comolli too well because he has only been with Liverpool for a short time. But at least his appointment as director of football by the new owners made sense because he has worked in the sport for many years. He knows how clubs and players work. Purslow was not qualified in the same way and if anyone looks back at a lot of the football decisions that were made in the summer of 2010 it is easy to see that a lot of them were not the right ones for the club.

Despite all of this, and even though I was extremely worried at the time about the direction the club was heading in, I never actually got to the point where I felt I had to leave. At one stage there was a newspaper report claiming that I'd asked to go but that simply never happened. All that report did was make me angry because I did not want the supporters to think that I was pushing for a move.

But I'll be honest. My refusal to seek a transfer did not mean that the doubts went away.

Our form deteriorated under Hodgson and by the end of December, 2010, I was at my lowest ebb.

No matter how positive I tried to be, I just couldn't shake the feeling that we were going nowhere. We were even threatened by the prospect of a relegation battle following some really bad defeats to Blackpool and Wolverhampton Wanderers at Anfield, and a terrible run away from home. We lost at Goodison and at both Manchester clubs, not to mention suffering miserable trips to Tottenham, Newcastle and Stoke in the first half of the season alone.

I tried to put it all in perspective but things were bad, as bad as they had been during my time at the club. I was really struggling to come to terms with the fact that in no time at all we had gone from title challengers to strugglers at the bottom end of the table.

Because I was down and Liverpool were weak it was no surprise that clubs started to ask about me again. This time, though, the situation was a bit different.

After Arsenal came in for me during the summer and the club had told me that I could not leave, I had asked for – and got – a buyout clause inserted in my contract. This meant that I would be able to leave if anyone offered £20 million for my services.

I was thinking that if Liverpool were unable to improve and show that they were able to get back to where we belonged then maybe I would have to put my own career and my family's happiness first.

The clause was an insurance policy, nothing else. The idea was that if things got worse I would have the option of going somewhere else and the club would be able to get a big fee for selling me, more than three times the amount they had paid for me when I joined from Villarreal in 2005.

By the time winter came, I had become really tired of the lies, of the broken promises that we had all heard. After being told the previous summer that we would be building a team to get us back into the Champions League it really hurt me when it looked like the only league we had a possibility of going into was the Championship.

I was also unhappy with the style of football we were playing under Hodgson because it did not suit me.

I was considering my future again, only this time it was worse because it was getting harder and harder to find reasons to stay. It was a test of how long I was prepared to remain at a club which was in danger of losing its way altogether, and one that had been badly damaged by two years of problems. My loyalty was there, but I needed someone or something to show me that we still had a positive future.

Yet once more I pulled back from the brink and by the spring of that season I knew that I would be going nowhere. I could list countless reasons for my decision to stay, but the biggest one by far was the influence that my family had on me.

At times back then, my wife Yolanda was actually begging me to stay because she and the children are so happy in Liverpool.

We have met lots of good people since we came to the city, people who have shown us great kindness and who will be our friends forever. Our life is so good compared to when we first arrived in Liverpool. She was desperate for us not to walk away and leave all that behind.

I cannot understate the importance of this because maybe if my wife had been a bit unsettled and wanted us to try a new experience somewhere else, in another city or another country, then that could have made a big difference to my decision. But she didn't. She knew what Liverpool had come to mean, not just to her but to all of us. It is our home and it has become a special place for us. Even though she knew I was thinking of leaving because of what was happening at the club, she helped make sure my thoughts never became more serious.

There were other factors involved. Fenway Sports Group had finalised the purchase of the club, and our owners had an important role to play in my decision.

As well as taking over from the hated Hicks and Gillett, they began an overall improvement to the club, helped by the appointment of Kenny Dalglish as manager in January, 2011. That gave all of the players new hope for the future.

There are no guarantees in football, especially in England where the league is so competitive, but at least the improvements that took place on and off the pitch in the second half of the 2010/11 season helped to give me the feeling that Liverpool could be great again. That feeling had almost disappeared completely at times and I know I was not alone in that. I could see it on the faces of my team-mates, in the mood inside the club and in the desperation of the fans for things to change for the better.

So when I started to feel positive about things once again it meant a lot to me because I knew that the club was on the road to recovery. The owners proved this to be the case when they spent £35 million on Andy Carroll and another £23 million on Luis Suarez in the January transfer window, after my great friend Fernando Torres had joined Chelsea for £50 million. This was a real statement of intent, the kind that myself and a lot of people had been aching for and it showed that even after all of our problems, Liverpool could still compete in the transfer market. We could still attract top players.

Since then I have seen only positive things. The introduction of a new kit sponsor, Warrior, with a deal that will hopefully give us more money. More exciting new signings have been made and there has been a complete change in the mood at the club. If we can keep growing then that is what we all want, not just me, and maybe then we can live up to our history as a club and our own ambitions as sportsmen.

At one stage during that traumatic season, Damien Comolli had asked me to meet with him because he had read in the press that I was not happy and that I wanted to leave. He asked me: "Are you going to stay or are you going to go? Can you explain your situation to me because I do not think that you are very happy."

I was totally honest with him and I told him that he was right, I wasn't happy. I needed him to convince me of what his plans were and of how he was going to rebuild the club along with the owners.

I knew that other clubs were waiting for me, but I did not even want to give them an indication of what my plans could be before I had spoken to Damien first. In my heart of hearts I was desperate for him to convince me that I had to stay.

He told me about the ideas that the owners have, that they would be giving Kenny a three-year contract to stay as manager and that it was going to be a long-term project. I was happy with that and when he told me that we would be spending decent money during the summer transfer window and that our target was to get back into the top four and to keep rebuilding by retaining our place in the Champions League, it was the final justification I needed to stay.

Throughout this time, the only thing I ever wanted was for my future to be at Liverpool. I did not want to join Arsenal or anyone else. I did not want to walk away from a club that I loved and where I also felt loved, especially by the fans. I did not want to quit a city that my family calls home and where my children go to school. I did not want any of these things.

The only thing I wanted was for Liverpool to act like Liverpool, to be the fantastic club that they have been in the past and that they always should be. I was aware of the interest in me from other clubs, but I never once asked to leave.

So I have experienced both sides of the same coin. I have felt that I might have to leave Liverpool for the sake of my own career, and I have felt that I might have to leave for the good of the club.

Neither was a pleasant experience and I am fortunate that I have always had good people around me when I have been in these difficult positions. I could have left on three different occasions but I didn't.

In some ways that says more about Liverpool and the hold that the club has on me than it does about myself. Even in my darkest moments I have had an unbelievable urge to be here when we are successful again.

But I'm realistic, too. When it comes down to it, like all players I know that football can change and it will always be a matter of what the game brings to your table. In six months I could be out of favour here. I hope that's not the case and I don't think it will happen because I am fortunate enough to have a brilliant relationship with the supporters, but anything is possible.

This is why no player can say they will be at a club forever, not even one like Liverpool, or that they will never play for anyone else.

For the clubs it is a business and for the players it is a job, although being at Liverpool for me is a labour of love.

My family always has to come first, but Liverpool is my club and my family are happy here. Now I would not think about leaving.

Thankfully, that time has passed. I went to the brink, but I came back from it.

3

Father To Son

My story is my father's story and his is mine. It isn't just family and genetics that bind us together, it is our chosen profession. Like me, Miguel Reina was a goalkeeper. He played for Cordoba, the club of his hometown, before going on to star for Barcelona and Atletico Madrid. He won five caps for the Spanish national team, set a Barcelona club record of 824 minutes without conceding a goal and won the Ricardo Zamora trophy, awarded to the best keeper in La Liga, on two occasions. The narrative of his career is the kind of which a son can only be proud. Great clubs, great anecdotes and great performances. What more could a footballer's son ask of his father?

But that isn't the whole story because he also suffered the kind of bad moments that are an occupational hazard for a goalkeeper, and one in particular that could have derailed my own ambitions to follow in his footsteps. That it didn't was down to him and the way he responded to adversity. I will always be grateful for that.

My father's career was defined by one game, one final. It should not be this way but it is, and even a thousand clean sheets would not change that. The year was 1974 and he was playing in goal for Atletico Madrid against Bayern Munich in the European Cup final at the Heysel Stadium in Brussels, Belgium.

On the way to the final, Atletico had knocked out Galatasaray, Dinamo Bucharest, Red Star Belgrade and Celtic and the game against Bayern was their chance to finally emerge from the shadow of Real Madrid, who had already been champions of Europe on six occasions by that time. This wouldn't be easy as they were playing against a great Bayern team, maybe even the finest in the history of the German club. It included players like Franz Beckenbauer, Sepp Maier, Uli Hoeness and Paul Breitner, so it was always going to be a really hard-fought match that would be decided on the smallest details.

Ninety minutes came and went and the two teams could not be separated so the final went to extra-time. With only seven minutes remaining and a replay seemingly inevitable, Luis Aragones, who would later become my manager with Spain, scored with a beautiful free-kick, skilfully curling the ball over the wall from the edge of the penalty area and into the net.

This was it. This was the moment when Atletico would finally get their hands on the most famous trophy in European football; the day when the pain of being the inferior city rival of Real Madrid would not hurt so much. Except it was neither of these things because in the very last minute my father conceded a goal that took him from hero to villain in the blink of an eye. Hans-Georg Schwarzenbeck was the goalscorer, but in Madrid few people still remember his name. Instead they all remember that my father was the man who could not stop his long-distance shot from going into the net.

That is the curse of the goalkeeper, a curse which mattered even more in my father's case because Atletico lost the replay 4-0 and they have not appeared in a European Cup final since that day.

My father could have used this experience to put me off being a goalkeeper, but he did the opposite. He used it to inspire me. He always joked about it, telling me that if it had not been for that goal then the people would not have remembered him. It wasn't just that goal, either. He was also on the receiving end of one of the most famous goals in the history of Spanish football, a goal so incredible that it still gets replayed on television from time to time to this very day, and has become an internet hit even though it happened back in 1973.

If the Cruyff turn was the most iconic moment for one of the greatest players ever to play football then the airborne backheel that Johan scored for Barcelona against Atletico Madrid was arguably his most iconic goal. It had everything – grace, skill, audacity, athleticism, imagination – and it defied logic. It was like something out of The Matrix.

Whenever anyone looks at that goal on YouTube they see Cruyff doing something that only he and very few other players could even think of doing. They also see the goalkeeper, my father, powerless to prevent a footballing magician from performing one of his greatest tricks.

When people say that you have to be mad to be a goalkeeper this is what they mean – you can make a thousand brilliant saves in your career but if you concede a goal in the wrong game, or to the wrong player, then that is what you will be remembered for.

My father knew this when he was a player and I know it now, but like he said, it is always better to be remembered for something than not to be remembered at all. If you thought of it any other way then you really would go crazy.

So my father did his best to make light of such instances, probably out of self preservation as much as anything else.

That is not to say it was not a deeply troubling moment for my father when he was beaten in the late stages of a European Cup final, because of course it was.

It was very painful for him and for his team-mates because the trophy was so close but we always say that to lose a final you must first have won a semi-final and a quarter-final and he is rightly proud of that.

Every goalkeeper knows that this is their responsibility, that this is the burden we must all carry. The goalkeepers' union is built on this shared experience, one that means that we can be responsible for how our teams do, whether they win or lose games, on many, many days.

I like this pressure. I like even more having it at a great club like Liverpool where the expectations are so high and where everything that every player does is scrutinised right down to the finest detail. I am proud that I have been given this responsibility by one of the greatest clubs in football because it means that I am trusted and relied upon by them. That is where the burden becomes an honour and a privilege. My father had it for Atletico and Barcelona and now I have it for Liverpool. How many goalkeepers would have liked to have swapped places with us, to play in the finals of the most important competitions and to play alongside some of the greatest players in football?

When you are in this kind of position you have to realise how fortunate you are, no matter what happens. That is the lesson that my father was able to pass on to me from his experiences and because of his advice it has made me better equipped to handle the bad moments. It is only natural that you will be disappointed when you make a mistake. But you cannot allow the negativity to consume you, just as you cannot get too excited when you have had a special game or pulled off a great save. They are just two sides of the same coin and sometimes the coin goes for you and on other occasions it goes against you. I just know that I am fortunate that I have people around me – my family and my friends – who keep my feet on the ground no matter what happens; who are there during the good times and who continue to be there during the bad ones. They are the kind of people that every player needs around them.

My father had already retired from football when I was born so at first I did not know that he had been a famous goalkeeper. I did not get to see him play and he was not the kind of person who felt it necessary to tell me all the time that he used to play for this team or that team. That was good for me because it meant I did not have that pressure of being my father's son until I was a bit older. I just got to grow up and make my own way until I realised what I wanted to do.

The first time I realised that my dad was someone who had been an important player was when I went to school and people were asking me about him. They knew that he had played for great clubs like Barcelona and Atletico and because of that they wanted to talk to me about it. I must have only been six or seven years old but when people come up to you at that age because they want to talk to you about things that your father has done before you were even born, then it doesn't take long to realise he must have been a pretty important player.

That made me curious because it is natural when you are young to want to know about your parents and what they did before you were born. In my case, I knew there was a special story to my father's life. So in the years that followed I spoke to him many times about his experiences, asking him questions about the teams he played for, the teammates he shared dressing rooms with, the great games he was involved in, the funny moments and also the troubles.

There are not too many children who can grow up with that kind of opportunity, knowing that you have a father who is able to pass on his knowledge of football. I did not know it at the time, but now I look back at that time and I realise how important it was to me as a person and as a player because a lot of the things that happened to him, the highs and the lows, are happening to me now.

We have shared a lot of similar moments even though we are separated by many years and this is why whenever I am asked who was the biggest influence on my career my answer is always the same – my father. There is no doubt about that and it is not just on the field either, it is also in life. I want to be like my father was and to be the man that he is. He has been an example to me throughout. Even the bad times he had, moments in his career that could have made me think twice about becoming a goalkeeper, he used as an inspiration to me.

People tell me he was different to me, that he was quick, sharp and athletic. But I never saw him play live. I have not seen too many of the games that my father played in on video either because when he was a player it wasn't like it is now with three television channels showing the same game and football on TV all of the time. You could not go to the pub to watch a game on a satellite broadcast or stay at home and try to tune in to an internet stream. This was the era when television was still moving towards colour and away from black and white, when games were shown only occasionally.

This means that it is very hard to find video tapes of the matches that my dad was involved in so I have only ever seen clips here and there. It is a shame because I would have liked to have seen a lot more just to see for myself what he was like, what his strengths and weaknesses were, what great saves he made and maybe even the similarities and differences between the way he plays and the way I play. I can look in the history books and see that he earned five full caps for Spain, won three Spanish Cups and even a league title with Atletico in 1977. But I would love to see more of him in action. Maybe someone, somewhere, a football fanatic or TV executive has a load of tapes gathering dust in their attic. I certainly hope so because it would mean a lot to me to be able to sit down and watch the games that he played in.

There are those who say that I was born to play in goal because of my father so when I pulled on a pair of gloves for the first time there was no shortage of people who saw it as nature taking its course, the son taking up the same profession as the father.

But the truth is that it wasn't that natural for me because like all kids when I first started to play football all I wanted to do was score goals. Every kid wants to do that. If you go to a schoolyard or the playing field and you see young boys playing football for the first time their instinct is always to score goals, not to stop them. You just want to run up and down, chase the ball and enjoy playing with your friends. That is the way it is in Spain, the way it is in England and the way it is all over the world. When you see children on the schoolyard nearly all of them are pretending to be a goalscorer like David Villa or Fernando Torres or a midfield player like Steven Gerrard or Xabi Alonso. You don't come across too many who fancy flinging themselves around, diving at people's feet and imagine being Pepe Reina or Iker Casillas.

At first, I was exactly like them and my dream was to pull on the famous scarlet and blue colours of Barcelona as an outfield player, not the green worn by their goalkeeper. But because of my qualities and probably more importantly because of the influence of my father, one day I decided to try being a goalkeeper and quickly discovered that I was better than I was as a defender or a midfielder. It changed my vision for the future because although I was only eight years old, I realised that I was not going to be like all of the other kids. I was going to be a goalkeeper.

I have four brothers; Miguel, Paco, Javier and Manolo. My grandfather on my mother's side was called Manuel, so that is why it is my middle name. I'm not the only one of the five Reina brothers to have Manuel either, four of us have the name as a tribute to my grandad.

I suppose that by the law of averages it was pretty inevitable that at least one of us would follow in our father's footsteps, or try to anyway.

Just as some boys are born into families where the father is a carpenter, an electrician or a seaman and then follow them into their trade,

I was born into one where the father was a goalkeeper and followed him into his. It wasn't as simple as saying to myself that I wanted to be like him and then it happened. It was more because I liked playing in that position and also because once I started I did well. So while it was an influence on me trying to become a goalkeeper, the most important thing, as is the case for all young players, is that I liked being one and believed I could do it well.

The first time I played in goal was during half-time of a veterans' match that my dad was playing in for Atletico Madrid. It wasn't at the Estadio Vicente Calderon, it was on a hospital pitch in Madrid and I had gone along to support my father and his team. I also knew that there would be a chance for me to have a kickabout if there were any other kids around. I was stood on the sidelines waiting for the referee to blow his whistle for half-time and as soon as he did I grabbed a ball and ran onto the pitch. A guy who was out there sent me in the direction of the goal – I didn't think twice.

As I got there I realised just how high the crossbar was and no matter how hard I tried I could not touch it, even when I jumped. That is one of the first lessons you learn as a young goalkeeper, how high up the crossbar is and how hard it is to save shots that are fired over your head. As you get older and you grow you soon get to a stage when this is no longer such a massive problem, but obviously when you are only eight years old it is a weakness that you cannot do anything about. It didn't put me off though and I spent the half-time interval flinging myself at shots, diving all over the place to try and at least look like I knew what I was doing. I didn't, of course, because at that stage I hadn't had any coaching or training or anything like that. I was just pretending to be a goalkeeper like my father and trying to do what he did.

When I look back now it was arguably the most important 15 minutes I have ever had in goal because there was someone there from the academy at my school watching. He saw something in me that he liked and then gave me the opportunity to join the school team. It was all down to the fact that I had wanted to impress people by pretending that I was a good goalkeeper and also because I was the son of my father and wanted to be like him.

The only problem early on was that when I played for my local social club in Madrid as a child my team-mates did not want me to play in goal. It was not because I was rubbish. They simply saw it as a waste of a player because I was not bad with the ball. But I knew where I wanted to play and once I got between the posts that would be for good. The only time that I ever thought of changing was when I moved up from the small goals to the bigger ones. I looked at that crossbar so high above me and realised that whatever I tried I was never going to reach that bar. I could jump, I could stand on my tip toes, I could do whatever I liked but it was just too high. When you are a child that is frustrating because you never want to believe that you can't do something. That moment soon passed and once it had I knew that I would never be anything other than a goalkeeper.

Because my father played for Barcelona, they became my team. I lived in the city of Real Madrid yet it was their fiercest rivals that captured my heart. Whenever they played in Madrid, against Real, Atletico or Real Vallecano, my father would take me along to see them play.

We would even sit with the Real fans at the Bernabeu watching El Gran Clasico, one of the greatest and most passionate fixtures in football, without showing even a flicker of emotion when a goal was scored either way. That was the way it had to be. No matter how much I wanted to see Barcelona score I had to show respect to the supporters around me, the people that I was sharing a stand with and who I also shared a city with. It was like a Manchester United fan living in Liverpool or a Liverpool fan living in Manchester but Barcelona were my team, and the team of my father. Nothing – not even geography or historic rivalry – was going to get in the way of that.

I was fortunate because my father also used to take me to see the Barcelona players, to watch them train and to meet them after games. Every chance I had I was visiting them and it was not just any team either. This was Barcelona's dream team, the side managed by Cruyff that featured players like Andoni Zubizarreta, Ronald Koeman, Jose Bakero, Michael Laudrup, Pep Guardiola and Hristo Stoichkov, which won the European Cup for the first time at Wembley in 1992.

That was a great period in Barcelona's history and I was getting to spend time with some of their greatest players. You don't realise it at the time because you are so young, but that really inspired me. It made me want to be like them and achieve the things that they had achieved.

That I really started following football between 1990 and 1995 was another blessing because it was inevitable that the dream team would make a major impression on me. Between 1991 and 1994 Barcelona won La Liga four times in a row as Cruyff became the most successful manager in the club's history up to that point.

As a kid you love your team no matter how well they are doing simply because they are your team. But for my devotion and for the price of my support I was getting to watch a Barcelona side that set new standards and which made many people in football look to them as an example of how the game should be played. As a youngster about to enter my teenage years I could not help but be inspired by them. I could not have asked for a more positive early experience from the sport in which I would later make my name.

The difference between me and everyone else who watched that Barcelona team was that while they were all focused on Romario and Stoichkov, I could not take my eyes off Zubizarreta. Everything he did from the way he kicked the ball out of his hands to the position he took up for corner kicks caught my attention.

For me it was like being a young singer getting to watch Frank Sinatra perform at the Sands Hotel or a young boxer getting to see Muhammad Ali fight at Madison Square Garden. Zubizarreta was my idol, the person I wanted to emulate, and I wanted to take in every single thing he did, no matter how small, and then try to use it to my advantage. If you are going to learn you may as well learn from the best.

I didn't just follow his example either. I was also lucky enough to enjoy an encounter with him that gave me even more motivation to become a goalkeeper. It came after the Copa Del Rey final of the 1989/90 season. Barcelona had just beaten Real Madrid 2-0 at the home ground of Valencia and they had played really well.

I was in the stands and like all Barcelona fans I was really happy because not only had my team beaten their greatest rivals, they had done so playing excellent football. But during the lap of honour my mood turned from jubilation to fear as Zubizarreta was hit by a coin thrown from the crowd.

I was only seven years old and the sight of my hero bleeding and being led away for treatment was too much for me. I was so worried that I turned to my father to see if we could get to the dressing room area to check that he was okay. My dad must have realised how concerned I was and he arranged for me to go down to see what the situation was.

As soon as I got there Zubizarreta looked at me and realised I was worried about him.

He called me over and said: "Pepe, do not worry about me. I will be okay. I know that you want to be a goalkeeper like me so here are the gloves that I wore in the game and I wish you luck for the future. I hope that you get to wear them one day and then maybe then you can give them back to me."

Zubizarreta never did get them back. I had them on when I got home the following day and I still have them now. I have never worn them in a game because they are one of my most important possessions. His gesture meant everything to me and to see the man who was my hero in this kind of situation was one of the greatest moments of my life.

It is funny because the incident that led up to it continues to be infamous in Spanish football and whenever there is tension or problems between Real Madrid and Barcelona it gets dragged up. But, to me, it means something totally different – it was the bad moment that created one of the most beautiful situations of my entire life.

It also had another effect on me – it made me realise how important it is for players to give their time to supporters, especially the young ones. All players have been supporters before they became players so we have been there. We have to understand that the children have a tremendous passion for football. It meant so much for me to be able to meet my heroes and now that the shoe is on the other foot I have a duty to give something back. We all have to realise that we are lucky to be in the position that we are in.

But even Zubizarreta could not surpass the influence that my father had on me. That was something unique, a bond forged on trying to stop goals in different generations.

Now I have a son of my own, a wonderful baby boy called Luca to go with my two beautiful daughters Grecia and Alma, and I want the same things for him that I had. I want him to love football, to enjoy the sport that has given his family so much and I want him to be whatever he wants to be. I will not put a weight on him by telling him he has to be a goalkeeper, but between the influence of his grandfather and myself maybe he won't have a choice.

Maybe goalkeeping is in the Reina genes after all.

Band Of Brothers

Having taken me into the sanctity of the Barcelona dressing room to meet the legendary Zubizarreta, my father's next assignment was to help me open the door to the club. He had played in the same team as Charly Rexach, who by this time was assistant-manager to Cruyff. My father spoke to him to see if I could have a trial, just to see if I could be good enough for Barcelona to consider taking me.

Two weeks later, Charly rang my father to say that they would take me for a week of training and then they would take it from there. But there were no promises, this was no old pals act. Barcelona have not become one of the biggest clubs in the world by giving undeserved opportunities to the sons of their former players. I was going there to prove myself. My father had handed me the key, now I had to open the door and show that I could walk through it on my own.

I went for my week's training and it was decent. I was there with a couple of players from my team in Madrid and after only a few days my father received a phone call. It was Charly. He said: "Listen Miguel, you told us that your son could be good but he is better than you said. He is definitely going to play with us in the summer. We have a place in La Masia for him."

That was it. La Masia, the football school that would with time become known as the best in the world, had offered me a place. I had opened the door to Barcelona, the club of my dreams but entry came at a price – I had to leave my family behind in Madrid before I had even celebrated my 13th birthday. At that age it is normal to have mixed feelings, even about an opportunity as wonderful as this one. On the one hand you are excited at being offered the chance to become the best player that you could possibly be. On the other, you know that if you take it you will have to give up the family home and the comfort and support of your mother, father, brothers and sisters before you are even ready. That is tough.

However, after entering La Masia I quickly discovered that I now had another family, one that was made up of 34 boys who shared the same dreams, endured the same nightmares and who fought for one another. It really was like a band of brothers. We may have come from all over Spain and we may have also been fighting for our own futures, but the shared experience brought us all together.

The lads in my year even shared the same dormitory, sleeping in bunk beds on top of one another. It was so funny. When I look back on it now it was easily one of the best experiences of my life as I made so many friends there who are still my friends to this day.

We spent four years together under the same roof and it was a pleasure to be with them. It was competitive and even though a lot of players came through the training school, many more failed to make it. When I managed to fulfil my dream by playing for Barcelona at the Nou Camp I realised how lucky I was because so many of my brothers had fallen by the wayside. They had been part of something special but the pursuit of their dreams had come to nothing. That is why, when you look at the players who make it and the ones that don't, you have to realise the part that luck has played. Talent, hard work and mentality are all important, everyone knows that, but so is luck. I was fortunate that things came together for me at the right time and I was able to take advantage of that. We all started to climb a mountain and only a few of us were able to get to the top, but you should never forget the people who were there with you at the start.

I started at La Masia on August 28, 1995. It is a date that will be etched on my memory forever because it was one of the biggest days of my career. It was also just three days before I turned 13. Stan Collymore had just signed for Liverpool for a club record fee of £8.5 million, more than they would pay for me almost exactly a decade later, but I was not taking any notice of that. I was too busy coping with becoming a teenager and having a brace on my teeth – though at least I still had a full head of hair back then! I was still a bit shy, but one of the few things I was sure of was my manners.

On my very first day, all of the new boys were welcomed by the director of La Masia, Juan Ferrer, who was an old guy in his 80s, and he went around the table shaking hands with everyone. We were all seated and no-one stood up to say hello when he shook their hand, apart from me. It was a bit of a shock for him because I was the only one who did it.

"I have just noticed that the education of all of you is the same apart from that one," he said, pointing in my direction. "You are more than polite. You were the only one who stood up, shook my hand and looked into my eyes. You are not yet 13 but already you can appreciate the importance of good manners so it is very nice to meet you." On the very first day I had made a good impression and started off on the right foot. That was all because of my parents and the values that they had instilled in me.

My father had told me that he could not be sure that I would make it, but the one thing he did know for sure was that I would be at the best possible place for me, somewhere that would give me a good education and make me a good person in the future. In his eyes, that was what mattered most. His attitude was that if I turned out to be a footballer then that would obviously be good, but if I didn't then that would also be fine. The most important thing was how I turned out as a person.

La Masia was a tiny old house. On the ground floor there was a massive kitchen and a library with four big tables where we would go to study. There was a dining room where we would all eat, which also had space for a ping pong table and a television. Outside there was a really big garden where we could relax. Upstairs there were four dormitories full of bunk beds.

Each room had 25 beds all the same size, except for one room where the basketball players slept in really massive beds. There was nothing luxurious about the place, it was very basic and humble. But that was one of the best things about it. We might have had aspirations of playing for one of the greatest and most glamorous clubs in the world, but we were living the most normal life imaginable. We all had the same dreams, the same teenage problems and the same homesickness. We shared everything, the good times and the bad, and this brought us together in a way that nothing else could.

During the time when I was at La Masia I met more than 100 boys, including some from different years. Among them were Mikel Arteta, Carles Puyol, Victor Valdes and Andres Iniesta. It would be easy for me to look back now and say that they stood out because they have gone on to become great players for their clubs, but it wasn't like that. Just to get to the front door of La Masia you have to have ability and it is only as players develop and their careers progress that you are able to realise how good they are. People talk about the secret of La Masia and look for the reason why it has been so successful at producing young players and from my own experience I can only say that it came down to the feeling of togetherness that it brought out in all of us. We were all very young and we missed our families like hell. You are 14 years old and all that you want at times is a hug from your mother or your father, your brothers or your sisters.

There were times when you would hear people crying in corners because they were lonely or because things were not going well for them, and you had to be supportive of them. When people talk about team spirit this is how it happens. There is no magic formula and no one can make it occur. It happens when people share bad times and good times, highs and lows and at La Masia the spirit between us kids was as strong as anyone could ever imagine. For me, that is what makes it special. It undoubtedly helped make me the person that I am. Barcelona gave me that through these experiences and the principles that they instilled in me. It is a philosophy, a way of life, and it is one that is easier to follow when everyone is in it together.

Of course there were fights. There were 34 of us in the same room and we were all young boys becoming men so it was inevitable that every now and again there would be a big argument or a fight. But the thing about it was that whenever two of the lads fell out within 10 minutes or so the same two lads would be mates again, laughing and hugging. That was how strong the bond was between us. No one could be anyone's enemy for too long.

The window in our bedroom looked out onto the Nou Camp so I used to look out of a night and imagine what it must be like to play there. I could see the scoreboard clearly and I would visualise seeing my name up there in lights, even though I knew that was so far away. We could see our prize, we could even touch it. If that was not going to make me give everything to achieve my dream then nothing was.

I had to fight for it and I did. We were given complimentary tickets for all of Barcelona's home games and we used to all go together. I was even luckier than most, though, because along with fellow goalkeeper Victor Valdes I was selected to be a ball boy.

I can still remember sitting behind the goal with him as teenagers being just yards away from our heroes and learning from all of the goalkeepers that we saw. Those were key moments in my education as a keeper and the lessons I learned there were more important than any I ever had at school. I was picking up the tricks of the trade and benefiting from watching some of the best players in my position.

Even though I knew what I wanted to do and I was working towards that goal, I still had to go to school with the rest of the lads just in case I was one of the many players who do not make the grade at Barca.

We were at school in Barcelona city centre. It was a normal school and we acted normally. We knew that we were at Barcelona and we knew that we were playing football, but we also knew that the day after we could be sacked and we would be finished in football. So we had to act like normal guys which, of course, we were regardless of our talent.

We would wake up at around 7am and sometimes earlier. Then we would have breakfast and make sandwiches for our lunch before heading off to school, carrying our books and sandwiches with us. It took us about 25 minutes to walk there. We always went in a big group because we were all in the same class so we would have a laugh on the way. We would get back to La Masia from school at about 1.30pm and then go back at 3pm for more lessons.

We would return to La Masia at 5pm, have a snack and then do a couple of hours training before having our evening meal, doing our homework and finally finishing for the day.

I wasn't bad at school. I enjoyed most of the classes, but from the moment I realised I had a genuine chance of making it as a player I became lazier, especially when I got into Barcelona's second team at the age of 16. I didn't give up on school exactly, but by that time my focus was almost totally on football because I knew that I had a real opportunity to realise the dream that I had held since I was a child. If that meant I wasn't so good at studying then so be it. You never think that you might miss out. Probably every person at La Masia expected to be a footballer for Barcelona. We played against Espanyol, Valencia and teams from the same part of the country as us and also some smaller teams who played in testing, little stadiums. They all wanted to beat us. It was like a trophy for them when they did because we had the best team. It was still a challenge, though, because we were competing at a high level and we had to defend our status.

When you join a club like Barcelona as a teenager you don't realise how lucky you are to be there until it gets serious and you get into a position where you really have an opportunity to play for one of the greatest clubs in the world. When I was about 16 I realised that I was one of the best there and that I really had a chance of achieving my dream. So from that time on I took it more seriously until I played.

But there was time for fun also and the sleeping arrangements in the dormitory ensured that there would be plenty of opportunities to have a laugh with my team-mates.

I shared bunk beds with lots of people, but Mikel was probably the one I shared with most. He was my best team-mate at the time and he used to complain about my snoring all the time. I can't criticise him for that because he was right. I snored a lot and I was only 14 years old so imagine how bad it is now!

He should count himself lucky that he only lived in the same street as me in recent years and not in the same dormitory. It was funny – maybe not so funny for the other lads when I was keeping them awake at night and it definitely wasn't for Mikel, who was right underneath me. But at least it gave us all something to laugh at.

They all used to throw stuff at me during the night when I started snoring. It began with little things, a rolled up pair of socks or a scrunched up piece of paper or something. But when I carried on snoring, oblivious to what was going on, they got more desperate and even more determined to wake me up so they started throwing flip flops and slippers.

Sometimes when I woke up there was enough footwear on my bed to open a shoe shop! It was like a war at night, my weapon was my snoring and they would use anything they could get their hands on to stop me. But poor Mikel was in the line of fire and he got hit almost as much as me, which made it even funnier because he was being punished for my crimes. The following morning when we got up we would be surrounded by shoes, rolled-up jock-straps, everything.

Mikel was a really good player. As good as he is now. The proof of how good he was can be found in the fact that he was the earliest to leave. He was ready to move before anyone else. He left Barcelona when he was only 17 and went to Paris Saint-Germain before joining Rangers, Real Sociedad, Everton and now Arsenal. He has been so mature for his age and the level of his independence has meant he has been able to spend time in foreign countries at a time of life when many other lads of his age have not even left home.

We met as 14-year-olds and it was strange because we were very close until we were 17, but then we hardly spoke to each other until we were about 23 because he was playing in one place and I was playing in another.

Then when I was about to move to Liverpool, Mikel was the first person I spoke to and we came together again as friends in a different country. When he was at Everton, we lived in the same street. He played for Liverpool's big local rivals, but that didn't matter.

It wouldn't matter if he was with Manchester United, he would still be my friend. Whenever we are together we always remember the times that we shared at La Masia. We were among the lucky ones so we have to count our blessings.

There were so many players at La Masia who I thought would make it but for one reason or another did not come through. I sometimes ask myself why they didn't make it and I did. The only answer I ever come up with is that I had the extra bit of luck that they lacked. It isn't about talent because every single kid who walked through the doors of La Masia had the ability to become a footballer. They would not have been there otherwise. It is about being in the right place at the right time or not. I am sure that there were better keepers than me who never fulfilled their potential, and I did, so it can't be about being the best one, it is about being the luckiest one.

Mario Rosas, a midfield player with so much talent, was one who I really thought would make it with Barca. He made his debut when he was just 18, but that was the only game he played and he ended up going on to play for clubs like Alaves and Salamanca.

Haruna Babangida joined us from Ajax when he was 15 years old and was tipped to be the next big thing because he had so much talent. As soon as we saw him in training I said to my friends that he was guaranteed to play for Barca for years to come, no question about it. He did play for Barca, I got that bit right, but it was only in pre-season games and friendly matches and he ended up leaving when he was 22 without having made a single appearance in the first-team.

Then there was a player called Aleman, who had more than enough ability and everyone was expecting him to make the step up but he broke one leg and just when he was recovering from that one he broke the other during training. It was easy to see how good he was and how good he could be, but by the age of 17 he was limping already and it was a great pity that he never made it.

There were so many players with unbelievable talent who appeared to be destined to be a success for Barcelona, but for some reason it didn't turn out that way. I am one of the lucky ones, I know that.

With it being so tough to graduate for the first-team, that made it so special when any of us made the breakthrough. I remember when Francisco Rufete, who now plays for Hercules in La Liga, made his debut. It was towards the end of my first season at La Masia and he was called up to play against Deportivo La Coruna. The game ended in a 2-2 draw, but the result wasn't important. What mattered was that one of our own had come of age. Rufete celebrated by bringing us seafood back from La Coruna and we all had a feast to share in his happiness. This was one of our brothers making the grade and we were all so happy for him. It also showed us that the path for the first-team was open to us. Whenever any of us got to play at that level it was like a dream come true for everyone.

It was at La Masia that I got my first sight of players who would go on to become world greats, but it isn't their ability that I remember them most for. We were just kids and the things that stick in the mind most aren't always to do with their talent. One of the exceptions to that is the Spanish legend that is Andres Iniesta. He is a couple of years younger than me, but like me he arrived when he was just 12 years old. He was even whiter than he is now, like a ghost. He was quiet, but he was so brave out on the pitch and he was good at studying, always working hard. It was with a ball at his feet rather than a pen in his hand that he really came into his own, however. You could see his quality straight away.

Puyol had crazy hair even back then, even bigger than it is now. That was the first thing I noticed about him. He is Mr Barcelona these days, the symbol of the club, and that is probably because he actually carries a piece of La Masia in his body. We were playing football in the garden one day and one of us kicked the ball high up into a palm tree and it got stuck there. Because Puyol isn't scared of anything and he didn't want the game to stop just because the ball was stuck in a tree, he decided to climb up and get it. He got up to the very top, grabbed the ball but as he was getting it the tip of a palm leaf punctured his skin and got stuck in his arm. It has been there ever since. At first, Puyol played in central midfield and it was only later that he moved to right-back before finally becoming a centre-back when he was about 15. He had so much spirit. He gave everything in every single game and training session we ever had. He may have had different qualities than the ones which most people associate with Barca, but he turned himself into a top player by sheer force of will and determination.

Even to this day, there is a lot of talk about Valdes and myself being rivals because we play in the same position and were at the same club. But in a way this misses the point because we are friends too. We were sharing the same dressing room, the same school, everything. We are the same age and we joined La Masia at the same time. We were taking turns in the team, playing two games each to ensure that we both got enough minutes to allow us to develop and to give us the best chance of fulfilling our potential, without one being given an unfair advantage over the other.

I know the media like to build up rivalries in sport and it has been a similar situation with me and Iker Casillas throughout our careers, but in this case it really wasn't like that. There was a period when Valdes was not happy and he left La Masia. We must have been about 15 years old and because he left it meant I was playing all the time. Obviously that was better for me, but after two months he came back, saying that he was missing La Masia and from that moment we went on our own paths, with me playing in higher teams than him.

People often ask would my career have turned out different if Valdes had not come back, but it isn't something that I ask myself. The reason is simple – I had the opportunity to play for the Barcelona first-team before him. I think my time may have come too early and before I was ready but I got my chance first so I cannot look at what other people did or didn't do. All I can do is look back at what I did and I am happy because I know that my time at Barcelona gave me so much socially and also in terms of sport and education. How could I have any regrets about something as special as that?

If someone else has gone on to be more successful than me then good luck to them. In this respect I agree with my father. The most important thing of all is how you develop as a person and being at Barcelona as a teenager was crucial to what I have become. There is no need for me to be envious of anyone else.

I'm lucky because I played for that team, the team of my dreams, and to have the experience of playing more than 50 games for the club I supported as a boy is extremely valuable to me. I am very fortunate to have enjoyed that experience.

The most important thing about the coaching at La Masia is that they teach you common philosophies. What I mean by that is every team plays in the same style, with the same system. People tell me it was like that at Liverpool in the 60s, 70s and 80s.

The youth system influences the way the first-team plays – not the other way around. There is uniformity between the age groups so that there is no culture shock for a player as he develops and progresses to the next stage. They go up a level and they play in their position in the same way that they would have done in the level below. It is a very simple strategy, but it is very effective and that is because it is founded on common sense.

Nobody is blinding you with science or trying to be too clever by doing their own thing at the expense of the collective philosophy. Every kid at La Masia knows how to play, they would not be there otherwise. So what the club does is it channels your individual talent into a collective way of playing. When I was there we played 3-4-3, the system that Cruyff had introduced, at every level. We had a diamond in the middle and three strikers so we all got used to being in a team which kept possession and had lots of attackers at an early age.

It was not easy for me as the goalkeeper because while it was an enjoyable system for the outfield players it wasn't quite as enjoyable for me, with so many players going forward all the time. I was often left exposed and we would win games 6-3 and 5-2. The attackers would be really happy because they had scored goals, but I would be disappointed because I had let goals in. In a way, though, the keeper is the exception to the rule and it did not matter so much that we were conceding goals because the team was playing in the right way, in a fashion that gave everyone the best possible chance of developing.

What is happening at Barcelona now is the profit of 10-15 years of work. To bring your own players from the academy like they have there and into the first-team takes a lot of time. The plan doesn't start one day and finish the next. Liverpool are attempting something very similar now at the Academy in Kirkby and we are already seeing the results, with players like Jon Flanagan and Jack Robinson coming through into the first-team.

We have Rodolfo Borrell and Pep Segura at the Academy and having worked at La Masia they are now trying to implement the same strategies so that the kids play the same way in the Under-12s as they do in the Under-18s. It is common sense because it means that none of the kids will be surprised when they make the next level. That makes it easier for them to progress and takes away some of the fears that you get when you are about to make the step up. It has to be like this.

If I am ever coaching or working at any club I would want this strategy to be followed because it makes it easier for everyone. You have a programme to follow and you stick to it. It has worked for Barcelona, as everyone has seen with the success they have had in La Liga and in the Champions League so hopefully in the future it can work as well for Liverpool. If it does then the club will have a very exciting future.

The philosophy at Barcelona is unique – individual to the place for a lot of different reasons, whether they be political, social or sporting. There are similarities with Liverpool though, because of the club's meaning and relationship with the fans and the city. The people are humble and working class and they always try hard to achieve what they feel is right.

That has to be a good thing. But at Liverpool we have to find our own path to success. Rodolfo is always saying that we are too big a club to follow what another one has done. I agree with that. We have our own strengths which are unique for us, but if we can take the best practices from clubs like Barcelona and weave them into our own strategy then that can only be positive. There are things at Barcelona that any club could learn from. It is clear from my time there that they understand that everything begins at the base, at the very beginning. But identity is important and Liverpool is big enough to lead the way.

What I do know without doubt is that the system Barcelona have implemented has worked incredibly well for them and it has also had a really positive effect on the national team. It is incredible when you think about it that when Spain won the World Cup there were seven players in the squad who had come through Barcelona's youth ranks. There was Puyol, Iniesta, Xavi, Sergio Busquets, Gerard Pique, Pedro Rodriguez and myself.

We went to La Masia to follow a dream and the dream came true. We became champions of the world, champions of Europe and Barcelona became one of the greatest teams that football has ever seen. What else could you ask for from one academy?

What more could you expect from a coaching philosophy that exists with the aim of helping the most promising young players fulfil their potential? At one time we were in bunk beds, crying because we missed our families and training every day to get better. Then, there we were, part of the squad that was undeniably the best in the world. The work of La Masia could have no greater vindication than that.

For myself, I am proud just to have been someone who was on that incredible journey and when Spain won the World Cup I really believed that I deserved to be a part of it because I had been fighting for that since I was 13 years of age. I lived away from my family and the only relative I had with me was my grandad, who lived in Barcelona. He was the most important person of my life.

When my father played for Barcelona he moved the family over there with him and they stayed there after he left. His father and his brothers were there and they were my only family. My grandad walked with a limp because he had a bad hip so it was not easy for him to come and visit me and to come and see me training, but he did that.

No matter what the weather was like, if it was cold, wet, snowing or blowing a gale, he was there with me, always standing in the same spot watching me train. He was so supportive of me that he became like a dad to me. He did so much for me that it was unbelievable. Like my father his name was Miguel. He was one of the greatest men I have ever met. My father and him are so similar and one day I hope to reach the standards that they set.

My grandad made it easier for me than it would have been and if I'm honest about it I have to admit that I might not even have been a footballer had it not been for him.

He was always there when I needed him. Everything I've ever achieved in my career is dedicated to his memory.

Family Man

"To the prettiest face in the festival, a big kiss." It may be one of the most unusual autographs ever written by a footballer – it certainly wasn't the standard "Best wishes, Pepe Reina," anyway – but it was good enough to win me a beautiful wife.

I was just 20 years old at the time and back in Cordoba, the town where my parents are from. I was enjoying La Feria, a spring festival which is held every year. A grand fireworks display signals the start of the fun and then there are nine days of flamenco and salsa music, dancing, good food and carnival games. In the city, local people wear masks and take to the squares and streets to enjoy themselves.

It was after the season had finished and I was just minding my own business and enjoying the festivities when a gorgeous girl recognised me because I was in the Barcelona team. She came over and asked me for an autograph. I think she was just joking, but I gave it to her anyway just in case she wanted it and I left her that special message as well.

A few years later, Yolanda Ruiz became my wife when we got married in the same town. That has to be the best autograph I have ever given.

Yolanda is my link between Liverpool, the place I have come to regard as home, and Cordoba, my spiritual home. I knew that there was something special about her from the very first moment that I met her and the best thing was she felt right with me. I had always said to my mum that I wanted to marry a proper Cordoban woman with the beautiful dark hair, long legs and so on and luckily that happened. I was aiming high, but not that high. I got lucky.

After giving her my autograph I asked her out the following night. She probably expected me to ask her to go to the cinema, for a drink or even a romantic stroll in the moonlight, but I had other ideas. The 2002 World Cup was taking place in Japan and South Korea and Spain were playing, so I invited her to watch a game with me. How could she turn me down? For some reason she agreed to come with me and that was the start of a relationship that has been the most important of my entire career. There are so many managers, coaches and team-mates who I owe so much to, but it is the support that my wife has always given me which has been most crucial. Whenever I have had doubts about my future, she has been the one who has helped me the most. That is why I love her so much – for putting up with me when things are not going well. She is there for me during the good times. She is there for me during the bad ones. She is the only one who I can always say that about.

I proposed to Yolanda in a tapas bar in Villarreal. I had bought a typical ring and built myself up for the big moment. While we were having our dessert I got down on my knee and said: "Do you want to spend the rest of your life with me?" She must have misheard me because she said yes and we were married on May 19, 2006, just six days after I had lifted the FA Cup with Liverpool. Yolanda was a greater prize than even one of the most famous trophies in football and like everyone else who has been married, I have my own special memories of my wedding.

When the big day arrived I woke up and looked outside. The sun was shining. I did not expect anything else, this was Cordoba, one of the hottest places in Spain, after all. But as the day went on so the temperature rose and by the time I got to the church for the service it had reached 44 degrees celsius. I was wearing a black suit, a shirt and a tie and, needless to say, was sweating like mad. Less than a week earlier the tension of an FA Cup final meant I was having to wipe my brow, but even that could not compare to this, the biggest day of my life on one of the hottest days of the year.

It turned out to be the happiest day of my life and I cried like a baby. The minute I saw Yolanda coming up the aisle looking as beautiful as she has ever looked I couldn't do anything but shed tears of joy. A few of my Liverpool team-mates at the time were there, including Xabi Alonso, Fernando Morientes and Bolo Zenden. I think I was allowed to cry in front of them just once without getting any stick! It was my wedding day after all. Two days after the wedding I had to meet up with the national team to go to the 2006 World Cup in Germany, so I spent my honeymoon with 22 other guys.

It was fitting that we were married in Cordoba because that is the Spanish city to which my heart belongs. I was born in Madrid and I grew up in a suburb called Pozuelo De Alarcon, a posh area where a lot of footballers live. I spent almost my whole time growing up there with a football for company, kicking it around the streets and playing at a nearby social club. Madrid is where I was brought up, but when anyone asks where I am from I nearly always say Cordoba. That is where my parents are from, where my wife is from and it is where two of my children were born. Through my mother and father, Cordoba also gave me my principles and my belief of what life should be like. It is a place that means so much for me and the passion I have for it means I will always regard it as home, even though I was not born there.

I went to two schools in Madrid, one private and one public. The first one was called San Juan Bautista and then when my family was struggling for money a bit I moved to one called Pinar Prados. Just before I was 13 I moved to Barcelona and that was the end of my school days in Madrid. Even though I had been given a wonderful opportunity to learn my trade at La Masia it was still a big wrench to go to Barcelona because it meant I had to leave my family behind.

I am the second youngest in my family and I grew up in a household dominated by men. My poor mother, Concita, had so much to put up with. If we were not fighting, we were arguing. If we were not arguing we were messing about. It was totally normal. If you don't fight with your brothers when you are growing up then there is something wrong. Because there were so many of us there was never any chance that we could get bored, there was always something to do and even if I fell out with one brother I still had three others to get along with. That's why I have had three kids of my own. There is nothing better than having a big family to share your good times and your bad times with.

If there was one benefit from leaving home at so young an age it was the knowledge that I missed some fights – but I also missed my brothers badly after I had left. It would have been worth getting a few more black eyes and cut lips just to be able to spend more time with them. My mother probably had a bit of relief because she had one less to cope with after I had gone. She had enough to deal with as it was.

As the only woman it was some job for her. She was the queen of the house. Between our dirty clothes, our staying in bed when we should have been up and our laziness she had so much to deal with. It was a battle for her to make sure we grew up healthy and with the right principles, especially with my father busy with work. We owe her so much.

Sometimes it was really hard for me to be away from them. From my 13th birthday onwards all of my teen moments came away from home. I was missing my parents, I was missing my brothers and I was missing my friends. On a Friday night I could not go out because I had a game the following morning and on a Saturday night I could not go out because it was against the rules. There were plenty of times when it was tough and I was hurting but I fought for my dream to become a footballer because it had been my passion for all of my life. Everything that I did to achieve that dream, every sacrifice I made, every effort I put in, every night I had to stay in and every minute I spent away from my family was worth it in the end. When I became a player and even more when I got to the top of my career I was able to look back with pride at what I had done because I had given everything to get there. No-one had ever presented me with an easy route or a chance that I did not deserve.

In our own ways, all of the Reina brothers have gone on to be successful. One brother is a car salesman, another works in public relations and does everything well, one owns a clothes shop and the youngest one is a pilot. We were always very close and we still are.

My second brother, Paco, was an excellent goalkeeper, but he never took it seriously. He liked the girls more than he liked football and that was it. He had all the skills you would need, but he wasn't interested enough. I was different. I could not get enough of playing football. I suffered for my art, too, picking up injuries all the time from diving on the pavement to stop shots from becoming goals. It got worse when I had to have a brace put on my teeth. That meant that whenever I got smashed in the face with the ball my teeth and lips would bleed, but it never put me off. I loved playing in goal so much that I was happy to suffer the cuts and the bruises. Nothing was going to get in the way of me doing what I wanted to do.

I was a cheeky kid and I haven't changed that much since then. I like people who have a lot of life in them, who try different things and are always looking to have fun.

It is the same with the players I like the most. They are the ones who love to entertain the crowd, who do things that no-one is expecting and who are always trying to do tricks.

I loved Luis Suarez from the moment he first trained with us at Melwood. I could tell straight away that he had a bit of the devil in him and that he was going to be really exciting to watch. I don't like cold players who have no blood in their veins and no passion.

All I wanted as a kid was to play football whenever and wherever I could. Now if I want to play in the street where I live in Liverpool I would be able to have an all-star game against some of the greatest players in England. If anything shows how far I have come since I was growing up in Pozuelo De Alarcon it is this.

My neighbours now include Maxi Rodriguez, Luis Suarez, Martin Skrtel and Fabio Aurelio. We could have a great five-a-side team. Since I have been here, Albert Riera, Luis Garcia, Mark Gonzalez, Milan Baros, Fernando Torres, Bolo Zenden, Djibril Cisse, Fernando Morientes and Mikel Arteta have all lived in the same street as me. There can't be too many roads in all of Europe that have hosted more football talent than that.

Even though we live so close, we can go a week without seeing each another. It is good for the wives and the kids that we are in the same stree because it means they have a community network to help when we are away either on international duty or with the club. It may sound like a glamorous set-up with so many footballers living in one place, but when it comes down to it the situation is very normal and there have been many times we have had to knock on the door of a neighbour because we've run out of milk. Usually I go to Maxi. He never seems to run out of anything.

Mikel used to live around the corner from our house before his move to Arsenal. As soon as Mikel arrived he started having barbecues at his place so that we could all get together, eat good food and relax. The only problem was that he was borrowing my barbecue all the time and in the end I left mine there and bought another one. If people could see us sometimes they would think we are crazy because there have been occasions when we have had barbecues when it is freezing cold. I can remember being at one in March and it was no more than eight degrees. I was stood there turning sausages over dressed in jumpers, coats and all kinds because it was so bitter!

It did not matter that Mikel played for Everton at that time, of course. It was great that we could share these kinds of moments, even though we were rivals.

The only time we made sure we didn't see each other was in the run-up to the derby. That wasn't because we would fall out – our friendship is far too strong for that to happen – but we realised that three or four days before the game we were probably better off giving each other a bit of space so we could just focus on our own teams.

It was through Mikel that I got to know Tim Cahill who is a really, really good guy. We went to a Formula One Grand Prix in Valencia with Mikel a few years ago and had a brilliant time. James Beattie was with us as well. Any friend of Mikel's has to be a good person and since then I've got on really well with Tim. He's been to my home and I've been to his.

One time, we had a couple of days in Madrid for the Champions League semi-final between Real and Barcelona. I consider Tim to be a really good friend, but I know that in the derby he would kill me to win and he knows that I would kill him to win.

That is what rivalry is all about. There is a time to be friends and there is a time to fight for the honour of our clubs. None of us would have it any other way.

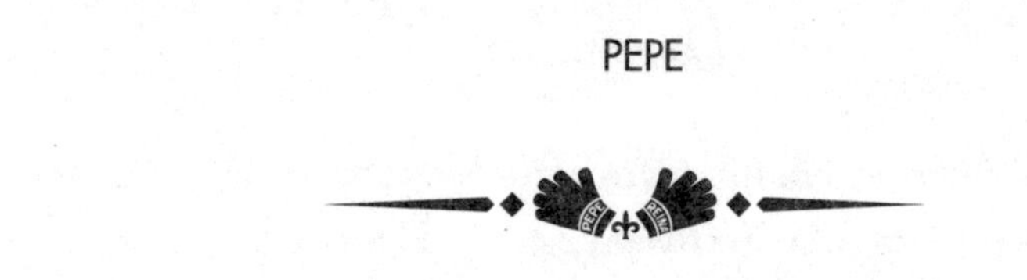

Not all of my neighbours are Premier League footballers, and there is one in particular who I owe a debt of gratitude to. Julian, who lives next door to me, played a really important role in the birth of my first child, Grecia, just a couple of days after we had beaten Barcelona in the Nou Camp in February 2007.

Maybe it was the excitement of that fantastic victory which made her come into the world earlier than had been expected, but whatever the reason her surprise arrival created a drama for me that I will never forget. Her early entry also meant that we had a little Scouser, rather than a Spaniard because our plan had been for Yolanda to return to Cordoba to have the baby. In the end the choice was made for us and Liverpool was her place of birth.

With the game at the Nou Camp being so important, Yolanda had travelled out to Barcelona to support me. It was a big occasion for me to travel back to my former club and we needed a good result in the first leg of the first Champions League knockout round. But because it was pretty late in the pregnancy, Yolanda had to receive permission from the doctor to make the trip.

The baby was due three weeks after the game so we were focusing on that date and preparing for the new arrival, thinking we still had plenty of time. But it didn't turn out like that. I think everything that surrounded the Barcelona game – the nerves, the excitement, the travelling, the happiness, the getting on and off planes – brought it forward.

We famously managed to win 2-1 in the Nou Camp, which was a fantastic result. The game was on the Wednesday night and we got back to Liverpool on the Thursday. My wife was due to depart for Spain on the Sunday, but then in the early hours of Friday morning her waters broke. I have to admit I was terrified.

I had never experienced this before and had not been expecting to be in this situation for another few weeks so I was nowhere near prepared for it. I headed next door and started hammering on Julian's door, even though it was 1.30am.

He was asleep in bed and as soon as I saw him I started shouting like a mad man.

"Julian, we've got a problem," I screamed.

"My wife's waters have broken and I haven't got a clue what to do or where to go."

We had nothing ready for the birth – and I mean nothing. Even our scans were in Spain.

Luckily, Julian was calm and in control. He said it was no problem and he told me to relax. He said we needed to pack some things because it could be a long night – some magazines, food and spare clothes just in case. I was running all over the house, wearing just a pair of jeans, trying to find what we needed to take with us. I didn't have a clue. We didn't even have any clothes for the baby because everything was in Spain. It was crazy.

Thankfully, Yolanda kept calm too, even though I couldn't. If it had been me having the baby then the doctors would have had to control my blood pressure – but my wife was the opposite. While I was running up and down the stairs, going in and out of rooms and generally not having any idea of what I should be doing, she was in the shower shaving her legs. I was sweating with panic and she was just normal, behaving like this kind of thing happens every day.

Looking back now, it was funny. I realise now that with the first child you can still have a lot of time after the waters have broken, but I didn't know this and I was thinking the baby could appear at any second.

Fortunately, we could not have asked for a better place to have our baby than the Liverpool Women's Hospital, where the staff cared for us like friends – even though they hadn't even set eyes on us before.

Once we got to the hospital we were in the hands of the experts and they took control. If I had needed to do anything more than get a bag together and sort out a taxi to take us to the hospital then God knows what would have happened. Julian has remained a close friend after helping me through it all.

What a week that was – winning at the Nou Camp on the Wednesday, my wife's waters breaking on the Friday and becoming a father for the first time on the Saturday. I will probably never have a better or more dramatic one, that's for sure. I had a great 10-day spell when we beat Real Madrid 4-0, United 4-1 and Villa 5-0, but that was just sport and no matter how special it was to be a part of that it cannot compare to when a child is born. That was just incredible, the best feeling I have ever had.

We have had two more children since then, and all three births were so special. But the first one was always going to be that bit more memorable because we hadn't experienced anything like that before. When Grecia came into the world and looked at me with her big, open eyes it was a moment I will never forget.

We now have three children with Alma, our second beautiful daughter, having been born in the aftermath of Euro 2008. Our family was made complete by the arrival of Luca, a son, at the end of the 2010/11 season.

For a daddy to have a boy is one of the greatest things of all. It feels special because I have the hope that Luca could one day follow in my footsteps and maybe become a goalkeeper like me. After two generations of keepers in the Reina family it would be great if he could keep up that tradition. But that doesn't really matter. The most important thing is that he is a good person with good principles and hopefully a good education. If he has these things then that will be more than enough for us. After that he can be whatever he likes. The same goes for Grecia and Alma.

The girls both speak English and Spanish yet it doesn't matter which language they talk in, they always sound Scouse! When Grecia says "daddy" no-one would believe that her parents are from anywhere but Liverpool, that is how strong her accent is. I heard her speaking to her teacher one day and she sounded exactly like any other Liverpool girl of her age. It is normal because she is a Scouser and she will become more Scouse with the more time that she spends here.

Even I feel like a Scouser now. I understand the people better now than I ever have. They have always been good to me from the moment I first arrived here so I like the idea of being one of them, even if I am from another country.

I have got so many good friends in the city now and they all mean a lot to me because they are all part of the Liverpool chapter of my life. There are too many to mention, but there are a few in particular who have been extra special and who I owe a lot to.

Julian runs my house like it is his own and if it wasn't for him it would not be anything like it is now. Carl Spelly, the driver for Liverpool, is a great person who has done so much for all of us and we love him. Ann Clayton, who works for the Flannels clothes store in Liverpool city centre, has been so kind to Yolanda and the kids that we all call her Auntie Ann now. Amy, the English teacher, who taught us all; Donna, who used to clean our house when we first arrived; Norman from Liverpool who helped us to settle in; Owen Brown, for being there for me during some of my lowest moments and for always supporting me.

I consider myself someone who remains close to my friends and I am fortunate to have so many good ones in Liverpool.

I might be more than one thousand miles from Cordoba, my spiritual home, but Liverpool now feels like the place where I belong. It means so much to me that when I was thinking of leaving the club one of the things that kept me here was the thought of leaving behind a city where all of us enjoy living.

All of my family are happy here and the only way I could make it better would be a few more days of sunshine every year and Liverpool winning more silverware.

Only one of them will ever happen though, so I suppose I better get used to the wind and the rain.

Barca Dreams

I could feel the collective breath of 12,000 people on my neck and I could sense their desperation for me to fail. All that was standing between them and a place in a major European final was me, a potential villain in the making.

At just 18 years of age, this was my first experience of the Kop, a young goalkeeper trying to make his way in the game thrust into the spotlight as the crucial examination of a UEFA Cup semi-final between Liverpool and Barcelona arrived.

There are still those who were present at Anfield on that unforgettable occasion in April, 2001, who don't realise that I was the man in goal for Barca that night; that I was the one who was beaten by Gary McAllister's decisive penalty. They recall a keeper with a full head of hair and think it must have been someone else!

I can remember them, though. Their passion left an indelible mark on me and it changed my opinion of Anfield. Before then I had wondered what all the fuss was about when people talked about the incredible atmosphere and the famous 'twelfth man'. As I left the pitch with my ears ringing and my tail between my legs I knew what all the fuss was about. I had learned the hard way.

As a child growing up I had dreamed of playing at football's greatest stadiums for Barcelona and here I was, still a teenager with hardly any experience, running out at the most famous ground in England.

I admit that I did not fully appreciate either the size of the occasion or the magnificence of the venue. I knew, of course, that Anfield was a great stadium, one of the most famous in football. But nothing, I mean nothing, could have prepared me for what I encountered that night.

In my mind, I was a Barcelona player, my home was the Nou Camp and the way I looked at it, European semi-finals were a pretty normal experience for my club, even if it was my first. There was nothing to get too excited or worried about. We were going to be playing in a stadium which held only half the number of supporters as my home ground after all. Maybe it was because I was too young to appreciate it or maybe it was because I was so focused on my own team, but whatever the reason, the enormity and the privilege of playing at the home of Liverpool Football Club did not hit me. That soon changed when I stood on the pitch before kick-off.

Like every fan I knew all about 'You'll Never Walk Alone' and what it means. I had heard it while watching games on television and I thought it was a good song with a nice tune, but when I was stood there, hearing the Liverpool supporters sing it with such passion, I was awestruck.

I can remember thinking to myself, 'Wow. What the fuck is going on?' It was really impressive. I looked around the ground and realised that it had become a sea of red, not just the Kop, all four stands, with people holding up scarves and flying flags and banners. This would be a famous season for Liverpool, Gerard Houllier's Reds marching on to a famous treble after a few barren seasons, roared on all the way by the fans. I had never seen anything like it in my life and I knew then, even before the game had kicked off and even accompanied by team-mates who could get into any team in the world, that we had a major task on our hands. Not only did we have to overcome Liverpool, we also had to overcome their supporters.

This was the second leg of the semi-final and having drawn the first leg 0-0 we arrived on Merseyside knowing that we needed a big performance to qualify for the final.

The action on the pitch revolved around one incident. When Patrick Kluivert was adjudged to have handled the ball in the penalty area, the Swiss referee Urs Meier pointed to the spot. McAllister stepped up. I tried to narrow the angle by coming off my line but he kept his cool and sidefooted it past me into the top left-hand corner of the goal before celebrating with Stevie and the rest of the team. The Scot will always be credited with taking Liverpool into the final at our expense, but the record books should give the crowd an assist because they made a crucial difference.

I actually made a couple of decent saves from Michael Owen on the night and in some ways that was enough for me because I had played well in a massive game at such a young age. Owen was well established as the main striker back then and had scored both goals when Liverpool beat Roma 2-0 earlier in the competition, so it was nice to deny him a goal. But obviously I was really disappointed because we had lost the match and missed out on the chance of playing Alaves in what would have been an all-Spanish final in Dortmund.

If I'm honest, the whole experience was intimidating. Now I am lucky enough to have the Liverpool fans supporting me and backing me all the time, even when things aren't going well. I know, as someone who was once an opponent, what an effect the Anfield crowd can have on you. This is why I wish it could always be like it was on that night. I know that isn't really possible. I also know that it is up to us as players to inspire the crowd and turn them into the beast that they were on my first visit there. But when they are at their most ferocious I can guarantee that it can scare the hell out of opposition teams and players. How could it not? You can't even hear yourself think, never mind shout encouragement or instructions to your team-mates. It is managers and players who win football matches, but Anfield is one of very few stadiums in the entire world where the crowd can be so special that the supporters can inspire their team to victory. I have benefited from this passion and I have also suffered from it.

Another positive I took from the experience was the reaction of the Kop to me. Again, I did not know anything of the tradition that sees the supporters on the Kop applauding opposition goalkeepers. That doesn't happen in Spain and it probably doesn't even happen anywhere else in football, so how could I have expected it at Anfield?

I can remember running from the tunnel towards the goal and the supporters started clapping. I didn't know what it was for so I was looking behind me to see where the Liverpool players were, but I could not see any. It made no sense. As the clapping got louder, I looked behind me again thinking Owen, Stevie or McAllister or someone must be there, but they weren't. I kept looking and looking, trying to see any Liverpool player, but there were none on the pitch and it was only then that I realised the applause was for me! I'd never been in a situation like that before. In Spain the opposition fans are more likely to throw stones at you than applaud you and at first I did not know how to respond. But I made a good decision – one that I am grateful for to this day. I returned their applause and the Liverpool supporters gave me a massive cheer. That is something special I took with me from that night. It is something I will never forget.

That was a good Liverpool team. Stevie was the emerging player who everyone in football was starting to take notice of, but there was also Owen, John Arne Riise, Sami Hyypia, Emile Heskey, Carra, McAllister and others. There was no shame losing to them, but I am sure that they would admit that the crowd helped them that night.

I came away thinking that Anfield was a special place to play football and wanting to go back there. Little did I know that one day a phone call would come that would give me the chance to call it home.

That is the thing with football, you never know when opportunities are going to come your way. One of the lessons we were always being taught at La Masia was that we always had to be prepared because in football you can never tell when circumstances can change and you can find yourself thrust into the limelight in the blink of an eye. That advice was drummed into all of us from the word go. I suppose it is the same for young players at clubs all over the world, but few can have had the kind of rapid, unexpected promotion that I had when I was just 18 years of age. One day I was playing for Barca B in the knowledge that there were two senior goalkeepers blocking my route into the first-team, the next I was making my debut for one of the most famous clubs in football and I would end the season having played in a European semi-final.

As is so often the case in these situations, it was injuries to others that gave me my chance. Like every other player, I never want to see anyone get hurt, especially if it is one of my team-mates who is suffering, but if it does happen and you are the one who stands to benefit from it then you just have to make the most of the opportunity. It is the same for every player and we all know that if you come in and do a good job then there is always a chance of keeping your place. It seems ruthless, but there is no other way. You have to take advantage whenever and wherever you can.

In my case, I found myself on the substitutes' bench for Barcelona because of an injury that Francesc Arnau, the first choice goalkeeper, suffered during a UEFA Cup tie against FC Bruges of Belgium. Arnau actually suffered a broken knee in the game, so it was clear that he would be out for some time. This was obviously bad news for him, but it meant that Richard Dutruel would take his place in the first-team and I would move up to the bench. So while I was sorry for Arnau I was happy for myself because I was taking another step closer to realising my dream of playing for Barcelona.

Not in my wildest dreams could I have imagined just how quickly my big chance would come. Just a couple of weeks after the Bruges game, we were away to Celta Vigo in La Liga. I went into the match expecting just to pick up some more experience and learn from the way the senior players prepared for games, but I soon found myself playing a central role.

I was sat on the bench watching the game when Dutruel went down with a knee injury. Something like 42 minutes had gone and I was sent to warm up. Even then it didn't really dawn on me that I could be about to make my debut for Barcelona, one of the biggest clubs in world football. I thought it was a bit of a knock, that he would be able to carry on and I would be running up and down the line and doing my stretching exercises for nothing, apart from being professional.

I was expecting to be sat back on the bench in a couple of minutes, but as the treatment continued I realised I could be coming on.

My first thought was 'fuck me!' It is one of those moments that I will never forget because it was so exciting, but it was also scary at the same time. Anyone who has ever been in that kind of situation, especially goalkeepers, will tell you that your imagination goes wild.

You are picturing the brilliant saves – and mistakes – you could make; what it would mean to your family; what the papers will say the next day if things go well and what they will write if they go badly. Everything goes through your mind all at once. All you really want is to go out there and not let yourself down. It is unrealistic to expect any heroics. The best you can do is keep things simple and get the basics right. Anything better than that is a bonus.

While I'm still visualising tipping a shot over that is destined for the top corner of the goal or, worse, letting one in that I should save, the manager, Serra Ferrer, is beckoning me over to him.

"Shit," I thought. "This really is it."

My heart raced even faster. It was obvious that I was nervous, but Ferrer made things worse because as quick as I was putting my goalkeeper's jersey on, he wanted me to get it on even quicker. He was shouting at me and between my nerves, the situation of the game – we were losing 3-1 at the time – and him screaming down my ear, I was shitting myself.

Fortunately, Dutruel managed to get through until half-time, but it was clear that he would have to go off and that I would be coming on. At least I had a bit of extra time to compose myself and get mentally prepared for my biggest test yet.

I can't have done too badly when I did go on because I didn't concede a goal and we scored two to grab a 3-3 draw. Because of this I always say that we won my debut 2-0. I never had any big saves to make because we played much better in the second half, but I was involved a bit. For me, it was just good to be part of the team and involved in a good comeback. It was only after the game that the enormity of becoming a Barcelona player really hit me. This was the club of Cruyff, Romario, Maradona and of my hero Zubizarreta. But it was also the club of my father. I had followed in his footsteps.

Everything had happened so fast. It really was a case of playing in the Second Division with Barca B one day and playing for the first-team in La Liga the next. I expected my spell in the side to only last for four or five weeks until Dutruel was fit again, but things went better than I had allowed myself to imagine and I ended up playing 31 games in a row. That was a big achievement for me because I was part of a Barcelona team that was winning games. My arrival in the team had coincided with our good form and the newspapers started saying I was the talisman. Imagine what that felt like for me! It wasn't down to me, of course, but if people want to say nice things about you then you are never going to complain, especially if it helps you keep your place in the side.

There was a problem, however, before I had even made my debut which could have stopped my promotion to the first-team. It revolved around my relationship with Ferrer.

I had difficulties with him on some occasions because he was strong with the weak people and weak with the strong people. At one point, I really fell out with him because I had appeared in a couple of adverts. I didn't realise that by appearing in a television advert it would cause me any problems, but he had other ideas. He wasn't happy at all and he summoned me to his office to see him and Jose Bakero, his assistant. This was a month-and-a-half before I made my debut and I was playing for the second team, but training with the first-team.

He said: "Listen, I don't want to see you on the television any more. I know you more for what you do off the pitch than what you do on it. I'm not happy at all and I have decided that you are not going to train with us any more and you will be playing with Barca B."

I felt that wasn't fair because every time I had trained with the first team I had given everything and yet here I was being punished for something that hadn't even caused anyone any problems.

Somehow I handled it and did not let it get to me. I carried on training hard, hoping that I would be given the opportunity to prove that I had the right qualities to play for the first-team.

Then the injuries happened and he had no choice but to pick me. I will always be grateful to Ferrer for being one of the people who supported me most at that time, but I had also proven a point to everyone else. That was very important to me.

I didn't really appreciate at the time what it meant to the people around me that I had made the big breakthrough and become a Barcelona player. I was so focused on making sure that I was ready for games and that I was training well enough to keep my place that I didn't really think about anything else. It is a bit like when an athlete says they are in the zone. The intensity may not be the same because it is over a period of days and weeks rather than just a couple of minutes, but you do subconsciously shut out everything in your life that isn't football.

That was the way it had to be at that stage because I had to give absolutely everything. I knew that I could not afford to be distracted in any way because if I had been and I'd allowed my standards to drop by even just a little bit then I could have found myself out of the team as quickly as I had got into it.

It was only later on in my life, when I had more experience and became more mature, that I was able to look back and appreciate how important it must have been for my father, my grandfather and all of my family to see me play for Barcelona. I recognise it even more now that I have a son of my own, Luca. My father must have been even prouder than I was because it must be amazing to see your son do something that you had done 25 years earlier. It was probably a bigger dream for him than for me. He can now say that he played for Barcelona and so did his son. That is a special thing and it is only now that I appreciate just how special it is.

It was a fantastic team to go into. When I think back to the players I shared a dressing room with at that time then I realise how lucky I was. Carles Puyol was there, which is only natural because it seems like he has been with Barcelona forever. I don't know exactly how long he has been there, maybe 12 or 14 years. All I do know is that it's hard to remember a Barcelona team without him in it.

I have a lot of gratitude to the senior players who were there at the time, the likes of Abelardo Fernandez, Sergei Barjuan, Luis Enrique, Pep Guardiola and Rivaldo. Gabri Garcia and Xavi Hernandez were also there and so it isn't a great surprise that when people think about these kind of players the first thing that comes to mind is their talent, the wonderful things they could do with a football and their ability to win matches. But for me it is different. My memories of them are dominated by the way they are as people. They were really supportive of me and when you go into a team as a young lad and you see the senior players – now at Liverpool it's the likes of Stevie, Carra and me – you have an automatic respect for them, so it means a lot when they help you. It is so important because it allows you to settle in and become a part of the squad. In the case of players like Luis Enrique, Guardiola and Abelardo in particular, they were so easy to work with that it turned what could have been an intimidating experience into an enjoyable, natural one. They did not take advantage in any way, telling me to go and get their boots or take the balls or whatever.

I remember one day especially when I discovered how important the senior players can be. I was really struggling for form at the time. I was bad in training, bad in games and nothing would go right for me. It didn't matter what I did, I was in a slump and I couldn't find a way out. The harder I tried, the worse it got. I had hit rock bottom and I ended up breaking down in tears in the dressing room. As soon as I did, Abelardo came over to me and gave me one of the best pep talks I have ever had.

"Listen," he told me. If I wasn't listening at that point because I was too upset then what followed certainly grabbed my attention.

"I wish I could be you. You are going to win a lot of things and achieve so much in football. You have to realise that you are only 18 and you are already playing for one of the best teams in the world. At your age the only things you will get right now are good moments and experience. If you are good enough to play for Barcelona then you are good enough to play for any team in the world and you will see that with time. Trust me, you have nothing to worry about."

This wasn't just anyone telling me this. This was Abelardo Fernandez Antuna, the centre-back who had helped Barca to two Spanish league titles, two Spanish Cups and a UEFA Cup-Winners' Cup during the 1990s as well as being a regular in the national side. Of all the moments in my career, this was one of the most important. It reminded me of my talent, it lifted me out of a slump and it made me appreciate the importance of my team-mates, all in one short speech. Abelardo wasn't finished there either. Within weeks I was getting better and better and every save I made either in training or games he was there telling me how well I was doing and clapping every little thing I did. He was supporting me all the time. That is something I will never forget.

It wasn't just Abelardo who showed leadership qualities either. Guardiola was a manager already. He was the captain and the extra responsibilities that come with that role aren't always easy to take on, but in his case it was like asking a fish to swim. He was an absolute natural. He understood Barcelona as well as anyone else because he was a Catalan who had come through La Masia. He knew everything about the club. He was the inspiration for the young players who were coming through the ranks and you could see even then that one day he would be a manager. He had everything you need – intelligence, knowledge and an understanding of the game. So it was no surprise to anyone who shared a dressing room with him when he took charge of Barcelona. It seemed totally natural. It wasn't even a big surprise that he was so successful straight away, although no-one could have expected or predicted that he would create a team that would make the football world ask if there has ever been a better one. That is beyond the imagination of everyone – but he has done it.

The experience of playing in that team was so valuable to me. It wasn't just my team-mates or the club that I was at that played a part in my development either, it was the games I was involved in and the level I was playing at.

A couple of years after I had been waking up surrounded by shoes at La Masia I was walking out at the Santiago Bernabeu to play in El Gran Clasico. That is some journey. It may have turned out to be my one and only appearance in a fixture that is watched by tens of millions of people around the world, but it is something that I will never forget, not least because I got caught up in one of the most controversial moments in one of football's most historic rivalries. I didn't do anything wrong, I was actually the innocent victim, but it gave me a place in the history of El Gran Clasico so I suppose I should be grateful for that, even though I knew nothing about it at the time. If I had, I wouldn't have been too happy about it.

The game, which took place on March 3, 2001 was a 2-2 draw at the Santiago Bernabeu. Real boasted players of the calibre of Roberto Carlos, Luis Figo, Fernando Hierro, Claude Makelele and Raul, not to mention two men who Liverpool fans know well – Steve McManaman and Fernando Morientes.

Raul opened the scoring for the hosts and then put them 2-1 ahead, but we were not to be denied and Rivaldo scored his second of the night in the 70th minute to get us a point. More than enough happened in the match for it to stick in people's minds for football reasons, but what fans tend to remember now is that this is the game when I was punched by a supporter.

At first I did not even have a clue what had happened. I had tried to keep a loose ball in the penalty box, but it went out for a throw-in. I went to get it to try and waste a bit of time because Real were chasing a winning goal. I moved past the security guards who were sat in their seats and got hold of the ball, but by that time I was really close to the stands. I felt someone at my back and I thought that it was Raul. I kept hold of the ball even tighter so that he could not make a quick play, but then I felt some contact. I was so focused on keeping the ball and preventing Real from having a chance to score that I did not notice that a fan had punched me. Not once either, he did it three times. But I was totally oblivious to it.

The game ended, I got showered, changed, got on the team bus and went to Barajas airport to fly back to Barcelona. I was still none the wiser. It was only when I was boarding the flight that someone told me what had happened. I could not believe it, not because I was angry about it – more because I had been unaware it had even happened. It has now become one of those incidents which is replayed on television and talked about whenever there are any controversial moments in the Clasico, but for me it was just one of those things that happens in the heat of a passionate game. The most important thing was that I kept hold of the ball and we came away with a draw. If I had to take a couple of digs from a fan along the way then so be it.

I'm proud to have played in the Clasico and the only disappointment was that I never got to play against Real in Barcelona. The 2-2 game was the only one I was involved in. We should have won that, too, because Rivaldo scored a third goal wrongly disallowed for offside.

Despite the talent in our squad, we had a bad run of form under Ferrer in the second half of the season and my own performances weren't the best during that spell. There was a run of three or four games where I conceded too many goals.

There were two 4-4 draws against Villarreal and Real Zaragoza and a 3-1 defeat to Osasuna. I wasn't good enough at the time. When I look back now I realise that, but the team was also struggling. When you are a goalkeeper and you are out of form you need the players in front of you to protect you a little bit. Because the team wasn't at its best that never happened. I got dropped, which was a big blow and by the time we ended the season I had become second choice. That was my first big disappointment in football since coming into the team, a personal setback that nothing could have prepared me for. It is only when you have endured this kind of experience that you really become able to deal with it.

Rexach replaced Ferrer as manager and I was hoping that this would give me a fresh start and an immediate opportunity to reclaim my starting place, but I continued to be understudy until Christmas 2001. When I finally got my chance, things were exactly the same as they had been the season before. The team was not at its best, I made a couple of mistakes and I got dropped from the team again with eight or 10 games to go. From that point on, it became increasingly clear to me that Barcelona did not rate me as highly as I needed them to and my future was already on the line.

I was with one of the best teams in the world and the club of my dreams, but in the end I knew I had to leave. When the time came to determine my future I had to decide whether I was happy to stay as second or third choice at the Nou Camp or go to Villarreal and play.

It was an agonising decision for me because Barcelona were in my heart, and had been since I was a kid. My father wanted me to stay, be patient and fight for my place, but in the end I was adamant that I wanted to go to a club where I would play every single week, not one where all I would do was sit on the bench and watch others play. Between myself and my agent, Manolo Garcia Quillon, we took the decision to leave. It is probably the best and most important decision of my entire football career.

The Yellow Submarine

I never knew who Pete Best was until I came to Merseyside, but his story is one that I can identify with. If he was the drummer who went his separate way from The Beatles before they became the biggest band in the world, I was the goalkeeper who left Barcelona prior to them becoming the best team in the world. Just as every time The Beatles had a number one hit people must have thought of Best and what he had missed out on, so whenever Barca lifted a trophy there will have been those inside and outside Spain who questioned my decision to leave.

Since my departure in 2002 they have won five La Liga titles, three European Cups, four Spanish Super Cups and one Spanish Cup. It is an incredible record of success. Had things turned out differently I could have been part of it, but I don't regret missing out on this golden period. Not even a bit.

In football you always have to do the right thing for your career. When the time came for me to choose between pursuing my dream at

Barca, in the knowledge that I would not be first choice, or accepting an opportunity to play regularly for Villarreal, I had no hesitation in leaving the club I had supported all my life.

So I have no regrets, but that does not mean that there is not a frustration, a feeling of what might have been that will probably never go away. That doesn't mean that I am unhappy at Liverpool or that I would prefer to be somewhere else because that isn't the case.

Frustration is not the same as regret and it is only natural that I should look at Barcelona with a bittersweet realisation that they are the best team that I have ever seen. From their point of view, they have Victor Valdes, a keeper who is now doing great for them. He is the lucky one who gets to play behind the kind of special team that makes a goalkeeper's job so much easier. But it could have been me, I know that.

My career changed course when Louis van Gaal returned to Barcelona as manager in 2002. He had managed the club before for a few seasons, but left in 2000 to become coach of Holland.

During his first spell at the Nou Camp I had worked with him and when I found out that he was coming back I did not foresee any problems for myself – but he had other ideas. Not only did he not want me in the first-team, he did not even want me to sit on the bench. When a new manager comes in and makes it so clear that he does not value you then he is effectively making your decision for you. He did not sit me down and tell me that I should leave and go to another club, but he may as well have done because by demoting me he put me in a position where I had no choice but to leave.

It did not take me long to realise that my time at Barcelona was up. When he took over, one of the first things he did was make it clear that I was going to be third choice at best. As a goalkeeper that is a disaster because if you are a central midfield player and you are third choice then all it takes is one injury or a suspension and you are back in the team. But there are second-choice keepers who never get to play so if you are third choice you may as well be retired because the chances of being involved are so slim.

I was really disappointed because the only time I had worked with Van Gaal was when I was 16 years old and he took me to train with the first-team. Yet here he was coming back to the club and killing my hopes of playing without even giving me a chance. Usually when that happens at a club it is because the manager has a personal problem with a player, but in this case the coach was making it clear that, for whatever reason, he did not fancy me as a keeper. No explanation was offered but when a manager does not rate you then it is obvious that you have a big problem. It is going to be very difficult to get any minutes on the pitch.

What I will accept is that at the time of Van Gaal's arrival I was not performing at my best and I could not have too many complaints about being dropped from the team. That's the way it goes and as a player you always have to recognise that the manager must do what is best for the team. If that means picking someone who is performing better than you are at that time then you just have to get on with it.

Yet this situation was not like that. I felt that this was a case of me being sent into the wilderness. I was a young keeper who had done well at first and then not so well and I did not expect to be killed over it. But the message I was getting was that my days as first choice were over and there was to be no opportunity to rebuild my confidence. There would be no travelling with the squad to make sure I remained a part of things. I just didn't matter any more, it was as simple as that. The team would play and I would not be involved in any way.

That is why when the opportunity arose to move to Villarreal I was more than happy to go. Every player needs to be appreciated and valued and with Van Gaal I knew that would not be the case for me. The writing was on the Nou Camp wall and all I had to do was read it.

When I first went to Villarreal the idea was that I was going on loan with a view to a permanent transfer. The fee was something ridiculous like 100 million pesetas, which is about €600,000, but Barcelona retained an option to sign me back two years later for €1.2 million.

Before I left I met with Joan Gaspart, who was the Barcelona president at the time. He told me that they trusted me 100 per cent, which I didn't believe. He said that they were treating my move away as a loan rather than a permanent transfer. At the end of the day it never was.

"You will be back at the Nou Camp in two years," he continued. "We are totally sure of this. So just treat it as a loan and enjoy your time at Villarreal. They really want you and it is a great club."

The only thing he was right about is that Villarreal are a great club. I will always be grateful to Barcelona because they made me the person I am and made a massive impact on the way I turned out as a footballer, but I regret the way it all ended.

Once my time at Barcelona was over I knew I had to move on, physically and psychologically. There was no point in me turning up at a new club wishing I was still at my old one because that would have been no good to me and no good to Villarreal. They had shown a lot of faith in me and now it was my turn to repay them.

In England, people may not know so much about Villarreal. Liverpool fans might remember that they defeated Everton in a Champions League qualifier in 2005 but in general it is Barcelona and Real Madrid that English fans know most about.

Villarreal's nickname is 'El Submarino Amarillo' – 'The Yellow Submarine' – because of their bright yellow kit. It is, of course, also the title of a famous Beatles song, so perhaps it was fate that I played there before joining Liverpool! Outside the stadium there is a statue of a yellow submarine, just like there is now outside John Lennon Airport.

It was a big change for me and a very different footballing culture to Barcelona. It was also a new place for me to get to know. The city of Villarreal is based in the province of Castellon, further down the eastern coast from Barcelona. The team had spent much of its history in the lower leagues, and were promoted to La Liga in 1998. Instead of Barca v Real Madrid, I would have to get used to 'The Valencian Derby' – Villarreal v Valencia.

They had just finished making some improvements to El Madrigal, their stadium, not long after I arrived – but even at full capacity, the Nou Camp could hold four times as many fans. It was a small club compared to Barcelona but I soon came to realise that it was also a family club, where the people at the top go out of their way to make every single person feel like they matter.

During my time there, the three managers I worked under – Victor Munoz, Benito Floro and Manuel Pellegrini – were great to me. It was a special time for me because it made me feel important as a player again. After the way my time at Barcelona came to an end, Villarreal became my refuge.

They were my sanctuary when I needed one most and they gave me the opportunity to fulfil my potential at a time when there was a real danger that it could have been squandered. I am who I am because of them and I will always be grateful to them for that, especially the board members who approved my transfer and who continued to support me after my arrival. If I was hurting when I got there, then by the time I left I was a much happier person and a much better goalkeeper. The three years I spent there were among the best in my career.

When we played for Villarreal against Barcelona it was always the most special game of the season for me. We always seemed to do well against them. Between 2002 and 2005 while I was there we beat them every time at home and made El Madrigal a bad place for them, a stadium where they knew they would have a very difficult game. It was always enjoyable to beat them, but not for personal reasons. This was not about revenge, it was about getting a result against Barcelona in the knowledge that if you could beat them you were beating one of the best teams in the world.

I matured at Villarreal and found my voice in the dressing room. I developed as a goalkeeper there to such an extent that Liverpool, the five-time champions of Europe no less, ended up signing me. I felt like one of the main actors every Sunday when we had a game and having become no more than an understudy at Barca this was really important for me and it made a massive difference to my self-esteem.

There is no comparison between the pressure at the club I had joined to the one I had just left. At Barca every single game felt like a test to me. Before matches I would have the same feeling that I get when I'm going to the dentist. My palms would be sweaty, my heart would be racing and all the worst case scenarios would be going through my mind. That's what it's like when you are under the microscope.

For a time, the press made my life a misery and I used to dread Sundays because I knew if I made even a little mistake it would become a massive story. No player should ever fear playing, but that was how bad it was for me at a time when I was still finding my feet in football. It is easy to say that I should have coped with the situation better. Now I would be able to do that because I have much more experience and far fewer doubts about myself, but at the time the pressure was made intolerable because Iker Casillas had just come into the first-team at Real Madrid and was proving himself to be a great keeper despite only being a teenager.

This became a burden for Barcelona, and for the goalkeepers especially, because we were expected to come up with our own answer to him. So I was going into games knowing that if I dropped the ball or failed to come for a cross I would probably get dropped – and I was still only a kid learning the game.

The spotlight was unbearable and there were times when it got so bad that I really did not want to play because I was scared of something going wrong during a game. I was expected to be like Casillas and the team was expected to be like Madrid. At the time this just was not feasible because they were the best team in Europe and we were struggling by comparison.

At Villarreal the levels of scrutiny and expectation were nothing like that. I was just able to play for fun and enjoyment, but with the ambitions of developing as a player and as a team.

That was despite the fact that Victor Munoz, the manager who took me to El Madrigal, was sacked just two months after I signed. Benito Floro took over from him and in his first four games he gave two matches each to myself and to Lopez Vallejo, who was the first-choice keeper at the time. Vallejo is now one of my closest friends in football, a really likeable guy, but I had to try and take his place from him or else get used to the idea of sitting on the bench again, as I had had to do at Barca. After the four games Floro had to pick one of us to be his first choice. He opted for me, I completed the season and in the next two I played every single game.

This was my big breakthrough but had Floro picked Vallejo instead of me, which he could have done because he was a really good keeper, then who knows what would have happened to me? My confidence would have been knocked at the very moment when my self-belief needed boosting and it would have been a long, hard road to get back to where I wanted to be. It is moments like these that shape your career and I was just fortunate that this one went my way as I never looked back from then. It was definitely a turning point.

Floro did not last too long. He was a bit of an annoying character with the goalkeepers, always on at us to change the way we did things and to adapt more to his ways, some of which were a bit strange. He will say he had his reasons and as players there may have been times when we doubted whether or not he did, but what I have to say is that I did learn from him and I came to appreciate this more as I got older.

After he left we had Francisco Garcia Gomez, "Paquito", a former Villarreal coach from years before, who took over for a short period, but he was an old man and even though we reached the semi-finals of the UEFA Cup with him, he was replaced by Manuel Pellegrini.

We made history with Pellegrini in charge, finishing third in the league in 2004/05, and it was during that season that I learned most because of his influence in the dressing room and on the training pitch. He had such a big impact on me that some years later I would find myself recommending him to a senior member of the Anfield board as a potential Liverpool manager.

We were a team which was playing really well. In two consecutive years we went to the semi-final and the quarter-final of the UEFA Cup. For a club like us to do so well was a big achievement. Our success was down to the players and the managers, of course, but the most important people behind our progress were the people on the board, especially Fernando Roig, the chairman and Jose Luis Llanez, the sporting director. They were the ones who made it happen, the ones who pulled all the strings.

In my first season there we fought against relegation, in the second year we fought to qualify for the UEFA Cup but just missed out and in the third year we fought to get into the Champions League – and we got it. We were a team that was growing and improving and the Champions League spot that we earned was proof of that.

As the team was growing so was I, and it was definitely helpful to me that I was at a club where I would no longer be in the spotlight as much as I had been at Barcelona.

It is a great club and a great city where the people are so passionate about their team, but it is also a place where a young player can develop at his own pace without the kind of pressures that you get at

Where did all that hair go? Me as a boy

Watching over me: My grandad was always there, from my early days at Barca's famous La Masia Academy

Teenage dream: About a month before my 17th birthday at Barca

Right: My dad training in England for the World Cup in 1966

I'm not the only Reina to have made a save at Stamford Bridge in a European semi-final. My dad punches one away from Chelsea's Bobby Tambling in the Inter-Cities Fairs Cup in 1966. Barca went on to win the final

El Gran Clasico: I'm proud to have played for Barca against Real Madrid – even if I did get punched by a fan

Right: My first appearance at Anfield, in the semi-final of the UEFA Cup in 2001. The next time I stood in front of the Kop it would be as a Liverpool player

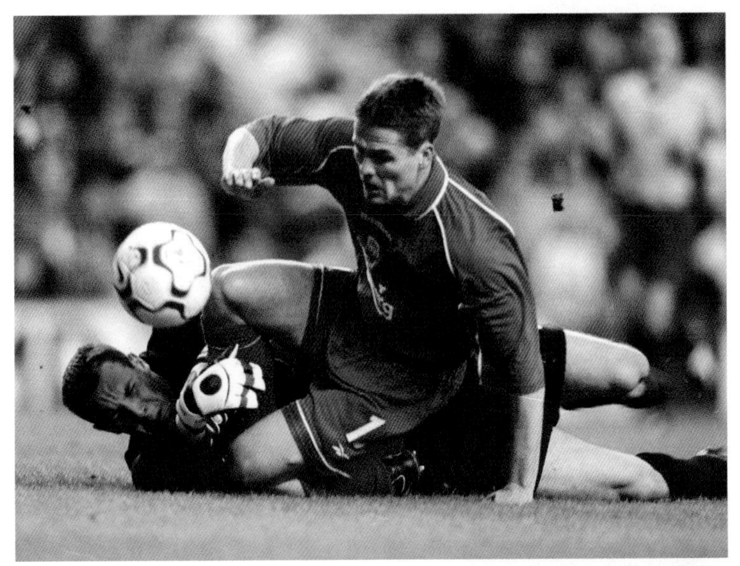

I made a few good saves on the night from the likes of Michael Owen, but there was nothing I could do about Gary McAllister's match-winning penalty

In action for Villarreal against Celtic in the quarter-final of the UEFA Cup in 2004

All smiles: Rafa's persistence pays off and I'm finally unveiled in front of the media as a Liverpool player in July 2005

Right: The only time I've been sent off, with a little help from Chelsea's Arjen Robben. Rafa's interview after the game said it all

It wasn't always easy in my first season in goal for Liverpool. This was our last game at the old Highbury stadium. Thierry Henry was in too quick for me to stop him scoring this one

One of my most important saves, in extra-time of the FA Cup final, to deny Nigel Reo-Coker

I saved three in the penalty shoot-out against West Ham including this one from Paul Konchesky

The moment we realised we'd won the cup. It really was a day of mixed emotions for me

Winning the FA Cup the way we did in 2006 masked over a poor display by me in normal time

Back in the dressing room:
Celebrating with
Fernando Morientes

Proud to be pictured with
the FA Cup and a hero of
Istanbul, Jerzy Dudek

I think that must be Fernando's sombrero, but Robbie seems happy to be flying the flag for Liverpool again

Happy homecoming: It was a great feeling lifting the cup on the bus in front of our fans. That's what it's all about

some of the bigger clubs. It was there that I became a footballer and I am proud of that – and also grateful for what they did for me.

But no matter how strong my feelings were for Villarreal I still did not have second thoughts when the opportunity came for me to leave. I felt that we had reached our limit as a team when we qualified for the Champions League because it was hard to see how we could go past Barcelona and Real.

In some ways it was unthinkable that we could grow any more. So when Liverpool came in for me, a club which is 100 times bigger than Villarreal and which has the potential to win so many trophies at home and abroad, my decision to leave was made for me.

Another reason behind my decision was that the dressing room that I was about to depart was not as healthy and happy a place as it was when I first arrived. When I got there it was predominantly Spanish and the squad was relaxed and enjoyable to work with. People like Quique Alvarez, Javier Gracia, Javier Calleja, Jesus Galvan and Jorge Lopez may not be that well known in England, but they are really good guys and I was lucky to be able to share a dressing room with them.

The atmosphere was always good and we had a lot of laughs, but the mood changed when we signed more and more Argentinians. When Juan Riquelme, Martin Palermo and Juan Pablo Sorin joined, the mood changed and it never went back to the way it was. I had a few bad experiences with Sorin, and a couple of run-ins with Riquelme.

They are different characters with different beliefs, and their influence was one of the reasons why I decided to leave when Liverpool came in for me. They did really well for Villarreal though, so from the club's point of view that is all that matters. It has to be like this.

Villarreal asked me to stay for one more year to help them in their first season in the Champions League, but my mind was made up.

It turned out that Villarreal didn't need me too much anyway because they reached the semi-final of the competition the year after I had left. They would have even have made it to the final if Riquelme hadn't missed a penalty against Arsenal. Villarreal had moved on without me, just as I had moved on from Barcelona. That is football.

The time I spent at Villarreal was crucial to me fulfilling my potential as a goalkeeper. I hope that I repaid their faith in me –I think I did. It was a transitional time and when I look back on the three years I spent there, it was probably my happiest time as a footballer.

But the plane to Liverpool was leaving and I knew that I had to be on it. It was too good an opportunity to miss.

Five Star Red

When Liverpool won the Champions League in Istanbul on May 25, 2005 there was one player missing from the celebrations – me. Not many people know this, but the £6 million deal that took me to Anfield was already done by then. It was not announced until July, but on the night that Liverpool won their fifth European Cup in the most incredible fashion imaginable I belonged to them. Villarreal had approved my sale and I had agreed terms, so on the greatest night in my new club's history I was at home, alone, watching the dramatic events unfold on my television with only some beer for company.

That game is one of the greatest examples of how beautiful football can be. It showed that nothing is impossible and that even the worst situations can be turned around.

I didn't see it that way at half-time, of course. With Liverpool 3-0 down and seemingly on their way to defeat I was absolutely gutted. Being a Liverpool player by then, my first instinct was that I was about to leave a club which had qualified for the Champions League for one who would not be in it. I called my agent and said to him: "We're fucked now. We are not even going to play in the Champions League."

The worrying thing about the whole situation was that going into the game Liverpool were not even sure that winning the Champions League would get them into the competition the following season because they had failed to finish in the top four in the Premier League. But the feeling was that if they won the trophy UEFA would have to give them the opportunity to defend it.

None of that mattered at half-time with Liverpool three goals behind. At that point UEFA being faced with a tricky situation didn't even look like a possibility. It was Liverpool who had all the problems and the question was whether they could even get a goal to make the scoreline more respectable. So I was really in a bad mood.

Then everything changed. After the three goals in six minutes I was back on the phone to my agent. "Manolo, Manolo, we are back," I shouted. Like everyone else I could not believe what I was seeing. Teams had come back from the dead before – but not like this. Not in European football's biggest and most important match – and certainly not against an AC Milan team which had played so well that the trophy could have been packed up and sent to Italy at half-time and no- one could have complained.

I was glued to the game as it went to extra-time and penalties. Everything turned crazy. I was so nervous that I kept on drinking and drinking. By the end of the final I was flat out on my bed after the 10 beers I drank. But I was happy. I had celebrated Liverpool's goals as if I was playing and when Stevie lifted the trophy I celebrated like the rest of his team-mates.

I might not have been out there, dancing around the pitch at the Ataturk Stadium and singing 'You'll Never Walk Alone', but in effect I was already one of his team-mates.

The deal to take me to Anfield was actually signed at the beginning of May. But Barcelona had a sell-on clause put into my contract when I moved to Villarreal and they were entitled to up to 40 per cent of any future transfer fee. That clause expired in July so the transfer was not formally completed until then to allow Villarreal to keep all of the proceeds. I eventually went to Liverpool to finalise everything on July 4. It is a date that is etched on my mind, and will be forever.

I had been aware of Liverpool's interest in me for some time before then, with the first contact probably being made as early as February that year. I share the same agent as Rafa Benitez, Manolo Garcia Quilon, and I became aware that Rafa was having a few problems with his goalkeepers and was not totally satisfied with them during his first season at Liverpool.

I was having one of the best seasons of my career at Villarreal and Liverpool made an offer for me in the springtime. They met with my agent and Benitez, being the annoying – in a good way – manager that he is, rang me every single day to convince me to make the move. Every morning when I was on my way to training my phone would ring and before I even answered it I would know who it was.

"Pepe, it is Rafa," the daily conversation would begin. "Things are the same as yesterday. I do not want to bother you because I know you need to focus on qualifying for the Champions League with Villarreal, but I just need to tell you that we are really keen to sign you and we are working very hard to make it happen."

I even ended up playing a part in the negotiations for my own transfer because Rafa was asking me to ask Villarreal if they could lower their asking price! He also asked me if I could get my agent to reduce my wage demands! It was an unusual situation but I just had to laugh about it. I was really grateful to Rafa because he wanted to take me to Liverpool so much. He gave me that opportunity, the chance of a lifetime. If I had to put up with a few phone calls and being asked to negotiate lower wages for myself then so be it. That's just Rafa.

This wasn't the first time I had been aware of Rafa's interest in me. He first wanted to sign me when I was with Barcelona B. I was only 17 years old at the time and he was making a name for himself as manager of Tenerife. With a team that included Luis Garcia, they enjoyed a good season in 2000/01 and ended up finishing third in La Liga. We were playing in a friendly tournament in Gran Canaria and before one of our matches I saw him standing behind my goal, watching me warm up and go through my routine. This was before the game had even kicked off. It was clear that he was keeping an eye on me as he didn't focus on any of the other players.

That made me nervous because I already knew that he was looking to sign me, but I came through the game with no mistakes and it wasn't long after that he tried to recruit me on loan. I turned the move down because at that stage I just wanted to stay and fight for a place at Barcelona. I wasn't ready to leave. Even that didn't put him off as a few years later he tried to sign me again, this time when he was in charge of Valencia. That move didn't happen either.

But anyone who knows Rafa at all will tell you that he isn't the kind of person who just gives up. If he wants something he will keep on going until it either happens or it is impossible to happen. His persistence is unbelievable. In my case it was a good thing because he came back in for me after he became Liverpool manager and this time he got me. It was third time lucky. I will always be grateful to him for not giving up on me, even after I turned him down a couple of times. He gave me the opportunity to play in England for one of the greatest clubs in the world and I appreciate that so much.

Because I knew Liverpool wanted me early in the year I was able to take an interest in their run to Istanbul in the knowledge that they were going to become my club. I was already interested because there were so many Spanish people there, but their exploits in the Champions

League meant I was getting more excited about the possibility of moving to Anfield with every passing round. The victories over Juventus and Chelsea in the quarter-finals and semi-finals stick in my mind, but as special as those occasions obviously were, they never made anything like the impact on me that the final against AC Milan did. I suppose that is the same for everyone in football. Whenever anyone mentions Istanbul it conjures up the most wonderful images.

I had spoken to Xabi Alonso about Liverpool beforehand because we were together in the Spain squad and I had a good friendship with him, but most of the conversations I had about the city were with Mikel Arteta. At the time, he was an Everton player through and through, but because of our friendship he was happy to help me and answer all of the questions that I had as I made my mind up about the transfer.

When it came down to it, it was definitely easier for me to make the decision to move to Liverpool because there were five Spanish players already there. The manager was Spanish, the goalkeeping coach was Spanish and so were a number of the staff. This wasn't crucial in my decision to join Liverpool, but it was definitely a factor because I knew it would be easier for me to settle in than it would have been if I'd gone to a very English club with a totally English mentality.

The way I looked at it, Liverpool were a Spanish English club and that meant they were perfect for me. By signing for them straight after they won the European Cup it made me feel that I was joining something special and that the work that Benitez was doing at Liverpool would have to be respected because they had lifted one of the most important trophies. Rafa had become an important figure at Liverpool in just one year and he would have the respect of the supporters forever, so when he came for me I knew that the time was right to sign.

I arrived thinking that even if this only lasts for two or three years it could be really good, but something inside of me was making me feel that I would be there even longer than that.

I was only 22 when I made the move, an age which some people say is too young to go abroad to a new league, particularly for a goalkeeper. But as well as Liverpool being too good an opportunity to turn down, I also had personal reasons for wanting to go.

At the time my girlfriend, Yolanda, and my parents were not getting on too well so I thought it would be best for everyone if we went abroad together as a couple and put some space between my family and ourselves, just to allow everything to settle down. It wasn't as if there were major problems, but when you are a young couple, sometimes it is a good idea to find your own way in life. The way I saw it, this would be a chance for Yolanda and myself to start a family together in a new country. It was as much about establishing our own independence and our own way of doing things. Whatever the reason it worked because I am now happily married to Yolanda. We have three wonderful children, and our relationship with my parents is better than ever. Whoever said a change can do you good was spot on because moving to Liverpool was the making of us as a couple and as a family. We have never looked back.

When we first arrived in Liverpool we stayed at the Hope Street Hotel, which is a beautiful place in the city centre where the staff were really helpful to us as we tried to settle in.

Despite this, we found the first 15 days really hard. In fact, they were absolutely horrible. This was the middle of July and every single time I looked out of the window it was pouring down with rain. Not just short, sharp showers, these were full on downpours that meant we could do nothing much apart from sit in our hotel room and think of the roasting hot summer we had left behind in Spain.

I can remember saying to my wife: "What the hell is going on? Is it ever going to change or are we going to spend the rest of our lives carrying umbrellas and staying inside so as not to get soaked?"

It is something that you cannot prepare yourself for when you leave a country with a hot climate and go to one where it feels like it rains all the time. Credit to my wife, though, because when we had these moments of doubt about the move she made sure that I never even got close to the point where I questioned my decision to come to Liverpool. Now, we look back on that time and we laugh. It is quite funny to recall because the whole family is now totally settled and my wife has become a proper Scouse mum.

I didn't really care about the weather or the food. I had no qualms about moving to Liverpool, despite some people suggesting that Liverpool had some problems. If you look at any place, anywhere in the world, you can find reasons why it might be better to go somewhere else. If anything, the idea of going to Liverpool excited me. I knew it was a city of fighters with people who are willing to stand up for themselves, even when it seems that everyone is against them. I liked that idea. It is easy to live in the richest city where you have everything on your doorstep and the politicians are helping you all the time. Liverpool is not like that and that makes it a challenge for everyone who lives there. There was something about that which captured my imagination. Then, when I looked at what the football club had achieved throughout its history, it made moving to Liverpool a no-brainer. The city and the club attracted me and no amount of rain or freezing cold summer days were going to put me off. Well, not in theory anyway.

Driving wasn't the problem that I had perhaps expected it to be. I got used to driving in the left-hand lane fairly quickly and my only trouble is that I still use a car that is left-hand drive because that is what I prefer. Whenever I pull over to get a ticket to go and park I have to throw myself across to the window on the opposite side of the car to grab it. It surprised me how quickly I got used to driving on the opposite side of the road, so much so that there have been a couple of times when it has almost got me into trouble when I am back home in Spain.

On a couple of occasions I have been driving along the road minding my own business and then all of a sudden a car is travelling towards me in my lane. 'Where the hell is this lunatic going?' I think and then I realise that it's me who is in the wrong lane and I have to get across to the right-hand side of the road before I cause an accident. That shows how much I have got used to the English way of doing things.

Sometimes people don't realise that a foreign player has to take all these new ways of life into account when they move to a new team. They look at the fabled lifestyle of a footballer, the kind that they see in the newspapers and on TV, and it makes them think that it must be easy no matter who you are or where you are from. But it doesn't matter what your job is, when you move to a new country your life changes altogether and that can be tough. You have to pick up the language, adapt your culture, get used to a new way of driving and adjust to a different climate – and you do all this without the support network that you had at home. Ultimately none of that mattered to me. I knew that I was going to a fantastic league and to one of the greatest clubs in the world. For all of the natural concerns I had about going abroad at a young age it was an easy decision for me to go to Liverpool.

My first impression of Liverpool Football Club was that it was totally different to Villarreal. It was a massive club that had been crowned champions of Europe only weeks before my arrival and it was based in the north of a big city. Villarreal has a population of only 40,000 people and every single person at the club knows one another. After six years at Liverpool there are still people who work for the club, particularly in the offices, who I do not know because the organisation is so big. So it was the size of the club that struck me first, but then I began to realise and understand its history, appreciate the supporters and started to come to terms with the expectations of playing for one of the most successful clubs in the history of European football. At Barcelona it had been different because I had grown up at the club. That meant I knew almost everything about it by the time I broke into the first-team. At Liverpool it was all new and it did take getting used to.

The first challenge I had was to establish myself in the dressing room. This is not as it easy as it sounds. When I first walked in, I saw Stevie Gerrard, one of the best players in the world; Sami Hyypia, a Liverpool legend; Xabi Alonso, a great player who had scored in the Champions League final, and so on and so on. Everywhere I looked there was a European champion and I was stood there with hardly a winners' medal to my name.

I had confidence in myself but I also knew that I could be punching above my weight so all I could do at first was keep my head down, work hard and try to prove myself. There were a few characters at Anfield when I joined. Didi Hamann was a very funny guy and we hit it off straight away. Crouchy joined the club in the same summer as I did and he was also funny, so it was good to be a part of a dressing room where there were people who would have a laugh. But this shouldn't give the wrong impression because that dressing room was also more professional than any I had encountered in my career to that point.

Every single player was more professional in the way they trained and the way they prepared for games than I was used to in Spain. That sent a message to me. I realised how serious football was taken in the Premier League and I knew that I had to reach that level. I had to look after myself and I had to give my all at every single moment because if I hadn't it would have been noticeable. The players didn't tend to socialise that much outside the dressing room – not because there was a problem or a bad atmosphere, it's just that we did not tend to go out for dinner or nights out together much. It was friendly but professional.

Like I say, there was a community of Spanish players there. Xabi, Luis Garcia, Fernando Morientes and Josemi were all at the club – and this undoubtedly made it easier for me to settle in. They were telling me everything that I had to do, all the rules I needed to follow and showing me where I needed to go. Thanks to them, the adaptation process was much easier than it might otherwise have been.

There was a massive interest in us in Spain. Liverpool had won the Champions League the previous year and because there were so many Spaniards in the team one newspaper even called us "El Benitels". Every single Liverpool game was shown on television in Spain and the people in my country were loving the club because they saw us as unofficial representatives of our homeland. That was really important for us because it showed that the project we were involved in mattered a lot. Had we been at a club that had no chance of success or that no-one was interested in outside of their own supporters then we would have been a curiosity in Spain, but not much else.

There are some things that even my compatriots could not help with though and the English language, or rather the Scouse accent, did take some getting used to at first.

I was looking around the city one time, seeing a few sights, and I thought I would go to see the cathedrals. I didn't know exactly where they were so I stopped someone in the street to ask for directions.

"Excuse me, can you tell me where the church is?" I asked in my very best English accent.

"The wha'?" came the reply.

"The church," I repeated, making a cross with my fingers to illustrate what I meant. Still all I got were more blank looks as if I was crazy.

"The church. You know, Jesus Christ and all that."

"If yer wanted to know where the cheerch was why didn't yer say?"

I'd stood there for five minutes repeating myself over and over again, doing hand signals and all kinds, but I still couldn't get across where I wanted to go because I couldn't say church like a Scouser says it.

Most of the staff at Melwood didn't speak English, they spoke

Scouse. It was very difficult to understand because it is so fast and there is so much slang. Now, when I speak with English people when I am abroad, they ask me if I am a Scouser. It is one of the best compliments I can have because it means I am a part of Liverpool and one of the people. I wouldn't have it any other way. Now even my daughters sound Scouse when they talk. Not Scouse like Stevie or Carra, but you can definitely tell that they come from Liverpool and that makes me proud. But it was hard to get used to at first.

I only spoke a little bit of English when I arrived – only as much as I had learned at school. It was a handicap for me to have so many Spanish speaking players and staff with me at Melwood because it was easy to lapse into speaking in our native tongue. Rafa kept on going on at us, telling us that we had to speak English all the time. Sometimes it was annoying because you just want to get a message across quickly and the easiest way would have been just to talk in Spanish.

But the principle that Rafa was trying to enforce was right. We needed to show respect to our team-mates by speaking in English, even if it was hard sometimes. We were playing in England so it was only right that we should do that. Still, there were times when no-one was around that we would have a chat in Spanish. We would always make sure Rafa couldn't catch us first though!

I was taken on a tour of Anfield and the museum at the stadium. When I saw the stadium without any people in it, it was still really impressive and it made a big impression on me. But it could not compare to my home debut which came against a team that I had never even heard of before I came to England.

Total Network Solutions, or TNS as they are better known, a team from the League of Wales, were my first opponents as a Liverpool player after we were drawn to play against them in the qualifying rounds for the 2005/06 Champions League. Because we entered the competition at such an early stage after UEFA had only allowed us to defend the European Cup on the basis that we started in the qualifiers it meant our season, and my Liverpool career, kicked off in mid-July.

The game was always going to be memorable for me, particularly as Stevie made my debut even more special by scoring a hat-trick in a 3-0 win, but there was another player who will never forget that night. The TNS game was the first time I had played alongside John Arne Riise – and I ended up punching him! He was a really good team-mate and I didn't mean it, of course. A cross came into the box and I punched the ball away, but I caught Riise as well and knocked him down.

As he was getting up off the floor he started laughing and said to me: "Fucking hell, what have you just done to me?" I said: "Listen, I shouted 'keeper, keeper' and when you hear that you have to move otherwise I hit your head." It was an important moment because it showed the way I was intending to go about things.

The main difficulty for me settling in at Anfield was that I was replacing one of the heroes of Istanbul. A few months earlier I had been dumbstruck when Jerzy Dudek made that save from Andriy Shevchenko in the Champions League final, and I had celebrated when he stopped a penalty from the same player to win the European Cup for Liverpool. But here I was taking his place in the team. It was a pressure for me, there is no question about that.

However, everyone knew that I was not coming into the team because of anything he had done in that game. I was given the opportunity because Rafa had not been convinced by his goalkeepers over the course of the entire 2004/05 season. The goalkeeper's position had been filled in turn by Jerzy, Chris Kirkland and Scott Carson. The stability was not there. It was clear that Rafa wanted someone to be his number one in every game and I was the person that he thought was right for that role. I could not do anything about the situation with the other keepers and I could not afford to worry too much about them, not even Jerzy, because if I had done then I would have been distracted and would not have been able to do my best. But of course I was a little bit scared because I was following in the footsteps of someone who had played a crucial role in Liverpool winning their fifth European Cup. It wasn't as if I was replacing a player who the fans did not like. I managed to get my head around it by realising that if the manager had phoned me 25 times in two hours telling me to come to Liverpool it was because he wanted me and trusted me.

My decision to join Liverpool was vindicated because in the first few years we were fighting for every trophy apart from the Premier League. We won the FA Cup and we were one of the teams to beat in Europe.

That Liverpool team is the one that the fans want to watch again and it is where we need to be. We need to be one of the best eight teams in Europe every year, not failing even to qualify for the Champions League. If you are lucky enough to be at a club that has set the standards for everyone else then you have to do everything that you possibly can to live up to expectations. We have to be fighting for the league every year and fighting for the European Cup. This is not optional at Liverpool, it is the way it always has to be and if it were ever to stop being like this then the club would be changed forever. It was once said that Liverpool Football Club exists to win trophies, but it is even more than that, as far as I am concerned – it exists to win big trophies. We are like Barcelona, Real Madrid, AC Milan, Juventus and Bayern Munich, giants of the game. When you are a member of the elite you have to act like one and this means competing for the biggest prizes.

I actually got my hands on a winners' medal just two months into my Liverpool career when we won the Super Cup against CSKA Moscow in the Stade Louis II Stadium in Monaco. It was another comeback in a European final. We went behind in the first half and took it to extra-time through substitute Djibril Cisse's equaliser late on. Another Cisse goal and one from Luis gave us victory without the need for any heroics from me in a penalty shoot-out.

The temptation may have been to think that this was what it would always be like, playing for a big club in a showpiece occasion and walking away with a trophy. But for me it was more about the past than it was about the future because I look upon the Super Cup, the Charity Shield and the World Club Championships as trophies for last year. What I mean by that is you only get to play in those matches because of what the team has achieved in the previous season. It is not like the FA Cup Final or the Champions League Final, which are your rewards for what you have done during that campaign. So while I was happy to pick up a medal in Monaco it did not satisfy my desire to win trophies in the slightest because I knew that the big competitions for that season – the ones that mattered most to the players, management and supporters – were still to come.

Even if I had thought that winning the Super Cup was a sign of things to come then I would have had my mind changed pretty dramatically just a month later when Chelsea beat us 4-1 at home in the Premier League. We had actually drawn 0-0 against them at Anfield in the Champions League just a few days earlier and there were no signs in that game that we were about to be on the receiving end of the kind of hiding that makes you realise how big the challenge is that you are facing. Chelsea were the English champions at the time and they were the most powerful team in the country thanks to the spending power of Roman Abramovich. It was a really bad day for us because Liverpool do not lose games 4-1 at Anfield, but after Stevie had equalised Frank Lampard's goal in the first half, Chelsea took control and we had no answers. It was a reality check for us and for me in particular because it showed how far we had to go.

Again though, the consolation was provided by our supporters because I did not see them being really angry with us, even though we had lost so heavily to one of our biggest rivals.

If that happens in Spain, then the supporters are outraged. While the Liverpool fans were not happy – they would have been crazy if they were – they still supported us all the way and did not turn on us. There are times when things go wrong on the pitch that you are still able to take something positive from the game. This was one of those occasions. It showed me that if we gave everything for Liverpool then the supporters would always be with us. That is a special feeling and it convinced me even more that I had joined a special club.

Sometimes it is the small things that help you realise that you have made the right decision. That was one of the reasons why I felt settled at Liverpool straight away. I had an instant sense of belonging and that was thanks to my team-mates, the manager, the staff and the supporters. I was more than one thousand miles away from my hometown of Cordoba, but I had never felt so at home.

I knew I had come to the right place.

Welcome To England

"I'm going to kill you. I'm going to come to your goal and I'm going to kill you."

The moment these words were uttered to me I knew the challenge of English football would be different to anything I had ever come up against in Spain. They were spoken by Danny Shittu, a massive centre-back who seemed to have trouble on his mind, before Liverpool played Watford in a Premier League game.

I had not met him before, never mind had a previous confrontation with him that made him hell bent on vengeance, but he was still talking about killing me – and this was before the game had even kicked off.

It was during the pre-match handshake between the two sets of players and as I loosened my grip and withdrew my hand from his, I looked into his eyes and quickly realised he was not joking or trying to wind me up. I thought for a split second about how I should reply and then instinct took over. "That's okay," I said. "I'll wait in my goal for you."

He was obviously trying to intimidate me but I couldn't allow him to do that. I was a bit scared if I'm honest because he is a big lad and if he was angry with me for no reason when the game hadn't even kicked off, what was he going to be like when the game got going? I ended up laughing because I did not want to show any fear, but I have to admit it was one of those situations when you wonder what is going to happen. He never did come to my goal, though.

Looking back at it now, Shittu was probably just trying to put me to the test, seeing if I showed a weakness that he could exploit. Had I said nothing back to him or looked scared then he would have had a psychological advantage over me. I knew I could not allow that to happen. I've got nothing against Shittu, he was just doing what most players do when they come up against a foreign goalkeeper by trying to take me out of my comfort zone. Many of the opponents I have come up against since moving to the Premier League have done this, although most of them have done it physically rather than mentally. From the moment I came into English football it was sink or swim and all I could do was paddle like mad until the danger passed.

On my Premier League debut in August 2005 we played Middlesbrough at the Riverside Stadium in a Saturday tea-time kick-off. Stewart Downing was in their team that day, but the man who gave me the most problems was Jimmy Floyd Hasselbaink. He was in my face all game long. To be honest, he was a pain in the arse because he was so physical. There were a couple of incidents where I went to claim the ball in the air and he led with his studs, which dug into my thigh. It hurt like hell but I took the rough treatment from him to be a normal occupational hazard. I knew if I'd reacted in any way then opposition players and managers might have thought that they could wind me up if they were over-physical with me. It was difficult to keep my cool though and it hasn't always been easy to make sure that I don't rise to the provocation in any way.

The ironic thing is that for all the intimidation and physical provocation that goalkeepers can sometimes receive, the only time that anyone was sent off for an incident involving me during my first season in English football, I was the one who received the red card.

We were playing Chelsea at Stamford Bridge in February. After losing 4-1 to them at Anfield we were keen to get a result in the return league fixture, but found ourselves 2-0 down. At a time like that, your frustration is massive because you are so desperate to get back into the game. It can be worse if you are a keeper because though you are stood in your own box you are still as determined to change things for the better. But you can only watch the outfield players on the ball. You can't play a part yourself.

There were only about 10 minutes left to go and the mood was getting more tense when Chelsea played a high ball over the top for Eidur Gudjohnsen to chase. Sami Hyypia was covering, but I could see that I had the best chance to get to the ball first and I came out of my area to make a tackle. I reached the ball but because it was strange to see a goalkeeper make this kind of challenge, every single Chelsea player raced over towards me.

The referee was Alan Wiley and to my mind he was partly responsible for what followed because he called me to the byline when I was in my goal. To defuse the situation, he could have come over to speak to me discreetly, but he called me over. I had to make my way through all of the Chelsea players and as I started to walk over, Arjen Robben was in my ear, saying all sorts of nasty things. I know I shouldn't have reacted but I did. I hardly touched him. I basically put my glove to the side of his face and he started crying like a baby. He went down like he had a broken neck.

Wiley called me over and I put my hands on his shoulders to plead with him, but with the crowd baying for blood, Wiley wasn't listening. He just reached into his pocket and pulled out the red card, pointing to the spot where I touched Robben by way of explanation. Harry Kewell, Steve Finnan and Sami surrounded Wiley, but his mind was made up and I had to take the walk of shame down the tunnel, much to the delight of the delirious Chelsea fans.

After the game Rafa made a crack on television about having to finish the interview early because he needed to go and see Robben in hospital. That summed it up because the whole incident was a joke. What disappointed me most was that I hadn't expected to see this kind of behaviour in English football, but then Robben is a player who has been punished before for simulation and this was one of those occasions. I was just unlucky that I was the one who suffered for it. It taught me a valuable lesson that it is better to avoid these situations altogether than run the risk of letting someone else get you into trouble.

There is a school of thought that foreign goalkeepers can be put off by the Premier League, that it can be difficult for them to cope with the physical approach of English players and the leniency shown to them by referees. Maybe I'm the odd one out in every sense of the phrase, but even though there have been occasions when I have been roughed up and when I have felt that I've been treated unfairly, I've still loved it from the first time I played in this country.

It is a proper test for a keeper because you have to expect to be challenged for almost every ball. In other leagues you can sometimes go up for a cross and not one single opponent will come near you. They just stand back and let you collect the ball. In England there are times when I'm stood waiting for a corner or a free-kick to come in and I am literally surrounded by players. One might be standing on my toes, another right in front of me and the rest all ready to charge in my direction the moment the ball is played into the box. It can be intimidating but that is the same for every keeper, regardless of where you are from. It doesn't matter if you come from Madrid or Manchester, when you are under this kind of pressure it can only be difficult. In my time at

Liverpool I have learned to live with it and there are even times when I actually enjoy the confrontation. In many ways, English football has helped me become the player that I am today.

Even before I had met Danny Shittu, Jimmy Floyd Hasselbaink and Arjen Robben, I was given a blunt impression of what English football would be like. I was left in no doubt that it would be more physical than what I had been used to in Spain.

In my first game as a Liverpool player we played Wrexham in friendly at the Racecourse Ground. It was a hot day in early July and the ground was full. An added attraction for fans was that the European Cup was being paraded. I saw a lot of red Liverpool shirts dotted around the stadium as the supporters took great delight in singing "We are the champions, champions of Europe!" Everyone seemed in a relaxed, happy mood. Then the match started and that all changed.

I can remember being absolutely stunned by some of the challenges. The game was only a few minutes old and a couple of really strong tackles had already been made. I can remember thinking, 'What the fuck is this?' In Spain you never see challenges like that – and this was only a friendly! When I mentioned it to a couple of the players afterwards they told me that this wasn't even the worst that I would see because the tackles would be even tastier when the competitive games began. I thought, 'Wow, brilliant' because it was so crazy.

As a keeper, one of the first things I also learned was that you do not get the same protection in this country as you do in Spain. That was the biggest difference I encountered and it was probably the hardest to come to terms with. But football is football. The only thing from my point of view was that I had to be prepared physically because I would have less protection from referees and also the players that I would be facing would be much stronger than the ones I had come up against in Spain. Most other aspects of the football are the same – the ball is still round and so on – but when you come for a corner and a forward impedes you, but the referee says that is okay, then you know there are differences that you have to get used to. The other noticeable change was playing in stadiums which were full every week. Wherever we went with Liverpool it was always a full house. That was how I knew that I had signed for a really big club.

It is always a learning curve when you are at a new club and in a new country. There was one part of my game I tried to adapt not long after I came because a lot of the Liverpool fans were telling me that I punched the ball too much when I came for crosses and corners. They knew English football better than I did and they had watched some great goalkeepers play for Liverpool, so I was happy to listen to them. But I also believed that the punch was an important weapon to have in my armoury because it meant that I could be safer by reducing the risk of dropping the ball when I came under physical pressure. It was a tactic and the key to any tactic is using it at the right time and in the right way. The experience I got in England and the more I came to understand the game in this country, the better I was at choosing when to punch and when to catch. I can punch the ball really far, but I know now that if I am able to catch it then I am better off doing that.

In the air it is harder for keepers in this country than it is in Spain. This means that you have to be as complete a player as possible. You cannot stay on your line and just stop shots or come for the easy balls. You have to dominate situations and show that you are in control, even though you know it is tough to be like that. I have no complaints about English football, but there are times when I wish the rules were enforced a bit more than they are where goalkeepers are concerned. If a player is stood on top of you in the six-yard box and stopping you from moving and coming to claim a cross then that is a free-kick all day long.

It doesn't matter if it is in England, in Spain or in Japan, it is a foul.

But the beauty of all these experiences, good and bad, is that they have undoubtedly improved me as a player. I do not see myself as a Spanish keeper or an English keeper, I'm more a fusion of the two. That is what modern goalkeeping is about. You have to be able to adapt to all kinds of different situations and learn to deal with different pressures. You cannot be just a really good shot stopper or someone who catches the ball well. You have to have so many different facets to your game because if you don't then you can be sure that your weaknesses will quickly be exposed, particularly in a competition as ruthless as the Premier League. I am fortunate because I have spent a similar amount of time as a professional in England as I did in Spain so this means that I am now able to cope with the demands of the game in both countries. Had I stayed in Spain for my entire career the chances are that I would be a different keeper to the one I have become in England. I certainly wouldn't be as prepared for forwards jumping into me and making life difficult for me.

I have definitely evolved but one part of my game that has remained pretty much the same is my sweeping behind the defence. When I first came to this country I already had a reputation for being a 'sweeper keeper' from my time at Villarreal, where I was asked to defend the edge of my box whenever possible to allow the back four to push as high up the pitch as they could.

This was a system that worked really well for us and it was one of the main reasons why we finished third in La Liga at the end of my final season there. For us, that was the equivalent of becoming champions of Spain because no-one ever expected us to finish so high in the table. It really was a major achievement. We did it by playing in that style so there must be something to it if it can help a relatively small club have such a big achievement. My physical attributes mean that this is the best style for me because I am quick enough to sweep up any ball that is played in behind the defensive line. I definitely prefer this way of playing and it was actually one of the key factors in my transfer to Liverpool because Rafa had seen me play for Villarreal and he wanted his team to play in a similar style. It was my ability to fit into this kind of system which won me my dream move to Anfield.

I know that in the past in England teams have tended to sit a little bit deeper. But the way football has changed, with the increased pace of the game, the changes to the back pass rule and so on mean that if a keeper is confident enough in his own ability to deal with a loose ball, then it allows his team-mates to push higher up the pitch and play with a higher intensity. This is what I prefer and during Roy Hodgson's time at Liverpool you could see that we were playing deeper and my performance levels were not the best. That is not to make excuses for myself because it is up to all players to adapt to whatever situation, but for me it was not a coincidence that as we got deeper as a team so my standards dropped. If you look at the most successful teams, the likes of Barcelona and Manchester United, they ask their keepers to act as sweepers and this approach hasn't done them too much harm.

The good thing for me is that at Liverpool I am playing for a club where this style of goalkeeping is a tradition. I did not see Tommy Lawrence or Bruce Grobbelaar play, but I know that they were the kind of keepers who liked to push up to the edge of their box and allow their defenders to play higher. It's good to be following in their footsteps because it means that Liverpool established their own style for goalkeeping. The only difference is that although I have done some crazy things when I have raced out of my goal I haven't yet got to the stage where I am trying to beat two or three men with the ball like Brucie used to! I try to keep things as simple and as safe as possible.

If I have to dribble an opponent then I will do so, but the less risk you take the better it is for the modern game. I would even go as far as to say that in the modern game goalkeepers don't have the right name because a better description of us would be goal-players. With possession becoming more and more important, all players have to play their part. It is no good having 10 outfield players who keep the ball really well all the time, but behind them they have a keeper who gives it away every time. That would defeat the object. Again, Barcelona set the standard because if you look at the statistics from their games Valdes hardly ever gives the ball away. He keeps possession, circulating with simple passes to players who are always available to receive the ball. We all have to be like that nowadays, it is part of our trade. Keepers have to play an effective role when it comes to keeping the ball.

That is why I try to play out as often as I can in training. It helps me to improve my technical levels because it means I have to get used to playing with the ball at my feet, even in difficult situations when I am surrounded by players.

No matter how much I enjoy it though, I still know that I would not have been good enough to make it as an outfield player. I found out the hard way just how tough that can be when I played in midfield for Liverpool in a pre-season friendly against Kaiserslautern in July, 2006.

We had run out of substitutes and Rafa asked me if I wanted to go on. I jumped at the chance, thinking I might make a great pass or score a goal. But I only played for 15 minutes and after 10 I could hardly breathe! It felt like I had been running for three hours. Even though I didn't move that much the experience taught me, if I didn't already know, that my position is in goal where I don't have to chase around so much. I came off the pitch that day thinking that if I ever had to play in midfield again it could end my whole life, so I'll stick with being a keeper and carry on taking my chances dealing with the big centre-forwards who want to smash me into the back of the goal. It's safer!

It is an honour for me to play in goal anyway, obviously because of my father and my predecessors at Liverpool but also because, as well as admiring Zubizarreta, I always wanted to be like Jose Molina, the Spanish goalkeeper, who made a massive impression on me when I was a youngster making my way in the game.

Molina played mainly for Atletico Madrid and Deportivo La Coruna, as well as Spain. He is an inspiration to me for many, many reasons. As someone who has fought and beaten testicular cancer he is also an inspiration to many other people. He is my reference point as a professional because for me he was the first of the truly modern keepers. By the time he won the Double with Atletico Madrid in 1996 he was already one of my idols because he changed the way my position was played.

I consider him the greatest and I tried to follow his style because he was a keeper who thought like a central defender. He would patrol his area but he wasn't waiting for something to happen, he was anticipating something happening and his ability to read a pass meant he was one of the best keepers anyone will ever see when it comes to closing down an attacker who is trying to race on to a through ball. By doing this, he prevented other teams even getting chances. He didn't have to make a save because he had already read the play, identified the threat and neutralised it. His starting position was always crucial to the way he played and I used to watch him and try to copy what he did.

I am so happy that I did because the demands of football these days mean that you have to be like this. If a keeper stays on his line then he has almost no chance and Molina was one of the first to realise that the higher up the pitch you played and the more you followed the play the better chance you had of preventing problems. I try to be like this, to do what he did, and if people think that this is one of my better qualities then that would make me very proud because all I ever wanted was to be like Molina. Fortunately, I played for Barcelona, a club where the coaches instilled in us the need to have the best possible starting position to prevent goalscoring opportunities and also to get involved in the possession game. This is why Valdes and myself are comfortable playing this kind of role for our teams.

Even though I have been in football for more than a decade, that does not mean that I don't look at other keepers and try to learn from them. You have to examine how the best players in your position do their job and pick up little lessons because this is one of the best ways of improving. Molina was my reference point in the past, but in more recent times, the goalkeeper who I believe has set the standard for all others to follow has been Edwin van der Sar. Along with Valdes, he has been the best and even though he played for Manchester United, our greatest rivals, I would have to have been stupid not to recognise how good he was. His retirement was a big blow to United because he brought so much to their team but by replacing him with David de Gea from Atletico Madrid, a player who I know well, they have recruited a very good goalkeeper who will only improve with time and experience in this league.

They are not my concern, though. All I am bothered about is to keep on doing my own bit for Liverpool, whether that means taking a high ball to relieve the pressure on my defence, saving a shot or just giving support to my team-mates. As long as I am contributing to the team, that is the main thing.

I have been building myself up and improving during my time in England and hopefully my best is still to come because the Premier League is a tough league where you learn things about yourself all the time. I have been fortunate enough to play in what I consider to be the best two leagues in the world and the combination of the two have made me the player that I am today.

They are both great leagues, but at the moment I would say that when it comes to organisation, television rights and supporters, England is better than Spain right now. It is a little bit more advanced. Even though La Liga has Barcelona and Real Madrid I still prefer the Premier League because it is so competitive.

The two giants in Spain only really have two or three teams who can compete with them to any kind of decent level but in this country you can go to places like Stoke City and be beaten easily. You can go to Sunderland and if you are not near your best they can get the better of you. You can visit Blackpool and West Ham United, teams who end up being relegated, and they can turn you over.

This is what makes English football so special and it is the physical intensity and competitiveness of the game over here which have made me the keeper that I am.

Maybe I owe Danny Shittu a debt of thanks for helping me along.

Bittersweet FA

They say that you never forget your first time and my first ever experience in the FA Cup is one that will undoubtedly live with me forever. When I was a kid growing up in Spain I had always associated the FA Cup with Wembley Stadium, magnificent occasions played in an equally brilliant setting.

But as I sat on the bench at Kenilworth Road on a bitterly cold evening in early January 2006, struggling to feel my toes in my boots and my fingers in my gloves and with Liverpool getting beat 3-1 by Luton Town, I would have strangled anyone if they'd even dared to mention the romance of the cup. This wasn't romantic – it was a nightmare in the making. We were the giants and we were about to be killed.

At that point, winning the competition wasn't even a consideration. The only thing that any of us could think of was getting back into the game and maybe earning a replay because the alternative did not even bear thinking about. Shocks are part and parcel of cup football, but when you are at a club like Liverpool then you are expected to beat teams from the lower divisions, even if you are having an off day. We were the reigning champions of Europe and yet there we were, with just over half-an-hour of the game still to go, on the verge of elimination and embarrassment. I don't know what it was – maybe it was the spirit of Istanbul from the year before – but something happened. It was something that happened so often during my first season at Liverpool that the press started to call us the 'Comeback Kings', and we fought our way back from two goals down to win the match. It was an incredible turnaround and it would not be the last time during an unforgettable cup run that we survived by the skin of our teeth.

I wasn't even playing at Luton, having been named as one of the substitutes. Perhaps that was a good idea because it meant I could come to terms with the FA Cup, its euphoric highs and stomach churning lows, before being plunged straight into the deep end. The TV people had chosen to screen the match late on a Saturday afternoon. Obviously they were hoping for an upset or a crazy game, but even in their wildest dreams they could not have imagined that the tie would turn out the way it did – I know I couldn't.

Eight goals were scored and we got five of them, including one of the most memorable in the competition's history. To say Luton gave us a massive scare would be a massive understatement. I don't know why but you could just sense that something thrilling was about to happen when we got to the ground.

Kenilworth Road is a really small stadium and nothing like what we were used to in the Premier League. The facilities were what you would expect from a club in the lower divisions and that immediately put us out of our comfort zone. As a player you know that in those kinds of settings you can lose if you don't have the right mentality, even if you are one of the best teams in the country.

The crowd was only small and though the weather was not the best, the atmosphere was cracking with the home supporters desperate for their team to claim our scalp. I actually thought the game would be straightforward when Stevie gave us the lead with a shot from the edge of the box, but from being in control we lost our way and somehow found ourselves 3-1 down, with Djibril Cisse having missed a spot-kick.

I was sat on the bench, gloomily thinking that I would have to wait another 12 months before I would get the chance to make my debut in the FA Cup. Scott Carson was in goal and he must have been saying to himself: "Why did I have to get picked for this game?" because things really did look that bad.

But we managed to turn things around and I think one of the main reasons for this was that we were so desperate to win the cup that year. I hadn't been at Liverpool the previous season, but I knew that Liverpool had been beaten by Burnley in the third round in controversial circumstances. The manager and the players did not want to suffer like that again. After that game the critics had rounded on Rafa and some of the players, accusing him of disrespecting the cup by fielding an under-strength team. No-one wanted that kind of situation again and the only way to ensure we would not be in the firing line was to make sure we had a really good run – hopefully one that would take us all the way to the final in Cardiff. So Luton was a crucial game for us to win. We simply could not afford to lose.

My strongest memory of our comeback was provided by Xabi Alonso, who scored a goal that only he could score. Xabi was always trying to score from the halfway line and when he did it in a game it was no surprise to me because he had already done it to me in training.

On this occasion, there was a funny side to it because when he got the ball 50 or 60 yards from goal you could see Stevie shouting: "Give it to me. Give it to me." But Xabi had other ideas. He had already recognised that he had a chance to score, even though he was miles out and he shot while Stevie was still demanding the ball. Stevie didn't look happy when he did that, but as it became clear that the ball was going to go into the net you could see Stevie changing his body language and starting to celebrate as if shooting from so far out had been a good idea all along. We were all laughing about it in the dressing room afterwards. Even now, when the goal is shown on TV it is one of those moments that all the players find funny because we have all been in Stevie's position, telling someone to do something and they do the opposite. The difference is that the ball hardly ever ends up in the back of the net in these situations – and you are even less likely to get caught on camera like Stevie did.

My first game came in the next round at the end of January and we were drawn away again, this time at Portsmouth, who were in the Premier League at that time. Again it was freezing cold and again we were on the television. It was as if the TV people were hoping that we would get knocked out just to boost their audience figures, but we used that to our advantage, telling ourselves that we would not be the sacrificial lambs for their benefit or anyone else's.

We won 2-1 thanks to a penalty from Stevie and a goal from John Arne Riise in the first half. From that moment on, we started thinking that the final is not so far away. But we could not have asked for a more difficult route to get to Cardiff. After surviving at Luton we then faced Manchester United at home in the fifth round before a trip to Premier League Birmingham in the quarter-finals and Chelsea, the reigning champions, in the semi-finals. The way cup competitions work means that sometimes you can get lucky and have quite an easy passage to the final, but in this year we were given one of the hardest routes imaginable and we still managed to get there. So when we won in Cardiff we were able to congratulate ourselves on the achievement in the knowledge that we deserved it. We had earned the trophy the hard way from the first minute of the third round to the very last kick of the final and when you win at a tricky venue like Fratton Park it gives you the belief you need to do that.

The day we knocked United out on February 18, 2006, is still one of the greatest memories of my time with Liverpool so far. To beat them in the cup is always going to be special because of the rivalry between the two clubs, but if you look at what happened in the matches that followed, it would be another five games before we even scored against them again. That puts that victory in perspective. It also spoiled their record against us in the FA Cup. I read in the newspapers afterwards that it was the first time we had beaten them in that competition since 1921, so we really made history. Not many, if any, fans will remember that, but many would have recalled the 1977 final that deprived Liverpool of a treble, and the 1985 semi-final defeat. So it was special.

Peter Crouch got the only goal of the game with a header from Steve Finnan's cross after less than 20 minutes. It is only now looking back that I realise how big and how important that result was because at the time you are caught up in the excitement of the occasion. The atmosphere on that day was something else so all you are thinking about is winning the game for the fans, not what the victory actually means. Just getting through to the next round, and at United's expense especially, was great for us, particularly as it meant we would eventually be going on to play Chelsea again.

It would be the fifth time that we had met them that season, but we had no fear of Jose Mourinho and his team, even though they were champions. It had been less than 12 months since Liverpool had knocked them out of the Champions League at the semi-final stage so though they were the best team in the country and we respected them for that, we went into the game knowing that in a one-off we could beat them. We had the manager who could come up with the right tactics, we had the players who had already proven that they could win the biggest games and the biggest trophies and we had the supporters who can inspire like no others. When you have all those things coming together at once, you have no reason for fear. It is exactly the opposite. You have reason only to believe.

I know that the rivalry between Rafa and Mourinho built up over time but at that stage it wasn't so bad. It is like Rafa has always said, there were no problems until we knocked them out of the Champions league at the semi-final stage for the second time in 2007. Then we started to see those famous confrontations between the two managers. Back in 2006 there was no sense that we were fighting against Mourinho, though our fans loved to get one over on him. It was just Liverpool against Chelsea and the prize of getting through to the final of the FA Cup was the major incentive that focused the minds of the players of both clubs.

As I have said, we had been beaten heavily by Chelsea in the league at Anfield earlier in the season and had lost at Stamford Bridge, but we did not have an inferiority complex. We were like rocks in the games that mattered most in the knockout competitions and we proved that in the Champions League, especially over the years, by winning games that most people expected us to lose. For some reason we found it much easier to compete in these games. It wasn't, like some people argued, that we were taking the cups more seriously than the league. It was just something that happened and in one-off matches we had no reason to fear anyone. It surprises me that more teams are not like this because if you don't go into a match thinking that you can win then what is the point? I'm sure that Luton believed in themselves when they played against us in the third round and through that they were almost able to make a big name for themselves on that occasion.

So for all Chelsea's wealth and despite the fact that they were going to end the season as champions again we arrived at Old Trafford on a warm spring day in April for the semi-final totally confident in ourselves and believing in our strategy. We won the game 2-1 with goals from Riise and Luis Garcia and ended Chelsea's Double dreams. But it wasn't about them. It was about us and our dreams of winning silverware. By getting to the final we had given ourselves a chance to win the FA Cup and give the club a second trophy in just two years.

I was alright in the build-up to the final. Everything was normal apart from a few nerves but you would expect that anyway. I had played in big games in Spain and in the main I was pretty calm, even though I knew it was going to be a big occasion.

For some reason, though, the game turned into a nightmare for me. The first 90 minutes I played against West Ham United were amongst the worst of my entire time in England. It wasn't just because of the goals I conceded, it was also because of the way I was feeling throughout the whole game.

For whatever reason I just wasn't right. My legs were shaking and my judgement was not like it is normally. This can happen to any player in any game and all you can do is hope that it doesn't happen to you when it matters most. Unfortunately for me, I was doing it in an FA Cup Final in front of a crowd of 71,000 people, with millions more watching on television and with my team-mates relying on me to be at my best in such an important match. I don't know why it happened, but somehow I managed to lose my confidence during the game. I was doing things that I would never normally do.

Carra scored an own goal to put West Ham in front, but if that goal had his name on it their second should have been put down to me because although Dean Ashton scored it, I was responsible, fumbling an easy shot by Matthew Etherington into the path of the West Ham forward. He could not miss. We got back into the game through Djibril Cisse and Stevie, but my worst moment was still to come.

Paul Konchesky's 64th-minute goal was a cross from the left wing and it was one of those situations where no-one says it publicly, but inside they are all blaming the keeper. The one type of goal that you never want to concede is one where the ball goes over your head from a wide area because that suggests that your positioning, a basic but crucial part of a goalkeeper's game, was not right.

Maybe there wasn't much I could do about it because it was such a difficult ball to deal with, but as it hit the back of the net I thought our cup dreams were over. It was a horrible feeling and I knew that questions would be asked about my performance and rightly so, because I had not been anywhere near my best. Worse still, five minutes later the same thing happened again with Konchesky crossing from the left. I could not get my steps right and I ended up on the ground with the ball running loose before going out for a throw-in. I just didn't feel right and even when I look back and try to understand why this was the case I have no idea. Whatever the reason, we were about to lose the cup final and I didn't need anyone to tell me that I would be as responsible for that as anyone else.

One of the problems with being a goalkeeper is that when your team needs a goal to make up for a mistake that you have made there is little you can do to help. It can be a lonely feeling. Unless you go up for a corner in the last minute and score you are totally reliant on your team-mates bailing you out. With time running out, West Ham still playing quite well and our players starting to tire in the heat, I started to accept that this would not be our day. I never gave up hope that there would be a dramatic rescue, but neither did I really believe that something incredible would happen.

It is at times like this that Stevie comes into his own. Look at the best moments of his career – and there are many of them – the number of times he has turned a game Liverpool's way with a moment of inspiration is incredible. What he did at the Millennium Stadium on that day was arguably the greatest of the lot. I did not know who Roy of the Rovers was before I came to England, I hadn't even heard of him, but when someone told me he did things in cartoons that Stevie does in real life I understood.

When the ball dropped to Stevie 35 yards out I was right behind it and I knew as soon as he made contact that it was a goal. There was no other place for that shot to end up than in the bottom corner of the goal and there was no keeper in the world who could stop it. For me, the emotion when the ball hit the back of the net was incredible. On the one hand I was elated because the game had been saved and we now had a chance to go on and win it. On the other, I was just so relieved because I knew that goal had prevented me from suffering one of the worst moments of my career. It was one of the best strikes of a ball that I have ever seen and also one of the most important. There are only so many players in the world who can do that and Stevie made the difference for us that day.

After the 90 minutes was over I went to Ocho – goalkeeping coach Jose Ochoterena – and he told me that all I could do was forget about everything that had happened and just to focus on the extra 30 minutes that were about to be played because I had to try and help the team. I think I did that by making a save in the last 90 seconds of extra-time. When Yossi Benayoun curled a free-kick into the penalty area, Nigel Reo-Coker managed to get his head on to it in the melee and it was heading for the net until I managed to get my left glove to the ball and deflect it on to the post. Sami tried to clear it but the ball then rebounded to Marlon Harewood. We all breathed a huge sigh of relief when he miscued his shot wide.

Without that save we would not even have had the chance of winning the game on penalties. That made me feel better. I felt I had contributed on the day, but I knew that my best opportunity to make amends came in the penalty shoot-out that followed. I was either going to be the hero or the villain.

I was desperate not to be the bad guy. I just wanted to help Liverpool to lift that trophy. I knew that I had made seven saves out of nine penalties the season before and I still believed in myself, no matter what had happened earlier on in the game. It was about using the skills that I had already used in Spain, the ones that meant I came to England with the reputation of being a good penalty saver.

Before the shoot-out started, Rafa came to me with a piece of paper and he showed me a list of West Ham's likely penalty takers, with information about their technique from the penalty spot. Teddy Sheringham was on the list, but even with the information about him he still scored. There was nothing on the paper about Bobby Zamora, Konchesky or Anton Ferdinand and I managed to make saves from all three of them! In the lottery of penalties I got lucky. Those saves meant that we won the game, but even though I was delighted for myself, for the team and for the fans, I still did not appreciate what it meant to win the FA Cup.

Even as we were celebrating with our fans I still had this nagging feeling that I had almost cost us the game. As we were doing a lap of honour one of the supporters gave me a massive mask of my own face to put on and I could not help thinking that had things turned out differently I might have needed something like that as a disguise, but with someone else's face on it maybe. Thankfully, I was wearing it in celebration and not because I needed to hide my face.

It was while we were on the homecoming parade the following day that it began to dawn on me just how important our victory had been. I saw the people on the streets of Liverpool who had all come out to see us with the trophy and it was clear that this was a very special moment for them. It was pouring down with rain – as usual – and still thousands upon thousands of people came out to see us bringing home the trophy that we had won the day before. Twelve months earlier I had watched Liverpool's homecoming after winning the Champions League on television and there I was on the same streets parading another trophy for those same supporters. That was the most important thing for me. I had come to the club to win trophies and in my very first season I had one.

In the days after the final, I was still really disappointed with my performance. Straight after the game I had given a TV interview where I said that I had been absolutely rubbish and even though I had enjoyed some good moments in the shoot-out I still saw no reason to change my opinion of my display before penalties. After half-an-hour of the game you could not have predicted that things would turn out so well for me and the team and with us parading one of the most famous trophies in football around Liverpool. It could have been such a bad end to the season for me. A really bad end.

At that point I probably realised more than ever before what my father must have gone through after his European Cup final experience. The difference for me was that I got away with mine. I have to give thanks to someone up there who must like me because before the penalties I was talking to my friend in the sky and asking him for some help. I don't know why but he did and it helped us to win the cup.

Having said all that, even to this day it is difficult for me to accept that the FA Cup is treated with such importance in this country. I have a winners' medal that means so much to me, but I really don't understand how anyone could think that the FA Cup is more important than the league title.

I recognise the history of the competition. It has a romance that few other tournaments can match, and I know that it is the oldest competition. But to me, being the oldest does not make it the best.

It is certainly the best domestic cup competition that is staged in any country in the world, but I would swap one Premier League title for 200 FA Cups without any hesitation. The league always has to be the most important trophy for any club to pursue and that is even more true when you are playing for Liverpool, who expect to be challenging for the title every single year.

I loved winning the FA Cup, I loved the occasion and I love the medal but I would give it all up right now just to get my hands on a league title winner's medal because that is the one that matters most. It means that you are the best.

The Golden Glove

When I first moved to Liverpool, Xabi Alonso thought it would be a good idea for me to visit the club museum so that I could better understand the history and spirit of the club. I saw all of the trophies, including the European Cup that had been won in Istanbul just a few months earlier, took in the photographs of some of Liverpool's greatest moments and learned about the legendary figures – and equally legendary supporters – who have made the club what it is.

There was one exhibit that really captured my imagination. To some it would just be another football shirt, a piece of fabric of no great significance. But as soon as I saw Bruce Grobbelaar's bright yellow goalkeeping jersey, the one that he had worn in his record-breaking 310th consecutive appearance, it really caught my attention. Because he played in the same position as me I could not help but admire Grobbelaar's achievement and it made me want to get my own place in the museum, to show I had done something important for Liverpool. It was only early days but already I had a personal ambition.

The funny thing is, while I was stood looking at the shirt, someone asked me if I would donate something to the museum. "Not until I have done something to deserve a place in here," I replied. I wasn't being unhelpful. I just wanted to be clear that I had to earn the right to have my own exhibit, as all the other players had.

Five years on and I finally had something worthy of that kind of treatment when I kept my 100th clean sheet for Liverpool, a total I reached in fewer games than any other goalkeeper in the club's history. That kind of record is not really important to me as an individual, it is just numbers not medals after all. Being part of Liverpool's history mattered to me. It mattered a lot because I had come from another country and tried to establish myself in a new country, in a new league and at a club which has set standards in England and abroad. So to reach my own personal milestone meant a lot.

I donated the gloves that I wore in that game, a 3-0 home win against Aston Villa, to the museum so that everyone could see them. It is nice for the fans to be able to see them, but I would much prefer to leave another trophy there that the team has won collectively rather than something personal to me. That is my new ambition.

It is strange as well because clean sheets are something that have only come to mean a lot to me since I moved to Liverpool. It isn't something that matters as much in Spain as it does here. There is a different culture there and it wasn't about keeping clean sheets. It was more about the average number of goals that you conceded.

From my very first official league game in England I realised how much importance is attached to a shut-out and it was Stevie who opened my eyes. On my debut at Middlesbrough, I was a little bit disappointed we drew 0-0 because I had been hoping to mark my first league game with a win, but it was a decent point against a difficult opponent. As we were going off the pitch at the end of the game, Stevie made his way over to me, gave me a high five and he said something that I didn't really understand. I honestly didn't have a clue so I spoke to him again in the dressing room and he told me that he was congratulating me on keeping a good clean sheet. That had never happened to me in Spain, so for it to happen on my Liverpool debut and for Stevie himself to be the one who did it made me realise straight away how much value is placed on clean sheets in this country.

It is not me who keeps the clean sheet, though, it is we. The team allows me the chance to keep a clean sheet through the way they defend and the way they play. It is not as if I'm stood there making save after save and my team-mates are nowhere to be seen. They are there protecting me and without them doing this it would have been impossible for me to keep one clean sheet, never mind more than a hundred. There is no doubt about that.

It is the same for a forward relying on service to get goals. I need protection to keep clean sheets. I do my job, that is my part of the bargain, but anything I achieve can only happen because of them. It means a lot to all of us, and for the back four and myself in particular, when our opponents fail to score against us because it shows that we have done our jobs well. For this reason, I would always prefer to win 1-0 than 2-1. Even in games when I don't have that much to do I still get a lot of satisfaction from keeping a clean sheet and I always will do.

I am superstitious about it as well. If I have kept a clean sheet in a game then I have to wear the same gloves in the next one. The only time this ritual has ever caused me any problems was during my first season at the club when I kept 11 clean sheets in a row. My gloves were completely destroyed by the end of that run and were so wrecked that I probably would have had to change them anyway if Sao Paulo hadn't scored against us in the final of the World Club Championship. It was a nice problem to have though and even battered and torn to shreds, those gloves were still better than the first pair that I ever bought. Those ones were called Mauro Silva. They had spots on the palm and they were black and yellow. They weren't the best but I was more than happy with them because they were my first ones.

When I reached my 100th clean sheet, the record I set meant I had got to the landmark quicker than any of my predecessors of the past, goalkeeping greats like Ray Clemence, Elisha Scott and Grobbelaar. That caused a debate about who is the best Liverpool keeper of all time, but I do not think it is fair to compare us because we are all of our own time and football is constantly changing. All I know is that I'm just happy to be mentioned in the same breath as them because when I first came to the club that was one of my dreams.

Now I have a record that will be there until someone comes along and breaks it, but it is not about comparing myself with anyone else. All I can do is continue to admire them for their achievements and particularly for the trophies that they won. If anything I am still jealous of players like Grobbelaar and Clemence because of the medals they earned during their time with Liverpool. That is what we are in the game for, and I want to taste the kind of success that they had.

I am in a country where the clean sheet is so significant that there is an award for the Premier League keeper who keeps the most each season so it is always a personal target for me. I have been lucky enough to win the Golden Glove award on three occasions, but I also claim a fourth because in my fifth year at Liverpool I got the same number of clean sheets as Petr Cech. Because he had played fewer games than me he was handed the award outright, even though it would have been fairer if we had shared the award.

When I started winning the Golden Glove, Owen Brown, who was Rafa's chief scout in England, started calling me 'The Glove' and the nickname stuck. It is a funny nickname and it is better than the ones I have been given by Carl Spellman, a driver for the club who has become one of my closest friends in England, most of which I couldn't even repeat. It was funny to me being called 'The Glove' because I knew it was just a bit of fun, but whenever I had low points, Owen would be there saying to me: "The Glove will be back. You don't need to worry about anything because you are the best."

I appreciated that more because it was coming from someone who is honest and who always supported me so it is a nickname I really like for this reason. I have a different nickname when I am with the national team – 'Fatty'. It doesn't mean that I am fat and the funny thing is it is something all the Spain players call one another. We call everyone that. I'm more or less average, I'm not fat. It's just a name we use for a bit of fun and it's always used with affection. Honest.

Clean sheets are crucial if teams want to be successful, it isn't just about keepers wanting to break records or win awards. That is why I get so angry when we concede goals that we do not need to, particularly in games that we have already won. There have been a couple of times when I have gone absolutely crazy about letting a goal in and I make no apologies for that. When we beat Man United 3-1 at home in the 2010/11 season we were absolutely coasting at 3-0 up after Dirk scored a hat-trick, but we let Javier Hernandez score a header at the very end of the game and I was furious.

It was the same the previous season when Portsmouth got a consolation goal against us in the 88th minute when we were 4-0 up. At times like this you want to kill everyone because these kinds of goals are so unnecessary. If you are playing a really tight game and an opponent does something that you just can't prevent then fair enough, that's just one of those things.

But when the game is in the bag you have to keep on being professional and see the game out because it gets you into a good routine and gives you the kind of good habits that are really important when the games are tighter and there is more at stake. In a way, it can also be a bit selfish when this happens because it sometimes means that we have kept attacking and looking for goals that we do not need and haven't cared enough about defending. It is a bit selfish on my behalf as well to think like this because I am so pre-occupied with keeping clean sheets.

I consider myself to be a winner and I also have hot blood, Latin blood. This means there will be times when I can explode because I am not happy about something we have failed to do as a team, but I leave my anger on the pitch. I try not to take it into the dressing room and all I do is remind them of the importance of maintaining our concentration for 90 minutes, even if we are winning five or six-nil.

A league championship, a Champions League trophy or a place in Europe can depend on having such high levels of concentration so this is always what we must all aspire to. Anyway, we don't give away cheap goals at Liverpool too often and this is because I have been lucky enough to share a dressing room with professionals who go about things in the proper way.

There are times when we have fall-outs on the pitch, though. Of course there are. We are all passionate and we are all desperate to win so it is totally natural that there will be occasions when our emotions boil over and we take it out on one another. That happened once between Carra and myself and it wasn't even over anything major. It was just a difference of opinion over whether I should knock the ball long or he should give me an angle for a short pass.

I can't remember who we were playing, but I can remember the row we had because it started during the game, carried on in the dressing room and didn't come to an end until we sent each other text messages apologising. Our opponents had been pressing us high up the pitch and the game was tight so the pressure was definitely on. Carra passed the ball back to me and I wanted him to go out wide so I could have the option of playing it back to him instead of just launching it up the pitch. He wanted me to kick it long but that probably would have ended up with the ball being given away so I did not want to do that. I dwelled on the ball a little bit to try and give myself the time to make my mind up, but the opposition striker closed me down and I ended up kicking the ball out wide to where I thought Carra should be, but he wasn't there and it went out of play.

He went crazy at me, screaming at me and telling me I should have just cleared it, and I was screaming back at him. We were like that for fully five minutes shouting at one another and getting our point across. The people who sit in the seats closest to the pitch probably could not believe what they were hearing. We were on the same team but we were arguing with each other with real passion and neither of us was willing to back down. They will have thought it was all over when we stopped, but as soon as we got back into the dressing room we started again and it was even rougher than it had been on the pitch. If anything, the screaming was even louder and all the other players were just totally silent, watching us giving each other hell.

"You really think you're Beckenbauer and you're always trying to play short passes when you should just empty it," he shouted at me. "If I know one thing it's that you definitely aren't Beckenbauer, but just give me a bit of support when I've got the ball so we can try and play instead of just kicking it down the pitch," I responded.

The veins in our necks were bulging, our faces were red with anger and neither of us was going to back down. We both went home, allowed our tempers to get back to normal and then sent each other text messages saying sorry and admitting that we had both lost our heads. That was the end. These things happen in the heat of the moment.

There have been occasions when I have wanted the ground to open up and swallow me because when you mess up as a keeper, the ball almost always ends up in the back of the net. I know that I have made my share of mistakes so before I point the finger at anyone else I have to be aware of that.

As I have got older and become more experienced I have learned to deal better with the difficult moments and I accept that mistakes are an occupational hazard for any footballer, and particularly a keeper. I have learned to get over them but it still hurts a lot at the time.

There have been three or four bad, bad moments I can recall. One of the worst came against Arsenal on the opening day of the 2010/11 season when I bundled a Marouane Chamakh effort into my own goal. That was particularly bad because it came in the very last minute and stopped us from getting our campaign off to a perfect start so I felt really, really guilty about that.

I made an even worse mistake for Spain in Argentina on a night when we lost 4-1 and I could not wait to get off the pitch. I slipped trying to make a clearance and Carlos Tevez ran in to score an easy goal that put them 3-0 up. Seeing as I don't get to make too many starts for the national team it felt like I was messing up a rare chance to show what I can do and even though it was a friendly it devastated me. It was so bad that as I stood there kicking myself for my mistake I started thinking to myself that I did not even want to play the second half. Fortunately – and I use that word purposely – I was taken off at half-time anyway and left to lick my wounds.

The worst mistake I ever made is actually the funniest and the only good thing about it is that Fernando Torres reminds me of the two goals he scored against me in the game, rather than my howler. I was playing for Villarreal against Atletico Madrid at the Vicente Calderon and I came out to control a back pass but the ball went under my foot. As it headed towards the goal I turned and chased after it in a blind panic. I thought I was running really fast but when I saw a replay later it looked like I was running on ice. My feet were moving at 100 miles an hour but I was going nowhere. I got back to the ball just as it got to the goal-line and tried to clear it, but all I did was smash it against the post and into the net. That was unreal and the whole crowd were singing "Reina, Reina, golden boot" to me because I had scored for Atletico. We lost 3-2, and that made me feel even worse about my mistake.

Fortunately, Torres only ever talks about the two he scored past me after coming on as a substitute at half-time. That is what forwards are like. They only ever speak about their goals, even when they could be taking the piss out of you about something else. At least it happened in Spain as well and not so many people in England have seen it. Had it happened here then I might never have escaped it and it is difficult enough to adapt to English football as it is without carrying that kind of stigma with you.

It is easier to recall the mistakes than the great saves. I don't know why that is. Maybe it has to do with the fact that when a keeper makes a mess of things it gets replayed on the television over and over again. There are a couple of positive moments that stick in my mind, though, more for what they meant to the team than to me personally. It wouldn't make much sense to remember a save in a 5-0 defeat because it wouldn't have made any difference whatsoever to the outcome of the game. Anyway, I don't think any keeper would take fond memories from a day when they have conceded five goals.

In my opinion, great saves are usually – but not always – the ones that matter the most. The saves that can make a difference between winning and losing or that help to win a competition, they will always be the most crucial and the ones I cherish the most.

That's why the save I made from Nigel Reo-Coker in the 2006 FA Cup Final stands out. He must have thought he was about to become one of the biggest heroes in West Ham's history, but I denied him. Without that moment there would have been no penalty shoot-out for me to redeem myself for my poor performance in normal time and

Stevie would not have got to lift the cup as he so richly deserved to do-after his heroics in bringing us back into the game. It was a good save but it was made better by the occasion, the timing and the meaning.

There was a similar save from Morten Gamst Pedersen of Blackburn Rovers that gives me a lot of satisfaction because he is a player with an unbelievable left foot and if he connects as well as he can then more often than not it will result in a goal, no matter who the keeper is. On this occasion, he hit one from 25 yards and it was a sweet, sweet strike that was swerving into the top right-hand corner, but I just managed to get there and tip it against the crossbar. I also remember when I denied Marouane Fellaini with a double save in the Merseyside derby at Goodison Park in 2009/10.

Back in Spain, there was one I made for Villarreal against Real Madrid when Roberto Carlos took one of his crazy free-kicks that flies at a million miles an hour and swerves all over the place – but I managed to get to the ball and deflect it onto the post.

That was a funny moment because on the television replays you can see Fernando Hierro, Real's centre-back, jumping up and down, celebrating the goal because he thought there was nothing that could stop it and suddenly there I was.

Those last two were saves for me, ones that I like because of the technique they required rather than what it meant to the team. But I would rather have just one save that makes the difference in a big game than one that looks good on television replays so I would rank the Reo-Coker save in the cup final and the ones I made against Standard Liege in the Champions League qualifiers at the start of the 2008/09 season as being better and much more crucial. They helped us into the group stages, which was very important to the club and the players.

I don't have a save that I would describe as 'the special one' just yet. The one that will stand out above all the others when I get to the end of my career and look back at what I've achieved. That is still to come.

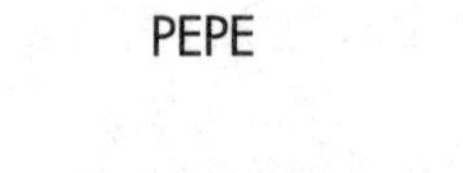

When I first came to this country everyone was talking about me being a penalty expert, but I never saw myself this way. I had done well with penalties on a few occasions in Spain and there had been a couple of times I had got a bit lucky. That seemed to give me a reputation of being some sort of specialist. I never bought into that idea, though, and it is just as well I didn't because after a good start to my Liverpool career when I did well in a couple of shoot-outs, I went a few seasons without saving a single penalty. So much for me being an expert.

It is a funny situation anyway because when I was at Villarreal and Benito Floro was the manager my penalty technique was a cause of conflict. Floro was always telling me that I had to wait as long as I could before making my move, because he believed that would mean I would be able to save all of the badly taken penalties that are going down the middle of the goal or whatever. "You have to wait, see what happens when the ball is struck and then react," he would tell me.

I agreed – but only reluctantly. It wasn't the way that I wanted to do it and it went against all of my instincts, but he was the manager and I had to go with his way of doing things. Inside, though, I was furious. The worst thing about it was that the only way I could show that he was in the wrong was by conceding penalties and I did not want that to happen in any circumstances. No matter how angry I was, my personal pride in the way I go about my job was always going to be greater.

There was one game when his technique really cost us and I will never forget it, even though it was only a pre-season tournament. We were playing Castellon, our neighbours and local rivals, and the game went to a shoot-out. They took five and they scored all five. I didn't save a single one and I went crazy afterwards, throwing anything and everything that I could get my hands on in the dressing room.

That wasn't the way I would usually react and it was out of character for me, but I was so pissed off because I felt that I was being prevented from helping the team by our own manager. I couldn't help myself. "This is shit," I shouted. "I don't do it like that." But it changed nothing. Floro had his way and I had to stick by it or else.

At the end of that season he left, Manuel Pellegrini came in and everything changed. Pellegrini gave me the freedom to do as I liked and he also arranged for me to watch video tapes of our opponents' penalty techniques before games, and this made a massive difference. That season I saved seven out of nine penalties through a combination of guessing the right way to go, being calm and having confidence in my own ability to get to the ball if there is a chance of saving it.

All this talk of being an expert is nonsense because, like every other keeper, I know that if a player takes a perfect penalty there is nothing whatsoever I can do to save it. It is impossible, simple as that. I am not a miracle worker or an acrobat and even if I guess the right way and time my dive to perfection I know that there are shots I cannot do anything about because of their power and accuracy.

I know this because when I have practised penalties in training for club and country I have been powerless to do anything to stop shots that are hammered into the very corner of the goal. Players like Dirk and Stevie for Liverpool and David Villa for the national team are capable of taking perfect penalties and when they do, you just have to wave bye-bye to the ball and congratulate them for their brilliance. They are so good that they can tell you beforehand where their penalties are going to end up and if they say it is going to be hit there, it is going to be there.

These three are probably the best who I come up against on a regular basis these days, but the best I have ever seen is Pep Guardiola. He was a phenomenal penalty taker and when I was a young player at Barcelona I wanted to know how he did it. He took me out onto the training pitch and showed me his technique. I won't reveal what he did that was so special because I still hope to get the chance to do it myself one day.

For all the talk about me saving penalties, the one thing I am desperate to do is to score one. I don't know how or when it will happen, but one day my chance will come and I will do it. I always have a penalty competition with the other keepers in training in which we take five penalties against one another. The winner gets to kick the five balls as far away, and in as many different directions as they like. Then the loser has to go and collect them all. I'm really competitive and I never like to lose, not even in a game in training so it means I have to keep my standards high or else I have to run all over Melwood chasing balls that the other keepers have kicked. I never want to do that at the end of a tough session.

Rafa actually put me on the list to take one when we played Everton in an FA Cup replay at Goodison Park in 2009. It was 0-0 after normal time and with the 30 minutes of extra-time about to run out I thought my big chance was finally about to arrive and that I would get to take a really important penalty.

I had been hammering Rafa and the coaches all the time, telling them that I wanted to be on the list to take a penalty if we ever ended up in a shoot-out. That night against Everton the chances of me getting an opportunity to show what I could do from the spot improved when we were reduced to 10 men after Lucas was sent off.

There would be five penalties and we only had 10 players on the pitch so I had a one in two chance of taking one.

Dan Gosling made all of that immaterial, though, when he scored the winner at the very end of extra time. It was a goal that I could do nothing about because it took at least two deflections. When the ball hit the back of the net, my own dreams of taking a penalty in a massive game did not matter. The pain of losing the Merseyside derby is much greater than any personal disappointment. But I did feel even worse when Xavi Valero told me after the game that I had been on the list to take one.

I also came close to taking a spot-kick at Villarreal when we played Atletico Madrid in the Intertoto Cup. The game went to a shoot-out and I was down to take the last one for us, but we won 4-1 before I got a chance to take mine.

My time will come though and I have absolute confidence in myself that I will score because I know the secret of Guardiola's special technique. If and when that happens I will donate the boots that I scored in to the Liverpool museum as well. It would mean a lot for me to have my boots and my gloves in such a special place.

Paradise Lost

Arjen Robben places the ball on the penalty spot at the Anfield Road End. I am standing in the centre of the goal watching him like a hawk as he backs away towards the edge of the area. Behind him the rest of my team-mates are lined up in the centre-circle with their arms linked around each other, a red blur bleeding into the Kop in the distance. Man for man they are praying for him to miss and are willing me on.

Rafa Benitez is sat on the touchline, cross-legged like a schoolboy, while Jose Mourinho is up on his feet. I do not see this. The Liverpool fans are whistling and jeering as loud as they can to put him off. I do not hear this. In my head I am creating a silence, a space to listen to my instinct as Robben starts his run-up. I look at his body angle and as he strikes the ball with the inside of his left foot, I dive to my left. I feel the leather of the ball strike my glove as I manage to palm it away. Anfield explodes, and I clench my fists with relief. I don't go mad though. After all, this is only Chelsea's first penalty of the shoot-out.

It's hard now, standing aside and watching Xabi Alonso step up. Much harder than standing on the goal-line trying to stop them scoring. All the time you are thinking we could be minutes away from reaching the Champions League Final in Athens, or we could be on our knees with our heads in our hands. You try to fight the intensity of it all and shut it out of your mind and stay focused on your own job.

Xabi scores, slotting the ball under Petr Cech's left-hand side, adding to Bolo Zenden's brilliant first penalty to make it 2-0.

I take my place between the posts again and as Lampard steps up I recall the videos I have studied, but allow myself to watch his body language. I guess the right way, but he puts it over me. There is nothing I can do. 2-1.

I see Stevie stepping up for the next one and I feel confident. There is no-one better to step forward, but the greatest players in the world have all missed penalties. Not this time. He calmly strokes the ball into the right-hand side of the net, sending Cech the wrong way. 3-1.

Geremi is next. As I start diving to my right, I am going the right way, but the ball comes quite central. I throw my left hand up and manage to keep it out. This time I jump up to celebrate a bit more, but again I have to hold back.

When Dirk walks up to take his penalty we know that if he scores, we will be in the final. I have the best view in all of Anfield, just to the left of the penalty area in front of the Centenary Stand at the Anfield Road end in the position where the referee has stationed me, just in case I have to face another penalty.

I crouch down as Dirk has to collect the ball from the far side of the six-yard box before he can put it on the spot. That extra walk can seem like forever and play on your mind. I am hoping and praying that I won't be needed, and he makes sure that I'm not as he smashes the ball into the bottom corner, giving Cech no chance.

We all go crazy. Dirk sets out to run towards the boys in the middle of the pitch, but then he sees me to the side and runs towards me first, pointing at me as I run to him screaming. We hug and then the rest of our team-mates join in, jumping all over us before we run down to the other end of the pitch to celebrate in front of the Kop. As we get there, 'You'll Never Walk Alone' comes on over the tannoy and I think to myself, 'This is why I came here. This is what makes Liverpool so special.'

It was the best night of my Liverpool career. Little did I know that the night of May 1, 2007 would also turn out to be my worst.

I left the stadium absolutely buzzing and as I was driving past the fans who were going out celebrating it made me even more excited. They were all singing in the streets around the ground, piling into the pubs for a party and having a great time. The best thing was I knew it would not be long before I would be enjoying myself just like them.

My team-mates were all heading to the Sir Thomas Hotel in the city centre so that we could all enjoy the moment together and I was on my way to join them. All I had to do first was take my wife and daughter home and drop them off before heading into town. Everything seemed right with the world. How could it not? The feeling I had is one that will live with me forever. I was excited, I was jubilant, I was proud.

As I headed up the road towards my house I told Yolanda that we would remember this night for as long as we live. I wasn't wrong because when we got home I quickly realised something was not right.

The first thing I noticed was that one of our cars was not on the driveway. I made a joke about it, thinking that Yolanda must have moved it. She said to me that she hadn't touched the car and it was then that it dawned on me that it had been taken. That realisation took me from being on top of the world to rock bottom in the blink of an eye, but that wasn't even the worst of it.

When we went inside we discovered that we had been burgled. Someone had got into my home and taken my possessions. It felt like I had been kicked in the bollocks. Whoever it was had actually been ransacking my home while I was making the saves from Robben and Geremi that helped take us to the final in Athens. I know that the break-in happened during the penalty shoot-out because the police told me there was a 40-minute period when the burglars were in the house and that coincided with extra-time and penalties. They probably watched the shoot-out on my television at my home.

They took a safety deposit box as well as the car and though most of the stuff that was taken could be replaced, they also got away with my wife's wedding ring and a couple of watches that meant a lot to us. We never got them back. The box was found but it had been blown up and the car was burned out. I didn't deserve it. Not that night. If they had chosen any other night it wouldn't have been so bad.

I had to stay in and take care of the situation even though I had family and friends over from Spain who wanted to celebrate with me as well. It was a disgrace that they couldn't. We ended up spending the night with the police who were speaking to us until about four o'clock in the morning. The burglars probably do not have a clue about what their actions did to me and they will care even less that they ruined one of the greatest nights of my life.

It was a nightmare but if there was any consolation to take from it, it was that there was nobody at home. My first-born daughter was only two-and-a-half months old and we had taken her to Anfield for her first ever game. It was a bad moment but, for me, it is like football. You have good moments and everything is great, but suddenly you can drop a couple of points and you hit the ground with a bump. The key then is how you respond and I knew that I had to put the break-in out of my mind, just like a bad result. If I'd dwelt on it I would have felt bad for even longer and I did not want the burglars to have an even greater effect on me and my family than they already had.

Where I was fortunate was that I could not have asked for anything better to help me bounce back than the knowledge that we were going to the Champions League Final. We had a good side that season, one that was good enough to make it to the Athens final and defeat some of Europe's best teams on the way.

Maybe we didn't have the kind of outrageously skilful players that some of the other teams had, like a Messi or a Ronaldo, but we more than made up for that with our work rate, togetherness and team spirit. By working together and believing in one another we became really tough to beat and when you play in a knockout competition this is one of the most important qualities you can have.

It was because of this that our opponents respected us. I won't say they feared us because that would be too much, but they definitely had a respect for us because they knew what we could do and that we would never be an easy opponent for them. We also had a growing maturity that came from our collective experience in the competition and this was one of the main reasons why we qualified from a tricky looking group with a game to spare having beaten Galatasaray, Bordeaux and PSV Eindhoven at home.

That wasn't all that normal for us because usually we would have to fight our way out of the group, sometimes waiting until the very last game to qualify. This year we were comfortable and this added to the growing feeling in Europe that we were one of the teams to beat, even though we were not champions of our own country. Some might have continued to view us as an ordinary, average team because we were not setting the world alight in the Premier League, but in Europe it was a different matter, as we proved by reaching the final.

We were accused of concentrating too much on Europe and not enough on the Premier League. It was never like this. It was more because of an accumulation of factors which on their own would not have made a massive difference, but when they came together they made us a force to be reckoned with in the Champions League.

The biggest one was Anfield itself. Mourinho got it spot on when he talked about the power of Anfield. No stadium or the people in it have ever won a football match, it is down to the players to do that, but in all my career in football I have never seen a stadium have as much influence on the outcome of games as Anfield did at that time.

The advantage our supporters give to us on European nights is huge. I say that as someone who has been intimidated by them when I was an opponent and lifted by them when I am on their side. Another factor in our favour is that it is always easier to be successful in 13 or 14 games than it is over an entire season lasting 10 months because you are required to be close to your best only occasionally, rather than week in and week out.

Tactically, we had few peers when it came to two-legged matches. These games suited us in a way that maybe games in the Premier League didn't. European football tends to be more about tactics than physicality, but in England it is usually the other way around and for me our weakness in the Premier League was that we were not always physically strong enough to compete.

We could have been as well organised as it is possible to be, but then we would get undone by a failure to win the first ball and then our opponents picking up the second ball. In England it really can be as basic as that, but in Europe not too many teams play this way.

Most of the teams we came up against in the Champions League tried to use the ball and this meant we could defend against them by sticking to the tactics that Rafa came up with. It is more difficult to do the same thing when you play against a team like Stoke City or Blackburn Rovers and they cross the ball from their own half. People think that it should be easier to combat because it is more basic, but the reality is that it is harder.

We were capable of beating the very best, as we showed on many occasions but if I had to pick one victory as my personal favourite then winning at the Nou Camp in the last 16 that season would take some beating. It is still one of the best results in my club career, if not the best. To win there is very rare, so it gave all of us great satisfaction to beat mighty Barcelona in their own backyard.

For me, it was more than just a win over a great side. The way I left there means it is always massively important for me to get a result against Barcelona whenever I play against them. I was lucky enough to be part of a Villarreal team that beat them three times in a row at home, but winning there with Liverpool was even better. It remains one of the happiest days of my career.

In football you always have a point to prove. It can be to your manager who picks the team, to the critics who doubt you or just to yourself, but in this case it was about showing a former club that I had moved on and had not suffered for leaving. I still have a lot of affection for Barcelona the club, and a lot of the players there are still my friends today, but that night I didn't have any sympathy for any of them. I just wanted to beat them. And we did.

It was like it was fate. You couldn't have written a script for the game that was more incredible than what ended up happening. People outside the club probably thought we had no chance when it came out that Craig Bellamy had attacked John Arne Riise with a golf club, because they will have questioned our team spirit and our focus. That incident was a one-off, though. We didn't usually have this kind of problem and if anything it brought the team even closer together because we were being questioned from outside the club.

It is unbelievable that it happened, of course, but afterwards destiny took control and a week later they both scored at the Nou Camp and we won 2-1.

The result speaks for itself because you don't achieve victories like that at one of the toughest venues in sport unless your team spirit is really strong and you have real togetherness. That night gave us the confidence to win through to the final because once you have beaten Barcelona away all you can do is believe in yourself. It is impossible to do anything else.

Bellamy and Riise took all the headlines for their goals and rightly so, but the game was also memorable for me because I witnessed one of the greatest debuts – and one of the best individual defensive performances – I have ever seen.

Alvaro Arbeloa had only been signed just before the game and when the manager told us the team beforehand, Arbeloa was picked – out of position, at left-back – to mark Lionel Messi. I have to admit I was not that confident in him because it was such a huge task for a new player and being totally honest I was worried about what was about to happen. I need not have worried though because Alvaro coped with one of the best players in the world as if he was born to do it. Wherever Messi was, Alvaro was there, tackling him, taking the ball from him and generally being a pain in the arse. Not many defenders have come out of a duel with Messi and been able to claim to have got the better of him, but Alvaro did. That was one of the main reasons why we were able to win the game.

We probably didn't get the credit we deserved for that victory, but we knew what a great achievement it was. Not too many teams ever win at the Nou Camp and Liverpool are still the only English club to have beaten Barcelona there.

That victory was part of a hat-trick that probably no club will ever repeat. We won at the Nou Camp in 2007, the San Siro in 2008 and the Bernabeu in 2009. Three of European football's greatest cathedrals conquered in consecutive years, an unbelievable achievement for Liverpool and one that was maybe taken for granted at the time. And we deserved every single victory. We were not lucky. We went to the most difficult venues in football and came away with three victories that we had earned.

When I am an old man sitting in my rocking chair boring my grandkids with tales of what I did in the past, the story of how we went to Real Madrid, to Inter Milan and to Barcelona and came away unbeaten will be one that I tell over and over again.

When we drew Chelsea in the semi-finals we all thought, 'Here we go again', but we were also confident because we had beaten them at the same stage a couple of years earlier. It was the same scenario, too, in the sense that we were away at Stamford Bridge first and then at home for the second leg. The only difference was that when we came back to Anfield we were a goal down, meaning we had to score once just to take the tie into extra-time.

Thankfully, Daniel Agger got the all important goal from a free-kick routine he performed with Stevie, finishing low in the corner of Cech's net with a left-footed strike at the Anfield Road end. It was something that we had worked on in training at Melwood in the build-up to the game, but to pull it off in the match itself was something else.

There was another similarity with 2005 in the Anfield atmosphere that night. In the days before the game Carra and Stevie had been telling us that the previous semi-final was the noisiest night they had ever experienced while playing for Liverpool. If the fans were louder that night than they were in 2007 then I can't even imagine what it was like because there were times out there on the pitch that I couldn't even hear myself think.

Even now when I see clips of that night on the television the first thing that hits me is the noise of the crowd. It doesn't matter how many times I have seen the game it is always the same. The eruption from all four stands when Dirk scored the penalty that took us to the final is something that will live with me forever. Burglars may have been ransacking my house at the time, but it still does not detract from

Through the wind and the rain: The weather certainly takes a bit of getting used to in England!

Below: Having fun in training is good for team spirit. Crouchy was always game for a laugh

It was actually sunny when this picture was taken. I must have needed something to cool me down, so I made an ice cream cone for myself

Back at the Nou Camp, and winning with Liverpool in 2007

Oh what a night: Celebrating our away-goals win over Barca with Stevie

Walking out at the Bernabeu for another victory to be proud of back on home soil in 2009

The penalty saves that helped us to Athens. Little did I know, the best night of my career would also be my worst

AC Milan had the luck in Athens that night and Inzaghi was the hero. We were the better side, but I suppose it was fate playing its hand after the way the drama had unfolded in Istanbul

I really believed I could bring a European Cup winner's medal back home for my father who had lost in the final himself back in the Seventies, but it wasn't to be

Enjoying a meal with the wives back home in Spain at the Euro 2008 victory party – myself, Fernando and David Villa. Yolanda was pregnant with Luca, who didn't turn up on the eve of the final after all

Trying to make an impression playing for Spain

My coaching soulmate: Jose Ochotorena

A lap of honour with the European Championship trophy and then it's party time at the homecoming

At least they didn't drop me off the bus like Madrid did with the Copa del Rey trophy

Left: Puyol lets his crazy hair down and so does Fernando

This is my famous Camarero routine, check it out on YouTube

It really was a never-ending party with singing and dancing that lasted for about 48 hours

our achievement in getting through to Athens – even if it does sour my memories of the night.

The night after we knocked Chelsea out, Man United played AC Milan in the other semi-final. In my eyes, United were the stronger team and I was expecting to play them in the final. Had I had my pick I would have chosen Milan because they were an older team and I thought we would have a better chance of beating them.

That doesn't mean I wouldn't have liked to meet United in the final because I would. It would have been the dream final then and it would still be a dream final now. It would be one of the biggest games football has seen and the beauty of it would be that the stakes would be incredibly high. They always are for a final, of course, but it would be even more so when the game features two of the biggest rivals, not just in football, but in sport. Lose and it would be a nightmare. Win and it would be one of the greatest nights in your history. One way or another it would be forever; pain or pleasure, desolation or delight. On this occasion I was happy with the idea of facing Milan and I imagine it was the same for all of the players and the supporters.

We looked forward to the final in Athens in the belief that we could win again. We were a better side than the Liverpool team that had won the Champions League two years earlier, with more experience and quality in the team, and if anything Milan had deteriorated since Istanbul with an ageing side and a few players that were not of the same quality as their predecessors.

It was just a case of preparing ourselves and making sure we were in the right frame of mind. Obviously, the manager has to do everything he can to get his strongest possible team on the field for such a big game. There was talk that I could have been rested on a few occasions, but I wanted to play to try and keep more clean sheets because I was in the running for the Golden Glove award. My ambition could have cost me because when we went to Fulham a couple of weeks before the final I was one of only a few players who Rafa did not leave out and I picked up an injury that could have ruled me out for Athens.

I went to claim a cross but as I caught the ball my thumb got bent back. It was really, really painful. My first thought was, 'Shit, I could miss the final' and I ended up being a doubt until just a couple of days before the game.

In the end, I had to play the final with my thumb strapped up. It meant I could only train the day before the game which wasn't ideal. I don't think it made any difference because I could not have done much about either of Milan's goals, but it certainly wasn't the perfect preparation that I had been hoping for.

It wasn't just me that struggled with the preparations. When we arrived in Athens in the days leading up to the final we ended up having to change hotels because the one that had been booked for us was no good. I don't know whether it was the club that booked it or if it is one that UEFA had designated to us, but it was not what we were expecting and we had no choice but to move to another one.

Again, this wasn't ideal but it made no difference in the grand scheme of things. When you are playing in a match on this scale you could sleep on the streets or in the stadium beforehand and it wouldn't matter. The excitement, passion and importance of the occasion would always mean that you could forget everything else and just get on with the game. We could not make excuses about hotels or sore thumbs for what followed. That had nothing to do with these minor distractions.

We really believed that we were going to win as well. If you go into a final thinking that you are going to lose then what the hell are you doing there? You may as well go home, not play the game and just watch your opponent collect the trophy on TV. Finals are to be won and we were confident that we would do that. We were the better team on the night, too, playing some really good football. We had some chances in the first half but could not take them.

For all our dominance it was frustrating that we went in 1-0 down at half-time after Filippo Inzaghi had deflected a free-kick past me with his chest. I don't know if he meant it. I doubt that he did. All the same, we still felt at the interval that we could get back into the game and go on and win it.

We also knew that because of what had happened in Istanbul two years earlier we still had a big psychological advantage over Milan. They could go two or three goals ahead of us, but still they would fear history repeating itself with us making a crazy comeback. We did not want to have to do this of course, but all the same it was nice to know that they could never feel secure when they were playing against us. Inzaghi got a second goal in the 82nd minute and I can still remember the noise in the stadium when he scored it. A dramatic sound effect was played over the tannoy. That sound will live with me forever.

Despite being 2-0 down, we kept on going and when Dirk got a goal back late on it looked like another miracle could be about to happen but it was too late, and Milan held on.

There is no doubt about it, losing was devastating even if I did not realise it straight away. Everything happened so quickly. It is hard to explain the emotions of the time because the build-up to the game and the action itself passed in the blink of an eye.

Because I was so wrapped up in the moment and so focused on winning the game I didn't stop to take in the enormity of the situation. When I look back on it now I realise that it could have been my last ever Champions League Final, my one and only. I didn't see it like that at the time. It was just another game and if I am honest I was probably expecting Liverpool to be in more finals in the years that followed.

Had I known then what I know now, I probably would have savoured the occasion more because just to get to the final is an incredible achievement. It is so difficult because it is so competitive and the standard of your opponents is so high. I was there with my Liverpool team-mates in 2007 and we were so close to achieving glory that it was almost as if we could reach out and touch the trophy. We could not get our hands on it though. It was Milan's turn to lift it and our turn to taste defeat.

Looking back, they certainly got a bit of luck. Maybe after what happened in Istanbul, fate went in their favour and Inzaghi's first goal started people thinking that their name was on the cup this time. Then when we were controlling the game in the second half they got a second and that turned the game totally in their favour. I know people say "what if we had done this differently" or "what if we'd done that" but it is difficult to see it in this way because we were the better team, we gave everything we had to give. It just wasn't our night.

It is a worse feeling when you lose a big game after being on top, especially a major final, as it is so difficult to be the better team on occasions like this, so when it does happen you have to try and make the most of it. Football isn't always fair. The best team does not always win on the day and just as Milan were the beneficiaries in 2007 they could claim to have been the victims in 2005. There is no point us looking for hard luck stories, what we should do is enjoy our achievement in getting to the final even if we could not win the trophy.

In fact, never mind the final, that season we could have gone out in the qualifying round when Maccabi Haifa gave us a proper run for our money back in August, 2006. It was a strange situation with the second leg being played in Kiev because of problems in Israel and we struggled to impose ourselves after winning the first leg 2-1 at Anfield. We thought we were safe when Peter Crouch increased our aggregate lead, but Roberto Colautti brought Maccabi back into the game after I was unable to hold on to a shot by Xavier Anderson.

That set the nerves jangling because we knew that one more goal from them would take us into extra-time although it was pretty normal for us to have our qualification hopes on a knife edge because we seemed to do the same thing almost every year. They had one big chance to put us under more pressure, but I managed to tip Colautti's shot over the bar and we went through – just.

If you look at any team that gets to a final there is usually a turning point on the way. Probably one of the best examples is Stevie's famous goal against Olympiakos in December 2004 because without that Liverpool wouldn't have been anywhere near Istanbul, never mind have the greatest night in their history there.

That's the way football is. You have big moments and you have to remember the ones that have gone your way when you are disappointed by the ones that have gone against you. That is why I refuse to get too upset about losing the final. I wish we hadn't and I would give anything to change the result in our favour, but I know also that when I look back on the earlier rounds there were times when things went our way so I can't complain when they went against us in the final. Well, not too much anyway.

It is always going to be a regret that I got to the final and then, like my father, did not win it. But the pain of defeat didn't hit me straight away. I know this because after I got back to the hotel I made love to my wife. I was happy because Liverpool had shown once again that we were one of the most important teams around. In hindsight, now I know that I was just covering up my pain. I had convinced myself not to feel too bad but deep down inside I must have been hurting. I know this because every single time I see those pictures of Paolo Maldini holding that beautiful big-eared trophy over the balcony at the Olympic

Stadium the first thing I think is 'that could have been me'. To come so close and then miss out has to be painful, but I guess that it doesn't really hit you until later. Maybe your body has its own anaesthetic to protect you from feeling too much pain straight away. Maldini did not need another winner's medal anyway. He already had enough. And his dad, Cesare, had one as well. Surely they could have allowed the Reina family to have just one?

In the week before the final we all did media interviews at Anfield and the press all wanted to ask me about what it meant to be following in my father's footsteps and I could not hide the pride that I had. The Reinas, the Maldinis and Manuel and Manolo Sanchis of Real Madrid are the only fathers and sons ever to play in the European Cup Final so there is a lot for us to be proud of. I told the press that after what happened in the 1974 final it had to be my family's turn to win the trophy, but I was wrong. It was Maldini's turn again.

I cannot feel any ill will towards them or be jealous of them though. My only feeling is that I have to say good luck to Maldini and his father. They were brilliant players, especially Paolo, who was one of the greatest in his position. His career is an example to everybody. No-one could begrudge them their success, even if their pleasure was our pain.

My father continually told me that to lose a final you have to be involved in one and after the game in Athens he said something to me which really made me stop and think: "No matter what happens now, you have played in one of the biggest finals, just like I did in 1974," he told me. "Maybe now the European Cup Final owes one to the Reina family and we will get it one day, but for now you have to be proud of what you have achieved and look forward." I know he meant what he said and it meant a lot to me, but I also know that he was suffering inside as a result of our defeat.

As a father myself, I know now how he must have been feeling when he spoke those words to me. It can't have been easy for him to support me like he did because I later discovered that he broke down in tears when we lost. He had been commentating for Spanish radio and he was so upset by our defeat that he could not hide his feelings.

He was right in telling me to look ahead and to forget about the past because just a year later I was part of the Spain squad that won the European Championships and the Reina family had another winners' medal to add to our collection. We may not have won them all and we may also have had our disappointments, but we're not doing too badly.

Born Winners

It was the night before the Euro 2008 final and as usual half of the Spain squad were in my room at the team hotel in Austria. It was an opportunity for the players who would not be starting the game to get together, relax and have a bit of a laugh. Iker Casillas was with us, even though he was definitely going to play in the final but he is so laid back that he doesn't need too much sleep. David Villa was there as well because he was injured and had been ruled out of the final.

Someone suggested we should have a game of cards just to pass the time. I pulled a deck out and we all began playing. Everything was going great until about midnight when Villa got a call on his mobile phone. He took himself away from the table to take the call so that we could carry on playing. I could see that he was getting a bit agitated while he was on the phone. I didn't think too much about it and convinced myself that he was just telling a friend or a relation about how disappointed he was to be missing such a massive game. When he sat back down and picked up his cards again he started acting really strange, and was sweating. It would come round to his turn to make his play with the cards and he would just be sat there looking blank.

"What the fuck's going on?" I asked him. "Just play your cards will you." This went on and on and on until he finally came clean.

"Okay, okay, okay. I have to tell you Pepe, your wife is about to give birth. I was told not to tell you because it could distract you, but I cannot do it. Yolanda is having contractions and she is on her way to the hospital in Vienna. I have tried to hold out, but I cannot keep something like this from you."

No wonder Villa had been sweating and acting weird. He had done well to keep something like that to himself for as long as he had, especially seeing as every time he looked up from his cards he could see me glaring at him. The news stunned me, it was bound to, and my mind started racing as I wondered if everything was okay and whether or not Yolanda was at the hospital yet. I rang her and she told me that she was nearly there. Yolanda was eight months pregnant and the idea had always been that she would have our second baby back in Spain, but babies do not stick to plans. They have a habit of arriving when they are good and ready, rather than when you are expecting it to happen.

This was our second child and we had already been surprised by the timing of the arrival of our first one a year earlier. It would have been par for the course if this one came into the world on the day of the Euro 2008 final, a whole month before the due date.

After she got to the hospital, Yolanda went in to see the doctors and got checked over. They did a thorough examination and decided that she was not going to have the baby there and then, but if she was determined to have it back home she would be best to fly to Madrid the following morning because it could arrive at any time. So Yolanda caught a flight on the day of the game while I stayed with my team-mates. It was a big blow for me that she wasn't there for the final because she had been there for the whole tournament.

If I am honest, though, it never crossed my mind to go with her back to Spain even though she had been having contractions. In a normal situation then obviously I wouldn't have thought twice about it. I would have just packed my bags and went with her, no questions asked. But I wasn't missing the final for anything! If there is one thing that you can miss the birth of your baby for then surely it is the final of the European Championships?

I had been at the birth of our first child and that was a wonderful experience, something that will live with me forever. This time I had to put my job and my team first. It will probably be the only time in my entire life that I do this and that shows how important the final was to me even though I knew I would not be playing. At the time it was the biggest night of my career and I had to be there for it. I am glad I was. Not only did Spain win our first major trophy since 1964, the baby did not arrive for another month. I definitely made the right decision.

One of the hardest things about being at a major tournament is that you get to see so little of your wife and family. It is the same for everyone, of course, and I come to terms with it by telling myself that it is one of the few occasions in my life when my family comes second. I am lucky that Yolanda understands this even though there are times when I am away for a month-and-a-half. At some points the monotony and the routine can really get to you, but I have really enjoyed being at every single tournament that I have been involved in. The Confederations Cup, Euro 2008, the World Cup. You name it, I've loved it. Surrounded by my mates, playing football, having a laugh – what is there not to like?

I know some players do not enjoy being away and I understand the reasons why, but I would not miss a tournament even if I was just going to be with the squad rather than a part of the first XI. From the minute I get out of bed to the minute I go to sleep at the end of the day I try to be positive with myself and everyone around me. Sometimes I can be over positive and the other lads will say: "What the hell are you on about, there's no point in making jokes now." But I still do it because I would rather be accused of being too happy than being someone who walks around with a long face all the time. That's the way I have always been and it's the way I will be all my life. What's the point in being miserable? I have nothing to be angry with the world about.

The press in Spain probably do not realise it but they were one of the main reasons why we arrived at Euro 2008 with a siege mentality, determined to fight for one another and not worry about what anyone else said outside of our group. They had given us some stick in the year leading up to the tournament, but instead of causing problems for us, it actually brought everyone even closer together.

After we lost two games against Sweden and Northern Ireland, the criticism was severe. According to the press we were all bad, Luis Aragones was 'stupid' and not good enough to be the manager of the national team and so on. One paper carried a front page with a picture of Aragones and a headline saying 'Imbecile'. I couldn't believe what I was seeing and how strong the over-reaction was to a couple of defeats. They could not have been more wrong. Aragones was one of the main reasons why we won the European Championships and he built the foundations for winning the World Cup two years after. He made us stronger as a squad and as individuals. This meant that when we got battered by the media we actually came through it with our belief and our team spirit enhanced.

Spain's record since 1964 meant that we could not afford to get too excited about our chances of winning the tournament beforehand. If anything, it created a dark humour amongst us with every victory being followed by jokes from the players about doing what Spain always do and getting knocked out in the next round, just when things are looking good. It was our way of coping with the pressure of playing for a country which is desperate for success after so long without it. It ended up working well. If we had taken it more seriously than that then maybe the pressure of carrying a nation's hopes would have got to us more and it could even have affected us on the pitch. One of the strengths of our group is our ability to have a laugh and make light of even the most serious situations and this really helped us.

I only played one game in the entire tournament and thankfully we won it because I wouldn't have wanted my sole appearance to have ended in defeat. There was a time in the game though when it looked like that could happen. It was our final group game and having already qualified for the knockout stage Aragones decided to change the entire team to give the players who were not involved in his regular starting XI a chance to play, just to make sure we had some minutes under our belts in case we were needed later in the competition.

We were playing Greece and we went a goal down when Angelos Charisteas scored a header past me from a set-piece routine. There was nothing I could have done to stop it, but as a keeper you are always disappointed when you concede any goal, so I was desperate for us to come back and win the game. Ruben De La Red got us back into the game just after the hour and then Daniel Guiza got us the points with a really good header two minutes from time. Even though it was a dead rubber for us, the result was an important one because it showed that we had quality throughout the squad and we were not just relying on the first-choice players.

Eleven changes had been made to the team that played the previous game and we had still managed to get a victory. This really helped our belief and gave us extra confidence.

Looking back, there is also a poignancy about that game because just a few months after being one of Spain's heroes, De La Red discovered a heart problem which meant he could never play football again. That is absolutely tragic for him. He deserved so much better than that because he was a really good player and a great person. He had so much to offer Spain and he would have been involved in the squad for years to come, but his health intervened and ended his career when he was in his prime. When he scored his goal against Greece it must have been a dream come true to make his mark for his country in a major tournament. Soon afterwards his career was put on hold when he collapsed at a Copa del Rey game in October 2008. He never played again and was forced to retire from the game aged just 25 in 2010. He did not deserve that and whenever Spain has any success we all know that we are fortunate to be involved because you never know when fortune can turn against you as it did for De La Red.

I never take my career for granted anyway. I know that I am very lucky to play football, and even luckier to play for Liverpool and for Spain. But it doesn't do me any harm to be reminded of this every now and again and whenever I think of what happened to De La Red I get all the perspective I need. It is exactly the same when I visit Alder Hey Children's Hospital at Christmas with my Liverpool team-mates and see kids of three or four years old who have cancer. That makes me realise just how fortunate I am. How can I complain about injuries or not playing or anything like that when there are people who have real problems in their lives?

We played really well in the first three games, but it was when we beat Italy in the quarter-finals that we really started to believe that this was going to be our year. The result was brilliant in itself. Italy were the reigning world champions, and we had defeated them after being the better side. The most important thing was the manner in which our victory was achieved. We won on penalties, the way Italy themselves had won so many crucial matches in the past, and in doing so we had beaten our opponents at their own game and proven to ourselves and everyone else that we had the mental toughness to come through even the most testing situation. If anyone asks me when the Spain team came of age I always think back to this game. It was a turning point for us and we never looked back after that day. Had we won the game in normal time then that would have been nice, but we gained more psychologically by winning the shoot-out than we probably would have done by recording a comfortable 2-0 win.

The national team had a mental weakness for many years in that whenever we got to the finals of a major tournament we would get knocked out in the last eight. It was a mental barrier that we struggled to overcome, but we managed to break through that wall when we beat Italy that night in Vienna. From that point on it was like a weight had been lifted off all of our shoulders – we had got past the quarter-finals, beaten really difficult opponents and most importantly we had proven that we had the bottle when it was needed most. The fear that had dogged the national team for years had gone and we were able to move on with the belief that this really was going to be our year. Something changed on that night and Spanish football would never be the same again. The days of Spain expecting to win tournaments, only to fall apart in the last eight were over.

Spain were very similar to England in that whenever we got to a major tournament, the expectation was always that we would win it. The people and the press would be over-optimistic and then when the national team got knocked out they would be over-pessimistic. It was black and white, never grey. That was part of the problem because the team was always under pressure due to expectations that were always going to be difficult for them to live up to. It happens with every team at club and international level. Whatever your target is you start the season or the competition thinking that you are going to achieve it, but sometimes after a few games you have to revise your targets. That is why it is so important that you go game by game and not look too far ahead. That was something I learned when I was at Villarreal and at Liverpool I know people can get bored when we say we will take every game as it comes but this is the way it has to be. There is no point in getting ahead of ourselves and then being unbelievably disappointed if we fail to achieve our targets.

So after reaching the Euro 2008 semi-finals the talk inevitably turned to us winning the competition, even though we still had to face a Russia team in the semi-finals that had just eliminated Holland in the previous round. But we also knew that we had beaten them 4-1 during the group stage so we had reason to be confident.

The combination of momentum and belief is a potent one in tournament football and we had both heading into the semi-finals. As I looked on from the bench at the Ernst Happel Stadion in Vienna that night I could only have sympathy for Russia. In the kind of form that we were in by that stage of the competition it was hard to imagine too many teams being able to cope with Spain. We won the game 3-0 with goals from Xavi, Guiza and David Silva and the margin of victory only added to the feeling that this was going to be our year. We would be up against Germany in the final, a really good team with a history of winning trophies going back decades, but not even that could change the way we felt. We were expecting to win and nothing was going to change our minds about that.

The big advantage that we had was that we were winners already. Just by getting to the final we had ensured that Euro 2008 was a major success and our achievement was being celebrated at home almost as if we had won the entire competition. So we went into the final with nothing to lose. Well, apart from the final itself, obviously. The pressure had been lifted and the weight of history was no longer holding us back. This was a new Spain, one that could not be burdened by a failure dating back to 1964 and one which had shown itself to have both the quality and the mental strength to come through every single test that had come our way.

When you go into a final with this kind of feeling then it is almost impossible to think that you are going to lose. Germany saw things differently, of course, and they knew that their experience could be important on such a massive occasion. Even that did not concern us too much because of the way we had performed throughout the competition. I hope it does not sound arrogant because that is not the way we were at all. If anything, we were totally humble. We were always respectful of all of our opponents, but our confidence was fuelled by the way we had played so far. We had no reason to fear anyone, even a team like Germany with a great history of success.

Throughout the tournament we had been really good defensively and special credit for that must go to Carles Puyol, Carlos Marchena and Marcos Senna, our holding midfielder, who, for me, was our outstanding player at Euro 2008. Wherever you looked in the team there was real quality. Alonso, Xavi, Iniesta, Torres, Villa and so on and so on. Because of this we were able to do a great job in the final and we deserved to defeat Germany 1-0.

Fernando's winning goal was a massive moment for him and for all of us. As the move developed it did not look like he would even be in a position to score because it did not seem possible that he would reach the through ball from Xavi. But he managed to get goal side of Philipp Lahm and once he got into his favourite position with the goalkeeper rushing out at him there was no doubt in anyone's mind about what would happen next. He flicked the ball like only he can do, spinning it over the keeper and making it bounce off the turf until it touched the back of the net. I was jumping all over the place, going absolutely crazy. It was the kind of goal I had seen him score so many times for Liverpool and it put him in the history books as the player who scored the goal that ended Spain's 44-year trophy famine.

That it was my friend and my Liverpool team-mate who created history made it even more special. I hugged him after the game and I told him: "You are in the history books now. You have done something incredible of which you can be proud for the rest of your career and for the rest of your life." Fernando is very humble but he probably already knew what he had done. He won't have needed me to tell him but I told him anyway.

When England beat Germany 5-1 in 2001 I can remember the headlines that followed, with 'Germany 1 – Liverpool 5' being one of the most common because all of England's goals had been scored by Liverpool players – Michael Owen, Emile Heskey and Stevie. I thought that was funny at the time and when Spain won Euro 2008 you could say we achieved something similar because we had four Liverpool players in our squad. There was Alonso, Torres, Arbeloa and myself. That is more than either Barcelona or Real Madrid had so the club can be really proud of this.

I know the Liverpool fans were happy because we were the second choice for many of them – and actually the first choice for those Reds supporters who do not care for the national team. With England having failed to qualify they were all supporting us and that is a special feeling to have. All four of us were getting messages telling us about the people in pubs going crazy when Spain scored goals and about Spain flags flying from the balconies of flats in town. Even Carra got behind us, having his restaurant covered in Spain flags, although I suspect he was trying to sell a few extra pizzas on the back of our success! So we knew all about the backing we were getting from the people of Liverpool, even though we were many miles away in Austria. After we won we all got bombarded with texts from friends and team-mates back in our adopted home town. Even Rafa sent us one. "Congratulations, RB," it said. Typical Rafa. No excitement, just straight to the point.

It was the biggest moment of my career. The country went crazy and the party when we got back was unbelievable. This was only natural. Spain had waited so long for success and suffered so much in the years when we could not win trophies and this was our big moment. The hoodoo had come to an end and the sense of relief was almost as great as the sense of joy. From the moment we won Euro 2008 we all knew that we could win again and that our success in Austria would not be a one-off. This wasn't the end of a journey – it was the start of one.

It felt even more special because we had waited so long for our success, but my feelings of joy and pride at our achievement was tinged with sadness and one very personal regret. Yolanda was not the only one who was not present who I would have loved to have been there.

But it wouldn't be until the celebrations after the game that my grandfather's absence would really hit me.

Party Man

"Here with you today, a genuine man without hands, the guy who made the dream possible by stopping penalties in the quarter-final, the Real deal, Iker!" That was how I introduced Iker Casillas, Spain's Euro 2008-winning captain, on stage at the Plaza Colon in Madrid as we showed off the wonderful trophy in our own capital. A crowd of one million people was gathered in front of me, hanging on my every word. I may only have played a bit-part role in Austria, but I was the centre of attention for the celebrations in Spain.

I learned 'Camarero' when I was at Villarreal and as soon as I got to know it I loved it. It is hard to translate into English but it is basically a celebratory routine to introduce your team-mates and whenever I have performed it, everyone has loved it. That night in Madrid I went through my brothers from the national team one by one and the crowd lapped it up. Even now when I look back at the video footage of my performance I get a buzz out of watching it. That was a crazy night, one of the greatest of my entire life. I see myself on that stage bringing out the players, shouting their numbers to the crowd before telling a little story about them with a microphone in my hand.

"The number two. The authentic and genuine longest sausage in the world – Raul Albiol."

"He is Tarzan, the man who eats pineapples whole – Carles Puyol."

"Here you have him, the man who struggles with the King of the Sky, the man who doesn't go well with the sunshine – Andres Iniesta."

"He's like a son of Johan Cruyff, the true and genuine Xabi Alonso."

"In tribute to our beloved Antonio Puerta, rest in peace, the legendary Sergio Ramos."

"And wearing number 23, a humble speaker, who is here with you with all his heart – Pepe Reina."

I went through the same routine for every one of our players and only finished after I had introduced our manager as: "The wise man of Hortaleza, the man who has made it possible to win the European Championship, the true, unique, Luis Aragones."

I was milking it, enjoying every single moment and the following day the Spanish papers crowned me king of the homecoming. I am shameless but that's the way I am. The people who know me were not surprised by what I did. My team-mates wanted me to do it, so I did.

The truth, though, is that I did not have a clue what I was doing. I'd had a few drinks and all I could say was whatever came naturally to me. This was not a prepared speech, it was anything but. All I was doing was having a laugh and a joke and it turned into one of the most memorable experiences of my life.

Everyone saw the funny side of me that night. I was a comedian for a million people in Madrid and many more watching on their televisions in Spain and all around the world. But what they did not see was what happened afterwards, the other side of me that only my closest friends and relations get to see. We were taken to the bus to travel to a restaurant to continue our celebrations, but as I was getting on I broke down in tears. I was crying like a baby. The reason? My grandfather was not there to enjoy the moment with me.

I was surrounded by my team-mates, my brothers in arms, but even that was not enough when the one person I wanted to be there more than any other was not. For him to die just a few months before the greatest moment of my career was one of the cruellest things that could ever happen. He deserved to be there. He deserved that moment. He was the reason I was there. After everything he had been through – supporting me in the worst weather, putting an arm around my shoulder when I needed it, coming to games even though he was in pain with his hip – this should have been his time to enjoy what I had achieved because none of it would have been possible without him.

Just thinking about that and the sacrifices he had made for me made me sad and by the time we got to the restaurant I was so upset that Fernando and Villa had to try and calm me down. They were both hugging me and telling me that it would be okay, but I just had this overwhelming feeling that it wasn't fair that my grandfather could not be there with us.

My grandfather was from Cordoba but he had to leave his family behind when he was young to go and work in Venezuela as a chef. That was typical of the man. Obviously he would have preferred to stay at home with his family, but he knew that they needed money so he went all the way to South America to try and support them.

My father was only very young at the time and when my grandfather came back to Cordoba he brought a football back for him. It was his first ever ball. It would be too simplistic to say that without that present my father maybe would not have gone on to become a footballer and that then I wouldn't have either. But that was the moment that my father's love for football really began because the gift was so precious to him and he passed that love on to me. That is just one reason why I have to be grateful to my grandfather. There are so many more.

As I came away from the stage in Plaza Colon, I had a picture in my head of him limping to the side of the pitch on a freezing cold day, coming to see me play for one of Barcelona's junior teams. He looked like a human beanbag because he had this coat which had a hood connected to it that covered his face. All I could see was his eyes. It had three holes to allow him to watch training and also to breathe. That was it. I would see him blink and I would see the hot breath come out of his mouth and hit the cold air, but that was all.

He was like the man in the mask. He looked really funny in some ways but by going to those lengths to watch me play, it showed how much I meant to him. He could have stayed at home, taking things easy and enjoying being in a warm house on a freezing cold day. But he didn't, he came to give me his support. For that alone, he deserved to be with me for my greatest moment.

He was the kind of person who never saw the bad in anyone. Even when I made mistakes he would pretend that he hadn't seen them to protect me. It's difficult to put into words exactly what he meant to me. The best way I can do it is by saying that he meant everything to me and he still does. I am always aware of my debt to him, but that night I felt it even more and I went from smiles to tears within seconds.

When I think of the celebrations we enjoyed after winning Euro 2008, it brings back some of the best memories of my life. After we had won the final in Vienna, Aragones asked us how we wanted to celebrate. He gave us the choice of staying with our families in the Austrian capital or going back to the national team base in Innsbruck. It was a difficult decision so we ended up putting it to the vote. Twenty-one of us voted to go back to Innsbruck, and only two voted to stay in Vienna.

It was the right choice. We had just won Euro 2008 as a team and the best way to celebrate that was to party as a team. This wasn't a snub to our families or anything like that. We really appreciated their support and everything they had ever done for us, but this was a moment for the team to be together. Aragones was delighted with our choice. "Thank God for that," he said. "If I win the European Cup then my children can wait to see me. I go with my team-mates and that is that. We have plenty of time to see them."

It ended up being a crazy night. Drinking and buzzing and more drinking and buzzing – the way it should be after something as special as winning one of football's biggest prizes. I actually ended up being drunk for 48 hours. It's not something that I am proud of but if ever there was a time to do it, it was then.

On the flight back to Madrid we drank all the beer that we had and Puyol had to go to the back of the plane to get us some more. As the plane entered Spanish territory we began to chant some of the phrases and sayings that Aragones had come out with so many times. We were also chanting, "We won't play without Luis," because he was leaving us to take a job with Fenerbahce. That moment remains the greatest connection I can ever remember a group of players having with their coach and it was the highlight of Euro 2008 for me. Aragones was touched and he tried to hide his emotion with laughter. "What sons of bitches you are," he said to us. "You remember everything!"

After the homecoming at Plaza Colon we held a dinner and party at the Buddah Bar, a club on the outskirts of Madrid. We knew that it would not be long before the location of our private celebration became public so we decided to create a password that our family and friends could use to get in.

The one we chose was "El Galgo de Lucas," a name that meant something only to us. It related to Aragones' last team talk with us before the final when he came up with a wonderful way of reminding us that in sport, only the winners are remembered. "Men, finals are to be won, everyone forgets the runner-up," he said. "Don't be like the greyhound of Lucas which decided to have a shit when it should have been chasing the hare." We all burst out laughing and we named the password in honour of that unforgettable speech.

I love being at the heart of the celebrations and having fun. It is the same in the Liverpool dressing room. I always try to have a laugh with my team-mates.

There are plenty of others in the squad who are similar to me. Glen Johnson, Andy Carroll and Dirk Kuyt are all really funny and so is Stevie, but we all know when to have a laugh and when it is important to be serious.

I always try to take control of the music as well but most of the lads hate my taste. During the 2010/11 season I was in charge of the music after our games and I was playing all kinds of great Argentinian and Spanish tunes, but it didn't go down well with everyone. So be it.

I love being in the dressing room and the only place where I am happier is on the pitch. My passion for playing is born of my love for football. I am desperate to do well in every single game I play and I want to enjoy every single moment so when the team does something positive I show my emotion.

It is not something I think about – far from it. Sometimes I look at videos of games and I am surprised when I see my own reactions. There is never anything premeditated about any of my celebrations.

One incident that everyone always talks about was when David Ngog scored against Man United in October, 2009 and I raced almost the full length of the pitch to celebrate with him. On that occasion everything came together at once. We had lost our previous four games so we badly needed a good win and Ngog's 90th-minute goal secured us the three points against our biggest rivals.

I was like a champagne cork out of a bottle. It is funny when I look back it at now because it is probably the quickest I have ever run, but I did give myself a head start. Everyone thinks I started on my goal-line but I didn't. I actually started walking towards the halfway line as the move built up, getting closer and closer all the time. So when David put the ball in the net I was almost up with play. If he'd hit the bar I might even have been close enough to score the rebound. It was a really happy moment for us and I did go a bit crazy, but I was only able to run past other players because they had all played a full match and were really tired.

That is why I play football. Moments like these that I am able to share with my team-mates are so special. There is nothing better than allowing your emotions to come to the surface and there is no better time for that to happen than when you have just enjoyed a great moment, either by scoring a goal, winning a game or securing a trophy. It is like a drug and you want it more and more. I am fortunate to be at a club and to be part of a national squad that give me the chance to enjoy so many highs.

Away from the pitch, when the occasion allows, I like going into Liverpool city centre for a meal with my family or even a rare night out. I have been in most of the top clubs and bars in town, not often by any means, but I have visited them. Mosquito, The Newz Bar, Baby Blue, Circo, The Sir Thomas and so on.

I always enjoy going out in town because the Liverpool people really know how to enjoy themselves and have a good time. In some cities a night out can be quite normal and maybe even quiet, but in Liverpool it is a real event and this suits me perfectly. Everyone has a proper laugh and even people who don't know each other at all can find themselves buzzing off each other. That doesn't happen in too many other places, especially in England.

My only complaint is the whisky. I do not drink it much, but when I do have one I want it to be really good. I have found it really difficult to find a bar that serves a top class whisky in Liverpool. It isn't served the same way as it is in Spain. The ice is different, the Coke is different, even the whisky itself is different. It just doesn't taste the same. That is why I drink beer on the very rare occasions when I do go out.

It didn't involve whisky, but I can still remember the first time I got drunk. I could never forget it no matter how much I might want to. It is something that most teenagers do, have too much beer and then regret it, and I was no different. The worst thing for me was not even the amount that I drunk – it was the type of drink.

I was only 13 years old and I was back in Madrid with my friends enjoying a break from La Masia. We were all together, just doing the kind of stuff that kids do and we all decided that the time had come to get drunk. We got a bottle of red wine and a bottle of Coke and mixed them together. It might sound a horrible cocktail but it is a very popular drink in Spain. We call it Calimocho, and the young people in particular like it a lot. But my first experience of it wasn't a good one. If it is ice cold, Calimocho can be okay, but if it is warm then it isn't the best. We had it almost hot.

We made things bad for ourselves. For me it was even worse because I had not had any dinner so I was drinking it on an empty stomach. I only had three glasses of it but that was enough to make me really drunk. My head was spinning, I was struggling to stand up and I felt sick. I managed to get myself home and had some dinner, but that only made things worse so I went up to bed to try and sleep it off because I was supposed to be playing football the following day.

As I lay down it felt like my bedroom was spinning around me so I closed my eyes as tight as I could and wished that I could stop, but it was too late. The damage was already done. When I'd got home, my mum hadn't even recognised me. I was like a monster. So while I was sleeping my dad came to my room to check on me and I woke up when he opened the door. But as soon as he came in I was sick all over the place. All the Calimocho that I had drunk came up and so did the dinner that I had hoped would soak all of the alcohol up.

My dad was worried about me but I managed to recover myself, as much out of shame as anything else, and then I went back to sleep thinking that the worst was over. I was wrong. At four o'clock in the morning I got up to go to the toilet, but I did not make it to the bathroom. I only got as far as the corridor before I collapsed in a drunken heap and all I could do was drag myself back to my bed, where I stayed for the next 12 hours until the effects finally began to wear off.

That was my first and last experience of Calimocho. It did not put me off drinking altogether though and it didn't reduce my determination to have a good time whenever and wherever I could. Life is for the living and mistakes are part and parcel of it, especially when you are young. Now I am older I know when and where to have a drink and how to enjoy it without ending up in a mess.

Having said that, there was an occasion as a Liverpool player where I'd had a few too many, as had a lot of the other lads – but it was our Christmas party after all and a chance for us to have a laugh and let ourselves go a bit. Someone who was great at that was Didi Hamann.

Didi is a one-off. I have been fortunate enough to meet so many different people in football with all kinds of qualities and characteristics, but there is only one Didi Hamann. He would do things that shouldn't make you laugh but because he did them you would be in stitches. There were even times when he would go a bit too far but I still couldn't help laughing at him. That is how funny he is.

As usual, the Christmas party was fancy dress. It was at John Aldridge's bar, 'Aldo's Place', in 2006, and the lads were wearing some really funny costumes. I think Luis Garcia came as Prince, Jermaine Pennant was Chewbacca and Fernando Morientes was Vicky Pollard from 'Little Britain'. I'm sure Stevie was a punk that year, with tartan pants and a red wig and he had all the safety pins on.

His best costume was a few years later at Carra's restaurant, Cafe Sports England, when he came dressed as a pensioner on a proper motorised scooter. I don't know where the hell he got it from, but it was very funny. I remember Carra had big blond hair and a silver suit for that one. He was that annoying bloke from 'X-Factor' who was in the news at the time. His name was Rhydian, I think.

Anyway, Carra was Spiderman at this party at Aldo's bar, Daniel Agger was Elvis, Stephen Warnock was a penguin, Dirk Kuyt – Superman, Peter Crouch was a giant multi-coloured parrot, Sami Hyypia – Zorro, Bolo Zenden – Captain America and Craig Bellamy lightened the mood by coming as a jester wearing a death mask.

I remember going as the Queen of England to one of the parties, but that year I was a zombie and Didi was dressed as a marine. The lads were buzzing all night long and we all ended up pissed, except for the ones who were not drinking, and as the party came to an end I sat down on the floor and fell asleep. I was well out of the game and didn't have a clue what was going on. I must have looked dead lying there in my zombie make-up.

The next thing I knew I was woken up, not by someone tapping me on the head and telling me it was time to go but by Didi, stood there in his army outfit, pissing on me!

At first I did not realise what was happening. I just thought he was spraying me with water, but then I realised that the thing he had in his hand wasn't a bottle. I said: "What the hell are you doing?" and Didi apologised straight away. "Pepe, Pepe, Pepe, I'm sorry," he said. "I was just having a laugh."

I wasn't happy for a moment, but then everyone just fell about laughing and I couldn't help but join in. I realised it was a joke, it was my turn to be on the end of it and I also learned a lesson – never to fall asleep when Didi is about.

He is a brilliant person and one of the funniest I have ever met, but I found out the hard way that he can also have a crazy sense of humour.

There are many ways to celebrate. I have really fond memories of special occasions when I was a boy. Christmas was massive for me. It always was from when I was a little kid, and it became even more important when I was at La Masia because it was one of the rare times that I would get to spend with all of my family.

We would all come together for dinner and enjoy each other's company. There was no turkey like everyone has in England. We would have lamb, angulas (baby eels), seafood, everything. It was a proper feast, but the company was better than the food. For me to be with my brothers and my mum and dad was really special because being apart from them was always difficult for me.

New Year was another one of my favourite times with my family. I would go out with my friends, have a drink and a laugh and then go home for dinner just before midnight. We have a tradition in Spain to eat grapes during the countdown to midnight.

We would all gather around the television in the living room and watch the celebrations in the centre of Madrid. As the TV cameras showed the famous clock in Puerta Del Sol we would wait for the bells to start ringing to signal the start of the New Year. They ring 12 times and after each one we would eat a grape. It wasn't just my family, everyone in Spain would be doing the same thing, and I used to love it.

Obviously, because I now live in England I am not able to enjoy events like Christmas and New Year in the same way, particularly as we have so many games during this period. But it is still a special time for me because I get to see my own children enjoying it just as much as I did when I was a kid, even if their experiences are very different to the ones that I had.

There is still one special party, however, that I am determined to be at – but more of that later!

So Close

When the referee blew his whistle to end a tense Saturday night game against Fulham in April, 2009, we celebrated on the pitch as our fans went crazy behind the goal in the Putney End. I thought they would stay for a bit and then go and get their trains and coaches back to Merseyside because it is a long journey and it had been a late kick-off.

But when we came out of the dressing room to go through our warm-down the stewards told us we had to wait because the supporters were still there, singing and dancing. I looked over at them and I could not believe what I was seeing and hearing. "And now you're gonna believe us, we're gonna win the league," they chanted, over and over again. If I did not already believe we had a big chance then seeing those supporters, who have waited so long to be champions again letting the world know that this could finally be our year would have convinced me. It would have convinced anyone.

That was the moment I really started to believe that we could actually win the Premier League. We had hit the woodwork on no less than four occasions during the 90 minutes – through Andrea Dossena twice, Xabi and Fernando – and it looked like it would be a frustrating night for us. Then Yossi Benayoun popped up with a goal in injury-time, firing a shot into the top corner. To score so late in such an important game was massive, particularly because it had looked like we were going to drop two points. It showed how it wasn't just the big names who were leading the charge for us. Even Rafa allowed himself a celebration on the touchline when that goal went in.

Players like Yossi, who is a really good friend of mine, made a huge difference in some really big games and it is when this happens that you start to believe that this could be your year, especially when they pull a victory out of the bag in the very last seconds as he did. And particularly with a win that takes you to the top of the league with just seven games to go.

We had gone into the 2008/09 season hungry for silverware. I had tasted success in the European Championships with Spain that summer, along with a few of the other Liverpool players, but after coming so close in Athens and winning nothing in 2008, we were all desperate to bring a trophy back to Anfield. There was no bigger prize than the Premier League trophy.

If that Saturday night at Craven Cottage was a high point, a moment when everything seemed possible, the next day proved to be a difficult one to handle.

Our title rivals Man United were playing Aston Villa at home and I decided that I'd be better off out of the house playing golf rather than sitting at home shouting and swearing at the television in front of the kids while I watched the game. I got to the golf course, but obviously I still wanted to know what was going on at Old Trafford, so I asked a couple of friends to text me if there were any goals.

I had only played a few holes and my phone buzzed. I read the text –

Ronaldo 1-0. No surprise. United were at home in front of their own fans with the title at stake and we'd beaten Villa 5-0 a couple of weeks earlier so this was par for the course. Then my phone went again, John Carew had equalised. 'Game on,' I thought, even though I still fully expected United to take control again. I was wrong because the next text told me Villa had taken the lead through Gabriel Agbonlahor.

At this stage my mind is racing, working out what it would mean if United lost. But there was also a voice nagging away in the back of my mind, telling me not to get excited because they would come back. They always do. There must have been about 10 minutes left when I got another text telling me Ronaldo had equalised. My emotions swung again as I accepted the inevitability of a United winner.

A hole later and I looked at my watch for the hundredth time in about five minutes. Ten to six, they were only going to get a point. "That's not so bad," I said to myself, knowing that I would have given almost anything for them to drop two points when I started my round. Then, as I was lining up a tee-shot my phone buzzed again. I couldn't believe it and part of me didn't even want to look. "Please tell me they haven't got another one."

I waited a couple of seconds and then I realised it must be full-time and the message was probably someone just letting me know that the game was all over so I opened the text message. '3-2 Macheda'. I smashed my ball into the water, turned my phone off and went home.

I came so close to getting my hands on a title winners' medal that it hurts. We were within touching distance of the Holy Grail but fell just short. It was the closest Liverpool had come to winning the league since their last championship in 1990, but when it came down to it we just didn't have enough to make the difference. It is painful, of course it is, because all of us are in football to win trophies and to add more chapters to the history of this club. The feeling was made even worse by the fact that we had been pipped at the post by Manchester United, our biggest rivals.

No matter how much it hurts, we must still take our hats off to United because they went on the kind of run that decides title races. From Christmas until the end of the season they won 18 out of 21 matches. That was a run that we just couldn't match. So hats off to them for doing that, it was an incredible sequence of results. It was going to take something special to stop us from winning that year and it is just unfortunate for us that they came up with it.

There were times in the run-in when it looked like we had them. When they were trailing to Tottenham Hotspur and Aston Villa at home in April I allowed myself to think that they could be about to slip up, but on both occasions they came back from the dead. Against Spurs they even ran out 5-2 winners after scoring all their goals in the second half. They were like the baddie in a movie that can't be killed off. Every time we thought we had them where we wanted them they found a way to wriggle free.

Ultimately there should be no recriminations for us, not when we ended the season with 86 points, a Premier League record for this club, having only lost two matches in the campaign. We shouldn't even have lost one of them. To this day, I still don't know how Tottenham Hotspur got the better of us at White Hart Lane in November, 2008.

The game was played on a rain-sodden pitch in torrential conditions and we took the lead with a great goal by Dirk Kuyt after just three minutes. After that we could have scored another four or five more but the ball would not go in for us. Spurs grabbed an undeserved equaliser with 20 minutes left when Carra rose above everybody from a corner. I think he got nudged in the air and somehow headed the ball down and it bounced past me for an own goal. Then they scored the winner that they deserved even less – in the last minute. I made a save from a powerful, swerving David Bentley shot, but the ball fell to Darren Bent out wide and he managed to whip it back in for Roman Pavlyuchenko and he got a foot in ahead of Daniel Agger to knock it beyond my reach. There wasn't much I could do about it. If we played that game another hundred times over they would not win.

That result allowed Chelsea to go top. We just had to accept that it was a one-off and that during the course of a season every team has a game that they're not destined to win. This was ours and had the luck gone our way instead of theirs then it would have given us another three points, which could have made a big difference.

The other game we lost was at Middlesbrough at the end of February when they beat us 2-0 a few days after we had beaten Real Madrid at the Bernabeu in the Champions League. That was a different story entirely to what happened at Spurs because we played really poorly, deserved nothing and got nothing. Even that, though, was one of those games that happens to everyone when it just isn't your day. There isn't much you can do to change that.

We took 14 points from our games against the other members of the top four, beating Chelsea and Manchester United home and away and drawing against Arsenal at Anfield and at The Emirates. That is a crazy total and it may never be repeated because to go unbeaten against your biggest rivals all season is hard enough. To win four games out of the six is something else.

This showed what a strong team we were during this season and it wasn't just that we knew we could beat anybody, we proved that we could beat anybody.

The problem for us was that we drew too many games, especially during a 10-week spell either side of Christmas when we dropped 14 points from nine games. We drew with Fulham, Hull and West Ham at Anfield and dropped points at Stoke and Wigan. When you do that the chances are that it is always likely to prove costly in the end and it did.

In every season you have a spell when you are not at your best and you are struggling to find your form. The key is to find a way to keep on winning during these periods. In the month or so after Christmas it felt as if we were not physically or mentally able to do this. I don't know why but we just couldn't get ourselves out of the rut that we were in. In addition to stumbling in the league, we drew Everton in the FA Cup and ending up going out in a fourth-round replay after extra-time at Goodison Park.

Sometimes the footballing gods were against us during that period and our match away to Stoke on January 10 was a good example of that. Although we did not play particularly well at the Britannia Stadium, which is always a tough venue for every visiting team, we still could have won the game if we'd had a bit of luck. We missed out on the three points because Stevie had two great efforts that hit the woodwork when they could so easily have gone in.

It had been a similar story when we played Stoke at Anfield earlier in the season because Stevie had a goal disallowed that should have stood and that cost us another couple of points. I think we hit the post and the crossbar more than any other team in 2008/09 and when you put all these moments together it makes a big difference, particularly when you consider that we finished off only four points behind United.

It is a pity we could not end as champions, but sometimes you just have to accept that you have given everything and another team has finished ahead of you. At least we gave them a hell of a run for their money. We should all be proud of that.

People talk about the signings that we made before the start of that season and though Robbie Keane didn't work out for us I was really keen on him when he first came, as were a lot of people at Liverpool. He was a really good player for Tottenham, a Liverpool fan and he had a lot of experience.in the Premier League so there was nothing in that signing that suggested Robbie would struggle for us in any way. In my eyes we had shown our ambition by paying big money for a player who was going to be really important for us and I was really looking forward to his partnership developing with Fernando.

But for whatever reason, and I certainly can't explain why, it just didn't work out in the way that we had all hoped that it would. This happens in football sometimes. It isn't a situation where the manager has gone out and signed a bad player. It was one where we brought in a proven Premier League striker and it just hasn't worked out. Keane ended up going back to Spurs halfway through the season and plenty of people were expecting us to struggle because we only really had Fernando as a forward, but in the months that followed his partnership with Stevie caught fire and we hit our best run of form at any time since I have been at the club. It just goes to show that football can prove anyone wrong. It can make mugs of us all because even sure things don't always work out as we expect them to.

We also brought in Philipp Degen, Andrea Dossena and Albert Riera that summer and though Albert did a good job for us, giving us a balance and a width that we hadn't had before, hindsight tells us that the other players struggled a bit. They were signings that did not really come off but Rafa and Eduardo Macia, his chief scout, had their own reasons for bringing them in.

Obviously, at the end of the day their performances were not the best, but it would be wrong to look at the transfers we made as the main reason why we did not win the title. We had opportunities to win more games and we did not take them. That was down to all of us as a group, not one or two players who came into the squad but did not set the world alight.

The team had so much quality during this season regardless. The performances of Xabi Alonso and Javier Mascherano in the centre of midfield were massively important to us. It was a great partnership, probably the best midfield pair I have ever been involved with at club level. They gave us so much balance, and allowed us to control games. There was no pairing as good as that in the Premier League. When people look for the reasons why Liverpool have suffered so badly in recent seasons then the fact that Mascherano and Alonso are no longer with us should be high up on the list because they are both special players. In the season when we finished second they were incredible.

Stevie and Fernando scored an unbelievable amount of goals that season and scared the hell out of our opponents. There were games when they were just unplayable. It didn't matter what teams tried to do they just couldn't stop them. I know Liverpool supporters talk of Kenny Dalglish and Ian Rush being the club's best attacking partnership, but if they were better than Stevie and Fernando were at times during this season then they must have been really special.

We also had Dirk on the right, in a new position for him, and he did really well in that role. I could go through the entire squad picking out individuals but when it came down to it the fact is that we had a proper squad and when we were able to name our strongest team for several games on the run we were really powerful.

A lot of the critics also claimed that we did not win the league because of zonal marking, but the evidence does not support this. The statistics show that this was an effective system for us and I certainly could not have won the Golden Glove award for the most clean sheets four times in five years if it had worked as badly as some people claimed. We have also conceded goals from set-pieces since then when using man-to-man marking so it is too simplistic to blame zonal marking.

At the end of the day, defending against set-pieces is much more difficult in English football than it is in any other country because of the size and physique of the players, it is as simple as that. All of the teams have problems in these situations, whether they decide to use zonal marking or go man-to-man.

Another myth is that we lost the league because of rotation, that the changing of the team disrupted our rhythm and cost us momentum. I was not at Liverpool in 2005, but rotation was one of the reasons why they won the European Cup that season. It has an increasing role in modern football with managers looking to utilise their squads to try and make sure that the players stay fresh and able to deliver. It is not as if we were the only ones who were doing it either.

Alex Ferguson was changing the United team all the time and this did not stop them from winning the league so anyone who claims that it cost Liverpool the title is getting it wrong.

We were even accused of being negative by some critics because we played with both Mascherano and Alonso in midfield. Yet we scored more goals than anyone else that season and nine more than United so how could we have been negative? It just doesn't add up. In fact, it's more than that, it is bullshit. We lost only two games all season and if United get 90 points to beat us to the title then you have to congratulate them for that. Of course we had games that we look back on with regret but that happens to every team, even United.

You have to put it all in perspective anyway. It is easy to look at the games where we were unlucky or where we dropped points that we shouldn't have. But there were plenty of matches, an incredible amount, where we took points after being behind to our opponents. The newspapers started calling us 'The Comeback Kings' again that season, a nickname that had been used for us in the season after Istanbul, and it fitted because there were so many games where we were trailing and we came back to win. Portsmouth away, Manchester City away, Middlesbrough at home in our first home game of the season, Manchester United at home and away, Wigan at home.

That was one of the great strengths of that team, we just didn't know when we were beaten and even if it took until the last minute of the game to get the winning goal we would keep on fighting until it came. All of us. The team spirit that we had at the time was crucial to this because it is impossible to keep on winning games after being behind unless you are all in it together. Once or twice, maybe, but to keep on doing it over and over again proves that there was a lot more to it than just a lucky comeback.

Our attitude was that we would keep on going until the 90th minute or until the referee blew the final whistle. It has to be like that out of respect for the supporters who travel all over the country to give you their backing and also out of respect for yourself and the club. There are times when part of you wants to give up because the situation seems impossible and you are ready to hold your hands up in defeat, but then something in the back of your mind tells you that you are a Liverpool player and throwing the towel in can never be an option. Maybe at other clubs it is easier to give in but this is Liverpool, the club of Istanbul and so many other brilliant comebacks. You have to be true to that legacy or else you are cheating the club and everything it stands for.

There were also times during that season when we reached unbelievable standards. The highlight for most people will probably always be the 4-1 win against United at Old Trafford, a really special day for everyone associated with the club. That it was their biggest home defeat for 17 years says it all. Teams don't go to Old Trafford and do to them what we did that day.

I can remember looking at the massive scoreboard after Andrea Dossena scored our fourth goal after coming on as a substitute and it just looked beautiful. Man United 1 – Liverpool 4! I took a picture of it in my mind and it has remained there ever since, a memory of a great day that showed just how good we were at that time. It wasn't as if it was all plain sailing either. Just before kick-off, we found out that Alvaro Arbeloa could not play and Sami Hyypia came into the side with only a moment's notice. It did not show.

Sami was a top professional, someone that we all looked up to, and he played as if he had been preparing for the game for weeks, when the reality was that it was only a few minutes before the game got underway that he knew he would be involved.

It looked like it would be just a usual visit to Old Trafford for us when the referee awarded United a penalty and they scored from it. I was actually at fault, bringing down Ji-Sung Park after coming off my line. I could do nothing to stop Ronaldo's penalty and at that point no-one could have predicted what happened next. But everything changed from the moment Fernando equalised after Nemanja Vidic failed to cope with his pace. Suddenly we took charge of the game and Stevie scored a penalty for us, Fabio Aurelio struck a beautiful free-kick for our third and Dossena completed the win with a lob from the edge of the box after I had set him up with a long kick.

I am claiming an assist for that one because even though I know it was poor defending by them, I just want to be able to say that I created the fourth goal in a 4-1 win for Liverpool away to Manchester United. That is something that I will tell my children and my grandchildren in the years to come.

It was one of the greatest days we have had since I have been at the club. I certainly enjoyed myself a lot anyway and I know the fans packed into the away end at Old Trafford did as well. What made it really special was that the stakes were so high for us because there were only nine games left and we knew we had to win to stay in the title race.

On the bus on the way to the ground I was looking out of the window at the police outriders and I saw all the supporters outside the stadium and it just struck me how big the game was. The scenario was simple – lose and go out of the title race, win and give ourselves a chance of winning it. So to come away from there, from this do or die game, not just with three points but having sent a message that we were back in the race with a bang was a really special feeling for all of us.

It was a massive, massive win and we came away from Manchester that March afternoon thinking that we could really challenge for the title. Our confidence was high and we felt that we could beat anyone. It is an unbelievable feeling when you go into games thinking like that because it is almost as if it does not matter what your opponent does and what questions they ask because you will have the answers. It was right that we should feel like that as well because that season we won at the Bernabeu, we ended Chelsea's 86-game unbeaten run at home when we won at Stamford Bridge and we won at Old Trafford. That is some hat-trick. You cannot win games against the biggest clubs in their own stadiums unless you are a special team and we were definitely a special team that year.

If anything, though, beating Real Madrid home and away was even better for me than the victory over United because over the two legs we gave them a lesson. My father had played for Atletico Madrid and Barcelona, Real's biggest rivals, so to beat them so comprehensively, 5-0 on aggregate, meant a lot to me.

Their chairman had been talking before the first game at the Bernabeu saying they were going to beat us easily in the first leg and even easier in the second so it was a matter of pride for us. We got it tactically spot on in the away game and Real hardly had a chance. We did not have too many either but creating opportunities was not our main concern that night anyway. When we did get a chance, Yossi Benayoun scored a great header from Fabio Aurelio's cross to give us a famous victory. I can remember seeing the ball go into the back of the net and trying to work out who had produced such a towering header. I thought it could be Dirk or Albert Riera and I could not believe my eyes when I realised it was Yossi. I think it was the only header he has ever scored in his entire life and what a time and place to do it.

The job was only half done and we knew Real would still believe they could win the tie, even though they still had to come to Anfield. On the day of that game, Marca ran a headline saying 'This is Anfield – So What?' Four goals without reply told them what Anfield is about. For me, it was a really special night because of what it meant for us as a club, but also what it meant in Spain.

We were unbelievable. We were sure about what we needed to do in the first 15 minutes or so when we knew we had to take the game to them and it was during these early stages that we made the difference when Fernando scored the goal that he so desperately wanted. The pace we played at was phenomenal and no-one could have lived with us that night, especially with Stevie and Fernando in such devastating form. In the days after the game I got lots of phone calls from my friends in the Spanish national team and they were joking about us, saying that when they watched the game on television they thought someone had pressed the fast forward button on the remote control. That was how high our intensity levels were. We were so determined to prove a point, not just to Real but to everyone else. We did that in the most spectacular fashion.

It was a perfect day. I even allowed myself to enjoy a little bit of personal satisfaction, but not because Iker Casillas, the player who has stood in the way of me and a place in the Spanish national team for so long, was in goal. It was nice to do a bit better than Casillas on this occasion, but I did not rub it in at all because he wasn't happy. The main reason it gave me a bit of extra pride was because I always want to win and beat the best teams and that night we did so in style. It was nice to do it against a team from Spain as well because I knew it would make the work that the likes of Alvaro, Xabi, Fernando, Albert and myself were doing at Liverpool seem even more important to people in our own country.

No team is ever unbeatable and we were not foolish enough to believe that we were, but we were really strong at that time and when we faced Chelsea in the quarter-finals after knocking out Real we were pretty convinced that we were going to go to another final – but it wasn't to be. It is a sign of how much belief we had in ourselves at that time that even after losing the first leg 3-1 at Anfield, we still believed that we could turn things around at Stamford Bridge.

We almost did as well but after going in 2-0 up at half-time we ended up drawing the game 4-4 and being knocked out of the Champions League. That was a big setback for us because we were in the form of our lives at the time and we had not been expecting to exit the competition at that stage. We were still in with a shout of the Premier League though on the back of four straight wins, starting with that famous victory at Old Trafford.

Aston Villa were our next victims after beating United. Again, this was another one of those days when it would have taken something special to beat us because we had so much momentum. We won 5-0 with Stevie scoring a hat-trick and I got an assist for the second game running, with a long kick to Albert Riera that he ended up smashing into the roof of the net from the edge of the box. It was just as well that I was contributing with my feet because the team was playing so well that I hardly had anything to do with my hands.

There are those who say this was our best performance of the season. I don't agree with them because if you score four against Real Madrid and four away to Man United they have to be your best moments, but I can understand why people think this is the case. It was more to do with the feeling of optimism that there was at Anfield on that beautifully sunny Sunday afternoon. You could almost reach out and touch the excitement. If that is what the supporters are like when we are just chasing the title, imagine what they will be like if we win the thing.

Our incredible night at Fulham followed, but that last-gasp winner for United against Villa the next day was probably what killed us.

We carried on fighting and beat Blackburn 4-0 at Anfield, but that Macheda goal turned out to be a real turning point in the title race. From that moment on we knew that United would have to fall apart to let us back in and that doesn't happen too often. We dropped another couple of points when Arsenal came to Anfield and held us to a draw in another memorable 4-4 draw.

People will never forget that night because Andrey Arshavin scored all four goals for Arsenal, an incredible achievement for him considering he only had four shots. Baptista did something similar for Arsenal when they beat us 6-3 in the Carling Cup in 2007 and when a player is on fire you just have to give them credit. Unfortunately for us, Arshavin's big night came against us and it damaged us. Three of the goals I could do nothing about, but there was one that I should have done better with.

If we replayed that game many times over and he had four shots he would never score four goals. That kind of thing only happens once in a career. It did not stop us returning to the top of the league on goal difference, but United now had two games in hand on us. They had the advantage and they were not about to lose it.

It hurt when United ended the race by winning the league, of course it did. I couldn't help but think how different things could have turned out if only we had not hit the post so many times and if only we had enjoyed a little bit more luck when it mattered most. But no matter what hard luck stories I came up with I knew in my heart of hearts that we had been beaten by the better team. If they had more points than us it was because they were better than us, it is as simple as that.

Some people try to claim that we were superior because we had beaten them home and away, but that kind of logic only applies to the

Champions League, a competition in which we had already proved that we could beat anyone over two legs. In the Premier League you have to be consistent over 10 months and up to now we have not been able to be more consistent than anyone else over the course of the season. That is why we are still waiting for the league title to come home.

It's not as if United only did it that year either. They have been doing it for almost two decades now. When something happens this often it cannot be put down to luck.

People complain because they will score a goal in the last minute of a game or a tap-in but that is because they have been hammering away looking for a winner and in the end their opponents just have to submit because it is so relentless. They probably took between 18 and 20 points that season just from the decisive goals that they scored in the last 10 minutes of games and that makes a massive difference to how the league table finishes up. It can be the difference between finishing seventh in the league and being champions.

It is about having the instinct of a big club and the unquenchable thirst for success that goes with it. I have been on the receiving end of it as a Liverpool player and it is like a hurricane coming towards you. It takes something special to stand up to them and not be blown away. There was also a spell when United kept 14 clean sheets in a row – they ended up with 24 in total – and it is so difficult for anyone to compete against that because it is such a phenomenal record.

Credit where credit is due. They have had that winning mentality for many years and that is one of the reasons why they have now overtaken Liverpool as the English team with the most league titles.

They took our record the following year. I call it 'our' record but it was the club's, not mine. I was not involved in any of our title-winning teams so I cannot claim to be part of it. But this is helpful in some ways because it meant that when United got to title number 19 in 2011, I was not gutted that the record had been broken. For those Liverpool players of the past who had helped the club become the most successful in the history of English football it must have hurt a lot because the record belonged to them and to their achievements.

For me and my team-mates, our pain is more about the situation we found ourselves in. It hurts when we are not involved in the title race and hurts even more when we are so far away from the top of the table that we cannot even qualify for European football, as we were during 2010/11. At times like that, losing a record or a title is secondary to the need to become competitive again. That is our priority. We cannot do anything about the failings since 1990 that have allowed United to edge in front of us.

What we can affect is our future and our ability to challenge them and the other big clubs. To do that, though, we must first accept that United have been much better than us for the last 20 years or so and winning the league has become a pretty normal occurrence to them. We can do that in the knowledge that it was different in the past when Liverpool were the team to beat and it can be different in the future.

This club has so much potential it is untrue and if it is ever realised then Liverpool can be the team that is winning titles all the time and setting the standards for everyone else to reach. It is up to us to redress the situation and I believe we can do it. We can do nothing about the past, but we can have a positive future.

World In My Hands

In the history of Spanish football only 23 players have ever won a World Cup winners' medal. I am one of them. As part of the Spain squad that defeated Holland in the 2010 final, I made my way up the steps at the Soccer City Stadium in Johannesburg with the rest of my team-mates and danced as Iker Casillas lifted football's most famous trophy high above his head. It was the most glorious and magical moment of my career.

When I arrived back at Liverpool after the World Cup, I took my medal to Melwood and to Anfield so that the stewards and staff could have their pictures taken with it. They were as proud to wear it as I am and that gave me a lot of pleasure because it made my personal success feel like Liverpool's success.

Of course, Carra was on my case straight away, joking that I hadn't earned the medal because I hadn't played, but that didn't bother me. I knew that like every other player who has played for England since

1966 he would have given anything to swap places with me, just to know what it is like to be part of a squad that wins the World Cup.

I had that feeling – I still have it – and it is something that will be with me for as long as I live. Even when I die, I will be remembered as a member of the first Spain squad ever to win the World Cup. There is so much that I still want to achieve in football, but even if I was to win nothing else that would be enough.

It was while I was in South Africa that I felt a tinge of sadness amidst all the celebrations. It dawned on me that Spain may never again be able to play in the free-flowing style for which we have become known. Our success has meant that teams now go to extraordinary lengths to try and stop us from playing. Some opponents get every single player behind the ball to try and deny us space and we then have to try and find a way of getting through them. Others let us have possession, but defend deep and try to hit us on the counter-attack.

Then there are those who go to really extreme measures, like Holland did in the World Cup Final, by resorting to being physical. That is the price that we are paying for our success, but it is the same challenge that all successful teams must face up to. It is up to us to find ways of making sure that we are able to impose our playing style on our opponents and not to become frustrated when they are making life difficult for us. What I can say is that we will continue to stick to our principles. Why wouldn't we when they have helped us become champions of Europe and the world?

When we arrived in South Africa our confidence levels were really high because we had shown that we knew how to win a major tournament. The World Cup is much more difficult to win than the European Championships.

There is an extra round to play and, of course, it also features the best teams from South America and other parts of the world. Still, it was there for us to win and we all knew that. In earlier years that knowledge would probably have added to the pressure on Spain, but our success at Euro 2008 gave us extra belief and also allowed us to relax a little bit more. We had achieved one massive success already and now we wanted another trophy.

The Confederations Cup a year earlier had been a wake-up call for us. Everyone had been expecting us to win that tournament. We were the reigning European champions, we had some of the best players in the world in our squad and we were in fantastic form. That feeling only got stronger after the group stages with us coming through with three wins from our three matches without even conceding a goal. We were drawn to play the USA in the semi-finals and they had only won one of their matches so it was all set up for us to reach the final and a probable meeting with Brazil – or so it seemed. I don't know what happened that night in Bloemfontein, but whatever it was, we were not able to reach our normal levels and the USA beat us 2-0 to knock us out of the competition. If it was a shock to the rest of football then it was an even bigger one for us.

We had not been complacent because that's just not the way we are as a squad. We go into every game knowing that we have to give our very best if we are to get a result, but it was just one of those occasions that every team has when nothing really goes right. It was an important lesson ahead of the World Cup and it might even have been a blessing in disguise for us because it showed us that if we were not at 100 per cent we could lose to anybody, no matter what our achievements had been the year before.

I know people think that the most important part of being involved in the Confederations Cup was that it gave us an early opportunity to get used to the conditions in South Africa and that was helpful to us, but when I look back on it that defeat was probably the most crucial lesson of all. We learned more from losing that one game than we did from any of our victories before then. It served us well.

It didn't prevent us from losing our first game at the World Cup, though. Despite producing one of our best performances of the tournament, Switzerland beat us. That setback could have really shaken our confidence but it did the opposite, even if it did take us to within one defeat of elimination. There was no panic or great concern amongst the management or players. If anything it strengthened our commitment to our system and our way of playing.

While others outside the camp were suggesting that we might have to become more direct and get more crosses into the box, we decided that what we had to do was to stay true to our principles and the methods that had already brought us so much success. It helped that we had played well even though we had lost because if we played the same way in the next 100 games we would probably have won 99 of them, so there was no need to go back to the drawing board or anything like that. We created 25 chances but couldn't take one of them, while Switzerland probably had only one but scored from it. That is the way it goes in football sometimes.

Our strategy was the right one, we had proven that in the past, and there was no reason why it could not work for us again. Had we changed the way we approached games at that stage, just because of one defeat, then I doubt very much that we would have gone on to win the World Cup. That we became the first team to do so after losing our first game says everything about the belief that we had in ourselves, in one another and in our philosophies.

We still went into our remaining group games against Honduras and Chile knowing that we would be on a flight home to Madrid if either of them beat us. After losing our first game we knew that one more defeat at any stage would be the end of our dreams. Most people will think that the pressure is toughest when you get to the latter stages of a competition, when most is at stake, but I can safely say that until Villa scored in the 24th minute against Chile and a path to the last 16 opened up to us, that they were the most testing moments of the entire tournament for us. That is why I charged onto the pitch to celebrate with the rest of the players after we had won 2-1 at the Loftus Versfeld Stadium. It was our last group game and we had come through a major test. The result ensured we finished top of the table and the sense of relief amongst all of us was there for everyone to see.

Vicente Del Bosque's cleverest move was to continue with the same mentality and approach that had been established by Aragones. He brought in some of his own players in certain positions and tinkered with the odd thing, but he resisted the temptation to make any major changes and that says a lot about him. A lot of managers might have been tempted to try and stamp their authority on the team and the way we did things, but he recognised straight away that there was no need to make too many changes. He put the team ahead of himself and to me that is one of the signs of a great manager.

It is one thing to know when changes are needed but it is another to know when they are not and by sticking with the philosophy that was already in place Del Bosque gave us the best possible chance of being successful. In some respects it could be argued that he had no choice as we were already playing good football, keeping the ball well and scoring goals, and we were getting good results. But it is still brave for a manager to stick with the strategy that he inherited, in the knowledge that he would get the blame for not making enough changes if things went wrong. Del Bosque deserves a lot of credit for that.

Del Bosque and Aragones are very different people – Aragones is cheekier and has a twinkle in his eye, while Del Bosque is more low key and keeps everything nice and everyone humble – but we were fortunate in that they have the same ideas about football.

That doesn't mean our players never kick the ball long or just smash it out of play for a throw-in. We try to play football as it should be played and possession is so important to us, even if there are times when you just have to play percentages and deal with a situation the way it is, not the way you might want it to be.

It is the same in training. We are not always trying to create the perfect goal with me or Casillas rolling it out to Gerard Pique so we can start a move of 20 passes or more.

Football is not like that. It's about doing the basics right and doing the right thing at the right time, although there are some of our players who are almost perfect in everything that they do, Xavi being the most obvious example. I have been lucky enough to play with some of the best players in the world and Xavi is undoubtedly one of them. When he works with Andres Iniesta and Sergio Busquets in training and in games it is special to watch.

In the rush to shower Xavi and Iniesta with plaudits, the role that Busquets plays is often overlooked and for me that is unfair because he is an unbelievably good player. He is so good. I love him. Everything he does is efficient and it is done for the team. There was a time when I hoped that he would become a Liverpool player. I thought that he would be perfect for us, but unfortunately it didn't happen. It was when Barcelona came in for Mascherano the first time and I told Rafa that if we were ready to sell him then we should tell them that we wanted Busquets and Pedro in return.

They were only just starting out then and not that much was known about them outside of Spain. I thought that seeing as it seemed Barcelona were so desperate to sign Mascherano that we could maybe get a really good deal out of it because I knew even then that Pedro and Busquets were going to be top players.

My idea was that we should offer Barcelona Mascherano plus £15 million for those two and I told Rafa that if we did it he certainly wouldn't regret it in any way. But the deal never took place, we ended up losing Mascherano and Barcelona kept Pedro and Busquets, with all three playing key roles in their Champions League success of 2011.

One of the most important decisions I made during the World Cup was to make sure I wasn't distracted in any way by what was going on at Liverpool. Rafa had just lost his job, the club was in the process of appointing a new manager and the situation with the owners was still dragging on. If that had caught my attention even a little bit then it would have made it harder for me to retain my focus on the job.

It wasn't easy. Liverpool are not the kind of club that you can just switch yourself off from, especially when things aren't going well. For one month of my life I knew I had no choice but to put everything that was happening at the club out of my mind. It was the right decision to make, it was the only decision to make. This was the World Cup and it was Spain's greatest ever opportunity to win it. I had a role to play within the camp, even though I knew I was unlikely to play, and if I'd been moping around the hotel thinking about Liverpool then I wouldn't have been any use to anyone.

In keeping with tradition, my room became the hotel's unofficial cafe the night before the final. More than a dozen of us sat there drinking milk and eating croissants – this is the way that the Spanish national team prepared for the biggest game in its history. It was keeping up with a ritual which dated back to a game against England at Old Trafford more than three years earlier. The night before that game we all met in one of the rooms, eating croissants and drinking milk and because we won the match 1-0 it became our superstition and one that we kept all the way to the World Cup Final.

The ritual was known as "The Croissant of Luck" and we would try to stick to it no matter where we were in the world. There was one time, we were playing in Belgium and the hotel we were staying at didn't have any croissants so we had to make do with slices of cake – at 30 Euros a slice! – but it was good enough. It was a superstition but it also brought all of us together and allowed us to relax in each other's company. That was so valuable to us when we were preparing for our most important games.

We already knew how big the World Cup Final was, but as we sat there just chilling out in my hotel room and trying to enjoy the moment it really began to dawn on us that this was a once in a lifetime opportunity and one we couldn't afford to miss. "We've come this far, we can't let this chance go otherwise we will regret for all our lives that we got to the final of the biggest competition in football and didn't win it," I told my team-mates.

The same kinds of things were probably being said in the Dutch hotel. In some ways, I didn't need to say it because I only had to look into the eyes of my team-mates to realise that they understood the enormity of what was about to happen. They were ready for it. The advantage we had was that we had been in a similar situation two years earlier before the final of Euro 2008, so our experience helped ease the tension. Not that I was feeling the pressure in any way. As usual, I slept like a baby the night before the final and I even had a nap before the game. If I can sleep before the World Cup Final then I suppose I can sleep through anything.

Of course, there was tension in the dressing room before the game. I could feel it as soon as I walked in there. It wasn't so obvious on the coach on the way to the stadium, but from the moment that we walked into the dressing room it was as if someone had flicked a switch. Again, the eyes of my team-mates gave away their emotions.

Every single one of them was totally focused and as Del Bosque was going through our tactical plans for the game you could have heard a pin drop as all of us took everything in.

I was sat next to Jesus Navas because he was number 22 and I was number 23 and I could sense his nervousness. That's nothing out of the ordinary. Navas is always nervous, it's just the way he is. I couldn't blame him for feeling like this and in my own way I suppose I felt the same, but as usual, I was the one making the jokes to try and relax myself and everyone else.

It was horrible to sit on the bench that night but it was also beautiful. Not many people will ever have been as close to a World Cup Final – in terms of playing in one and closeness to the pitch – without actually being involved. I was in the box seat watching history unfold and I knew it. Like I say, I am a bad watcher at the best of times and with this being such a massive game I was even worse. My own sense of tension was not helped by the way Holland played. They were nasty that night and in my eyes they played anti-football.

I don't think that was what the players wanted to do in the biggest match of their careers. I think it was what their manager told them to do to try and stop us from imposing our game on them. The way they kicked us was not normal. Every player goes into matches knowing that they will be fouled, probably on a few occasions, but this was more than that; it was happening every single minute.

The worst moment came when Nigel De Jong smashed Alonso in the chest with a karate kick. It is difficult to recall seeing a worse foul than this one and after the game Xabi told me that of all the kicks he had ever received in his entire career this was the most painful one. That may not seem like too big a statement, with fouls being part and parcel of football.

But when you consider that Xabi had previously suffered a broken ankle and yet De Jong's kick caused him even more pain, it gives you an idea of just how bad it was. Xabi thought he was going to have to come off because of it, but he managed to keep on going. I suppose this was the best way of answering their aggression, by refusing to give in to it.

I was not in the dressing room at half-time – I was out on the pitch warming up with the rest of the substitutes – but the message from Del Bosque was clear: we had to keep on trying to play the right way, no matter how strong the provocation was, and if we did the goal would come. It was the best piece of advice he could have given. Had we allowed ourselves to get drawn into a battle then we could have lost our way. A final is no place for us to abandon the principles that had got us there in the first place. Besides, that was probably what Holland wanted us to do. We had to play our game, not be reduced to playing theirs.

The belief was that if we kept doing the right things the goal would finally come. Waiting for it to arrive was not easy though, especially not when I was sat on the bench watching events, rather than taking part in them. It is occasions like this when being a non-playing substitute is hardest. In the games that don't matter anywhere near as much I am able to sit there and relax a little in the knowledge that Spain will more than likely win and then we can move on to the next game. A final is not like that. There are no second chances and every little incident on the pitch can be massive.

I said a lot of prayers that night, asking for a goal and for us to get it. My prayers were answered when Iniesta scored towards the end of extra-time. There are not enough words in the English or Spanish languages to describe my emotions when that shot went in. It was like an explosion of joy, something that is beyond description because it was so incredible.

The best thing about it was that everyone – the players and staff on the bench, the supporters at the stadium and all of the people watching at home in Spain – felt exactly the same way. This was Spain's greatest ever moment and I was privileged to share in it. It does not get any better than that. Well, it would have done if I had been playing, but when you are involved in winning something as special as the World Cup that does not even cross your mind at that point.

Iniesta even managed to make it even more special for all of us. After putting the ball into the back of the net he raced away to celebrate. Before anyone could get near to him to share in his joy, he pulled off his Spain shirt to reveal a top carrying the most poignant message imaginable. "Dani Jarque siempre con nosotros," it said, "Dani Jarque is always with us".

The previous August, Jarque, a player with Espanyol and Spain Under-21s, had collapsed and died while on pre-season with his club. It was a terrible tragedy and one which affected all of us because we all knew him. We had played with and against him and his passing was a great loss to his family, to Spanish football and to all of us. None of us had any idea what Iniesta had planned. The first we knew about it was after he scored the decisive goal.

That he had those kind of thoughts for someone who was no longer with us says everything about Iniesta and what kind of person he is. Hopefully none of us will ever have to wear that kind of shirt again because we do not want to be mourning the loss of any more players who die before their time, but Iniesta's tribute to Jarque remains one of the most emotional moments I have ever witnessed on a football pitch. I just hope I never have to see anything like it again.

It was a rollercoaster of emotions for all of us. I was excited, elated and overjoyed. But I was also sad for those who had been on the journey with me but who were not there when I was enjoying my greatest moment. It was a powerful concoction, but when I finally got my hands on the trophy I was totally overcome with joy. Not just because it was the World Cup, also because it is the most beautiful looking trophy you could ever wish to get your hands on. It is baldy – like me! – but it is still beautiful. I was stood in the stand with my hands wrapped around it just thinking that life does not get any better than this.

At that moment, the greatest of my career, it did not even cross my mind that I was not a world champion in the same way as Iker and the others who had played in the final. I was far too happy for all of us to consider my own situation. It was only when the celebrations had finished and everything that had just happened began to sink in that I started to see things slightly differently.

Yes, I am a world champion and I deserve to have that medal, but I cannot be as proud of my achievement as I would have been had I played. I contributed to our success in my own way but I was unable to influence the team on the pitch and I recognise that.

In some ways, I feel like a boxer who has become the best in the world only after the title has been relinquished. I did all of the training, worked hard every single day, rose through the ranks and did everything that is required – except I could not win the title in the ring, for reasons beyond my control.

Maybe I cannot be as proud of myself as I would have been if the Liverpool team I was a part of could have won the Champions League in 2007, because I would have played in that final and in all the other games leading up to it. But I still have my medal. I am a champion all the same.

In The Shadow

The trip back from South Africa after the World Cup was not as good as the journey home from Austria. It was longer and much more tiring. We had to sleep on the plane, otherwise it would have been impossible to keep on going when we got back to Spain. But the main reason why it did not feel quite as good was that nothing could beat the celebrations that followed Euro 2008. The first time is always the best and even though we had won the World Cup, the greatest prize of them all, the party that followed it was not as good.

Having said that, the flight home was an incredible experience. Almost two-and-a-half million people have watched the YouTube video of me, Villa and Ramos serenading Casillas and his girlfriend Sara. We wanted to give him a bit of stick. That was the way it was. Just a gang of mates having a laugh with each other. It could have been any football team, the only difference was we had just been crowned champions of the world.

The homecoming parade will also live with me forever. Travelling along the Gran Via, the biggest street in all of Madrid, I could not see even the tiniest speck of street below me because of the amount of people who had come out to welcome us home. It was unbelievable. Then I went through my Camarero routine again.

I was going through the players' names one by one. I got round to Cesc Fabregas, and as soon as I had started calling him out Pique and Puyol appeared from behind. They grabbed Cesc and pulled a Barcelona shirt over his head. I did not help them as they put it on him. All I did was realise what was going on and turned it into a joke. "The future of the national team," I shouted down the microphone, "and the future of Barca."

I hadn't prepared any of my speech and this bit was totally off the cuff because I did not have a clue what Pique and Puyol had planned. It wasn't my idea and I knew nothing about it beforehand, but it was just a bit of fun. Nothing more and nothing less. I know Barcelona were trying to sign Cesc from Arsenal at the time and that it was difficult for the Arsenal fans to accept, but this was only a joke between friends. Any supporters who found that offensive have got it totally wrong. I owe no apologies to anyone for what happened.

It is a pity that Camarero cannot be translated into English because when we win the league I would love to stand on the steps of St George's Hall in front of hundreds of thousands of Scousers and perform it for them, but it cannot be done. They will have to make do with me singing a song or making a speech. Whatever happens I will be at the heart of the celebrations. That is just the way I am.

It seems to some that my usual role for Spain is as cheerleader. Of course, I would prefer it if I was remembered more for what I do on the pitch. I don't like being stuck on the sidelines.

Like I say, I admit I am a terrible watcher. I get over-anxious, over-excited, over-emotional, the lot. There is no comparison with playing and if anything it is a hundred times worse. There is nothing you can do to influence the result, all you can do is sit there and support your team-mates in the knowledge that you are absolutely powerless to help them or to change the game.

If I am on the pitch then I am able to react and try and make things happen, even though I am a goalkeeper, but when I am on the bench I know that the best I can do is give everything I can in support of those who can make a difference. That's why it is so frustrating to be a substitute. Because I have hot Latin blood I am probably worse than most. When I see videos of myself as a substitute I have to laugh because I am everywhere except on the bench. I am jumping up and down, shouting encouragement to my team-mates, screaming at the referee, celebrating like a lunatic when we score goals, anything and everything apart from sitting there calmly watching the game. There are players who can sit and relax and just watch events unfold, but I am not like that.

The great thing from my point of view is that my team-mates know what I am like and they always try to involve me as much as they can. After scoring a goal, Villa often runs to me so that we can celebrate together. It is not only because we are really good friends, but it is also because he wants me to be included in what is going on and I really appreciate that. One of my favourite moments of the whole tournament was Villa scoring the winner against Sweden in stoppage time to book our place in the quarter-finals and him jumping on me like a madman.

In every international squad there are those who play all the time, those who play occasionally and those who make up the numbers. I don't really fall into any of those categories. I am the understudy to the lead actor, Iker Casillas, our first-choice goalkeeper and captain, and my status as back-up means I play only when he does not. He is the immovable object and the reason why I am on the outside looking in during games. I have been part of the Spain squad that won both Euro

2008 and the World Cup, but I only played in one single match and that was a group match after we had already qualified for the knockout stages of the European Championships.

I travel all around the world in the hope that I might get some minutes on the pitch, but more often than not all I get for my commitment is a place on the bench watching as Iker makes yet another appearance. If I was a jealous person then I would be really bitter, but I am not. I feel privileged to be a part of the greatest and most successful group of players that Spain has ever produced. I have no reason to be resentful no matter how many games take place with me consigned to the role of onlooker. I know my place and while I might not like it, I have too much respect for Iker as a person and as a goalkeeper to question it.

There are plenty who would like to think that our rivalry has made us enemies, but nothing could be further from the truth. My relationship with Iker is brilliant. I have known him for many years. We played together in the Spanish junior ranks, and the reality is that we are really close friends. I suppose that this kind of relationship does rely on the one who is not playing because it is always going to be tougher for the keeper who misses out than the one who is involved all of the time. I'm pleased to say that from the first moment I became part of the squad we have got on well.

It goes without saying that I would love to get picked ahead of him because I am competitive and I want to play for my country. I would be silly if I said Casillas is better than me because I have to have belief in myself. If I was picking the national team I would play myself in goal, no question. Casillas would also pick himself without hesitation. Valdes would pick himself without even thinking about it. We all think that we are the best and that is the way it has to be. Thankfully it is up to the manager to make a choice and not us because there would be a crazy fight for the goalkeeper's jersey if it was.

Iker also has the backing of the press and that is significant because for the manager of the national team to even consider replacing him in the team they would know that the media would give them problems. Even though I know that simply by playing for Real Madrid makes it easier for him to have the support of the press, I cannot use that as an excuse. I am also aware that from the moment I decided to leave Spain and come to Liverpool for the good of my career I made it more difficult for myself to be selected by the national team. That's the way it goes and I knew this would happen from the moment I decided to move to England. That's fine, though. I accept it and I take it.

What I simply have to accept is Iker is first choice. He has been for many years, and up to now there has not been a reason to change that. He is the man in possession and he has earned that right.

I cannot blame him for the fact that I am missing out on games or anything like that. It is not his fault in any way. It's down to the manager to pick the 11 players who start each game and all Iker can do is keep on playing as he has done and not worry about me or anyone else. It is tough for me, of course it is, but being a keeper I know that only one of us can ever play and I have to give him credit for keeping the position for as long as he has.

The situation has never divided us and if anything it has brought us closer because it is something we joke about all the time. When we meet up with the national squad one of the first things I say to him is: "Iker, you're here again. Don't you ever get a cold, sprain your wrist or knock your knee or anything?" It has become a running joke between us. But it's not just about having a laugh. He has always been really respectful towards me because he knows I will support him in any way that I can. I am not jealous of him and he is not suspicious of me. We train together, work together and if he gets picked ahead of me – as he

Playing for keeps:
My friend and rival
Iker Casillas

One of my
best mates:
David Villa

Work hard and play hard: A motto I try to follow in life and in training

Getting closer to the big day: In the team hotel with the Spain squad

World beaters: It doesn't get any better than this. Lifting the famous World Cup. When you see it up close it's beautiful and baldy – like me!

Uh oh, here I go again with the Camarero routine after winning the World Cup

Golden Glove: I'm proud of my clean sheet records with Liverpool

Below: Carra is as passionate about keeping clean sheets as I am. Sometimes that can lead to arguments but they are soon forgotten

A famous celebration when I ran down the pitch to jump on David Ngog after he'd finished off Manchester United in front of the Kop

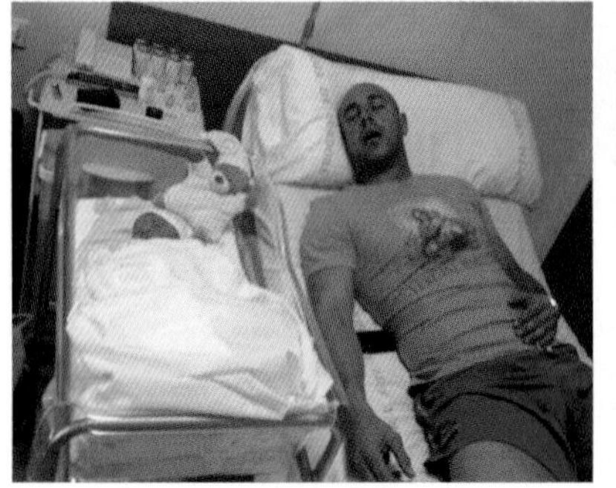

Like father like son, the next generation: Yolanda did all the work, but I slept like a baby myself, so happy and content after our little boy Luca came into the world

Our wonderful girls Grecia and Alma

My beautiful Cordoban wife, Yolanda on our wedding day. I was very emotional when I saw her walking up the aisle

Grecia enjoys scoring goals past me

I was sad to see Xabi Alonso go.
We definitely missed him on the pitch

Left: I have known Arteta since my teenage days at La Masia. He was a neighbour who I enjoyed barbecues with before he left to join Arsenal

King Kenny: Building a great squad. Hopefully we can win trophies together

© Andrew Powell / LFC

To have a banner created with me on it is an amazing honour – it makes me so proud to play in front of the Kop

always does – then I wish him luck for his own sake and for the team.

All I can keep doing is giving everything I have in training and do the same on the rare opportunities that I do get to play. If I am to become Spain's number one, then I want it to be on my own merits and not because the standards of my rival have slipped.

I made my international debut on August 17, 2005. For obvious reasons it is a date that I will never forget. We were playing against Uruguay in Gijon and we won 2-0. It was a really memorable occasion for me, not least because it was the first time I had played a game without any hair on my head.

That wasn't a deliberate decision and it certainly wasn't a fashion statement. It was because I allowed Ivan De La Pena to give me a haircut on the morning of the game and he shaved it all off. I think he must have wanted me to look like him. I had wanted at least a bit of hair for the game, but he left me with none. I looked ridiculous.

It brought me luck though because we got a good victory in one of my favourite stadiums, I kept a clean sheet and it proved to be a good night all round.

My big chance came because Casillas had picked up a knock playing for Real Madrid in a pre-season game and when I was called up I realised that it was recognition of what we had achieved with Villarreal the season before because we had managed to finish third in La Liga.

Jose Manuel Ochotorena was the goalkeeping coach with the national team and he was also working for Liverpool at the time. Seeing as I signed for Liverpool just before I was called up by Spain I have to presume that he played a big part in both decisions. I had been expecting to be selected as I had been playing well for Villarreal and there had been rumours in the press that I was about to be given my chance with the national side, so it wasn't really a big surprise when the call I had been waiting for finally arrived.

I had belief in myself, I was happy with the way I had performed for

Villarreal and I had also secured a move to one of the biggest clubs in the world so being involved in the international scene seemed a natural step, even though it was one of the most important moments in my career and a massive honour.

I was really calm about the whole thing and although I was under pressure I did not feel any. I had already been in the squad once before a couple of months earlier when we played a couple of games against Lithuania and Bosnia in Valencia. That helped me settle in, particularly as the people involved with the squad had made me feel really welcome from the moment I first arrived. I never felt like the new boy in school or anything like that. I was a part of things straight away and that helped give me the confidence I needed to deliver a good performance in my first appearance. From that point on I became a fixture in the national squad, getting picked all the time.

The next big tournament after I made my breakthrough was the World Cup in Germany in 2006. Spain had never taken more than two keepers to a tournament but this time, probably because Luis Aragones was finding it so hard to choose between Canizares and myself, we took three. The idea was that I was there as second choice behind Casillas, but when it came to selecting the substitutes Aragones ended up picking Canizares ahead of me, which was a big disappointment.

Canizares had more experience than me and he had just enjoyed a really good season with Valencia and I had to accept the manager's decision, but it was tough. I was angry. It was a big blow to me but I had to keep my head down and get on with things for the good of all of us. It isn't always easy for keepers to get on with one another because when it comes down to it we are in direct competition for just one place in the team. The relationship between Iker and Canizares didn't seem the best during that tournament. It wasn't bad, but it was more professional than anything else. With me being new to the squad and the other keeper, I ended up stuck in the middle.

To be honest, I felt that the squad at that tournament was not as united as it should have been and the team spirit certainly wasn't as strong as it would be at later tournaments.

It was a different kind of atmosphere to the one that would develop with the players being split into groups, a separation that was far from ideal. There was a group of experienced players including Raul, Michel Salgado, Santiago Canizares and David Albelda, they were a bit separate from the rest, and there was a group of young players as well.

We certainly did not have the kind of unity that would come to play a crucial role in our success. It wasn't that we were enemies and there were not any problems between the players, but there was a feeling that we needed a greater sense of togetherness. Despite this, it still ended up being a good tournament for me because I learned a lot just from being involved in it. I got to be part of a group of players that was growing all the time. It was also a significant competition for the squad as a whole. Aragones made some mistakes in Germany but he learned from them. This was crucial to us winning Euro 2008 two years later.

If I had to put my finger on one reason why Spain have been so successful in recent years it would be that the players who aren't selected are the first to give support to their team-mates. They are not selfish and they do not allow their own personal disappointment to get in the way of what is best for the team. There is a strong bond that exists between everyone in the dressing room. Team spirit is a basic requirement of any team, particularly one that wants to win things, and we have it in abundance.

For all the talk about the coaching, the level of the players and the overall quality of our team, I honestly believe that one of the main reasons why we have been so successful is the positive atmosphere that exists within the group. It is brilliant and the people are so humble, but it is hard work at the same time.

I have made friendships in the national squad that I know will last my entire lifetime. I have good relationships with so many of the players: David Villa, Fernando Llorente, Fernando Morientes, Albert Riera, Sergio Ramos, Xabi Alonso, Casillas, Puyol, Xavi, Busquets, Torres.

So many of them are good guys and although most people will not realise it, Xavi Hernandez is probably one of the funniest people I have ever come across in my career. Whenever I go to Ibiza on holiday in the summer the first thing I do is find out if Xavi will be there at the same time because I know that if I meet up with him and his friends I will have an unbelievable laugh with them. The banter between them is unbelievable and it never, ever stops.

Sometimes I have to pinch myself that I am sat with one of the true greats of world football, a player who maybe only Lionel Messi and Cristiano Ronaldo can claim to be better than and who, in my eyes, is the best player Spain has ever produced. But off the pitch he is the most down to earth person anyone could ever meet and that is what makes him even more special than he already is.

Villa and myself are very close. It dates back to our time in the Spain Under-21 team and we have been friends for over 10 years now. Even our families are very close. Our parents sit together at matches and get on really well.

After the Champions League final in 2011 Villa dedicated his goal to me and to my daughters, who he said were like nieces to him, and also to my new-born son. That meant so much to me and it says everything about him and about our relationship that after one of the greatest moments in his career he still thought about me. It was even more special because the goal was against Man United.

I do feel much more important when I am at Liverpool than I do when I am with the national team, there is no question about that. That is the difference that playing makes and it is the same for every player at every single level. At Liverpool I feel as if the club, my team-mates and the supporters are relying on me, but it can't be like this for Spain because I am sat on the bench when the games are taking place, unable to make the kind of impression that I am desperate to.

But within the dressing room it is different. That is my domain, a place where I feel totally comfortable because my team-mates have so much respect for me. I think I have earned that from being there for six years and it is a nice feeling to have, particularly seeing as I have had to earn their respect in other ways because of the fact that more often than not I am a non-playing player.

Any time I join the national team I am like a kid. I am so happy to go back to my own country, to see my friends and my family, to eat Spanish food and to speak my own language. This is something that I will miss when the time comes that I am not part of the national squad.

I can't understand why keepers retire early from international football because they don't feel they will have the chance to play too often. Just being in the national squad for any country is an honour and there is always pleasure to be taken from being involved with the best players from your country. There may have been other reasons why Paul Robinson and Ben Foster quit England while they were in the prime of their careers, but if the main one was that they thought it was pointless being in a squad if they aren't going to play then, in my eyes, that is not right. I would never do that, no matter what happens. I will not retire from international football no matter what. When the time comes Spain will have to retire me because I will not walk away from them.

I will never accept just being a back-up keeper and I wouldn't even try to pretend that I could because I am desperate to play. But I also know my place. I know that I am the understudy.

I would love nothing more than to carry the pressure of being Spain's number one goalkeeper, of going into big games knowing that I have to deliver if we are to stand a chance of winning trophies. I want to stand and fall by my own abilities, not rely on others to win medals for me. I want to be tested at the very highest level and show that I am capable of flourishing. All I can do is wait for my opportunity, and make sure that I am ready when it comes.

Only three goalkeepers can be picked and there are an unbelievable number of good Spanish goalkeepers around, so to be considered one of the best three in the country is a massive privilege. It gives me a great deal of pride.

Just look at the situation with my great friend Mikel Arteta. If he had been born in Southport instead of San Sebastian, he would be in the England team in every game they play. So many people ask me how it is possible that a player as good as he is has never even played a single game for Spain and it is something that is difficult to explain because there is no doubt that he is good enough to play international football.

Mikel has been unlucky not to be selected, there is no question about that. Maybe the fact that he left Spain at such an early age has not helped him because it can be a case of out of sight, out of mind when you are a young player. But the biggest reason why he has been overlooked is that he plays in a position where there is an unbelievable amount of quality around. There is Xavi Hernandez, Andres Iniesta, Xabi Alonso, Sergio Busquets and so on and so on. If I think it is hard to get a game as a goalkeeper then it must be even more difficult to break into the squad for a midfield player because the talent in that position is unbelievable.

Of course, when you do get a chance then you are under massive pressure to perform. That is the same for any player, although I know if I make a single little mistake as a keeper it will be highlighted and used as proof that it is right that I am second choice, not first.

Because I know the feeling so well and I understand the pressure, I have so much sympathy for the reserve goalkeepers at Liverpool when they come in for a cup game that I have been rested for. It is very difficult for them to show their level in a one-off game, no matter how good they are.

You could have a keeper who is one of the best in the world but if he does not play too often then it is going to be difficult for him to show how good he is. That is the burden that I carry when I join up with the national squad but, for me, it is a small price to pay for being part of such a special group.

My father had a similar situation to me when he was a player. During his era, Jose Angel Iribar, the legendary Basque goalkeeper, was first choice for Spain and my dad was his understudy. So we have both been unlucky in that our eras have coincided with times when Spain has had another great keeper. He could not complain about it and neither can I. All I can do is count myself lucky to be a part of the national team and I do feel that I am lucky, no matter what.

I cannot imagine that I will ever be involved in a better group of players than the national squad of recent years. Achievements like winning the World Cup and Euro 2008 speak for themselves. If I am ever part of a squad that does anything even more special than this then it would have to be one of the most incredible teams put together in the history of football.

The generation of players that won those famous trophies came through together. We already had experience of winning tournaments at a junior level and were used to winning with the national team, going all the way back to when we were teenagers. History is repeating itself now and there is another generation of young Spanish players coming through. They won the Under-21 championships, the Under-17s and so on. They, too, are in the winning habit.

The challenge for the current senior Spain team now is to try to keep on repeating our success, but we know how difficult that will be because no-one has ever won three massive tournaments in a row.

At Euro 2012 we will once again be the team who everyone else is desperate to beat. They will try to stop us playing in whatever way they can and we just have to make sure that we are as determined as ever to get the result, and to stick as close as possible to the style of football that has brought us so much success.

When I made my debut for Spain I was given a badge to mark my first appearance. In England, the players get a cap for every game that they play. We get a badge for our first game and then after every 25 matches we are presented with a commemorative picture showing all the games that we have been involved in.

I have been in the national squad since 2005, but I am still waiting for a picture. It is one of my biggest ambitions to get one. After six years, my running total was 22 games so I still have some work to do. That's rough because in that time I have been included in more than 90 squads. That speaks volumes for Iker, but it is hard for me.

Keeping The Faith

Of all the Liverpool players, I am the one who has the closest relationship with the Kop. I'm not saying that I'm their favourite, although I like to think that I'm one of them, I just mean that I am the one who is nearest to them during games. Stood in front of the most famous stand in world football, literally feet away from thousands of Liverpool's most passionate fans, there are times when I find myself singing along with their songs, laughing at the stick they give out to opposition players and managers and celebrating with them when we score goals.

When we run out onto the pitch before games I have the privilege of going to the Kop end. It doesn't matter how many times I do it, it is something that will always send a shiver down my spine, and I also get an incredible sense of pride when I see the flag that is flown in my honour behind the goal.

That flag means a lot to me. I first spotted it towards the end of the 2009/10 season and it has been there ever since. I used to wonder who had decided to make a banner for me and what I had done to be given that honour. It was only when a friend told me the story behind it that I realised just how privileged I am.

My flag was created and paid for by a disabled supporter called Dan Wakefield who goes to Liverpool matches home and away in a wheelchair, hardly missing any. Dan had my flag designed by a friend and then paid for it to be made in Australia and shipped to this country. He cannot fly it himself so he gets friends to do it for him. As soon as I see it I always give a thumbs up in its direction because I know how much effort has gone into getting it onto the Kop and I really appreciate it. For me, it typifies the level of commitment of the Liverpool supporters to their team and the lengths that they will go to just to show that they are with us.

When I found out about Dan and what he had done for me I knew that I had to meet him just to say thanks. So, just after I signed my most recent contract, I arranged for Dan to come to Melwood for the day. He brought his flag with him. It is so big that I needed help from Rafa and Owen Brown to put it up in the part of the building where we put our boots on before going out to train. It looks massive on the Kop anyway, but it seems even bigger when you are trying to put it up. Between the three of us we just about managed it. I wanted to show Dan my appreciation for what he had done for me so I signed a pair of my gloves and gave them to him and he also asked me to sign his flag which, of course, I was more than happy to do. It was only a small gesture, a token of my appreciation really, but I wanted to show him how grateful I am for the flag and how much it means to me.

It was during the same season that I realised just how loyal the Liverpool supporters are. We were playing Tottenham at home in a night game and we were under a lot of pressure because our form had not been good enough. There was a lot of talk about Rafa maybe leaving the club. At times like that you would expect the negativity to affect the fans and maybe make them a bit more critical of us because we are letting them down by not getting the results that they deserve. But at Liverpool it is different than at most other clubs. If the supporters feel that the criticism that is coming our way is unfair then they close ranks behind us, letting the world know that they don't care what anyone else thinks or says, they will always be there for us.

That night we were travelling to Anfield on the team bus as usual and I was looking out of the window watching the people walking to the stadium and seeing them clapping us as we went past. I had no idea what was coming, but when we drove up Anfield Road and approached the Shankly Gates I saw thousands of supporters with flags giving us a guard of honour. They just wanted us to know that they were with us and we got the message. Just seeing it made me emotional and there was no way we could lose after witnessing a scene like that. We ended up winning the game 2-0. It is these kinds of things that make Liverpool different.

The only time I have ever seen anything like it is when I have played at the Bernabeu in really big games and the Real Madrid fans gather outside the stadium to support their own team and to try to intimidate their opponents. But that is usually when times are good, when Real have a Champions League tie or have a vital match. In our case, it happened when we were struggling badly and things looked like they were going wrong. That is what makes it special and I doubt it would happen anywhere else.

I have never seen supporters like the Liverpool fans, in terms of travelling all over the country and Europe, supporting the team, backing the players even when things aren't going well. It is an incredible privilege to play for them and one of the best parts of playing in goal at Anfield is standing in front of the Kop for our home games.

One funny memory was the week after the famous beach ball goal at Sunderland in October, 2009. We were playing our next game against

Man United at home. It was live on Sky and they stationed all their TV cameras in front of the away end at the Anfield Road expecting the United fans to throw all kinds of beach balls onto the pitch to take the piss out of me. They could not have predicted what happened next.

Instead of the beach balls coming from the away end, they came from the Kop, one after another. I could not stop laughing and when the match kicked off I was still smiling to myself. There are no other supporters anywhere who would have done something like that. It defused the situation perfectly and took the pressure off me. I have always appreciated the Liverpool supporters, but this made me appreciate them even more.

I can't understand everything I hear when I am close to the Kop, but I am getting more and more used to the chants, the songs and the jokes. I was actually crying my eyes out when we were playing Sunderland for the first time after that beach ball goal. Their supporters were giving me some stick, but I wasn't distressed by what they were singing about me. I was in hysterics at the chant from our fans.

They had already sung a song saying that Steve Bruce had a 'big fat head' and the new version was saying that he had a 'head like a beach ball'. It was one of the funniest songs I have ever heard at a football ground and it took me about a minute to get my composure back. If Sunderland had gone on the attack at that moment we might have had problems because they would have come up against a laughing goalkeeper, but fortunately we had the ball at the time. To be fair to Bruce, I saw the pictures of his reaction on television later that night and he was buzzing as well. You have to have a good sense of humour in football, but even more so when the Kop are taking the piss out of you. There is no hiding place when that happens.

There have been times when I have caught myself joining in with the singing. I don't do it deliberately, but when you have 12,000 people stood behind you singing it can be hard not to join in, especially when we are winning a really important game and You'll Never Walk Alone is ringing around the ground. I would defy anyone to stand right in front of the Kop and not be moved when they are singing the club anthem. It can bring tears to my eyes. But even some of the less well known songs get me humming along with the tune. I might not know the words and I probably wouldn't understand half of them even if I did, but the tunes are really catchy. I loved the one about Fernando and the one for Crouchy – 'he's big, he's Red, his feet stick out the bed' – was really funny as well. I like mine too. It's 'Pepe Reina, Pepe Reina, ay! ay!' repeated over and over. I just think it needs more words now!

The supporters are always there for the team. I had friends over from Spain for our last home game of the 2010/11 season when we needed to beat Spurs to qualify for the Europa League. Spurs played really well on the day and beat us 2-0. We struggled to be honest and they deserved their win. It was a bad way to end the season for us and we were all disappointed because we had let ourselves and the fans down.

The worst thing about it is we still had to do a lap of honour, our traditional way of saying thank you to the fans for backing us throughout the season. I walked off the pitch after the final whistle thinking that I wouldn't blame the supporters if they had all gone home or to the pub by the time we came back out, but as we re-appeared a few minutes later, the stadium was still nearly full.

We had messed up but the supporters were still there, singing our names and showing that they will never give up on us no matter what. That is an incredible feeling.

My friends keep on reminding me of this moment, telling me that in Spain the only reason supporters would stay behind after their team had lost would be to give the players stick. They are right about that. The Liverpool fans are different. They have a code of honour that is unique and we are fortunate to play for them.

As a Liverpool player you always want to win for the fans. The importance of being like this is drummed into you from the moment you first arrive at the club. But there are occasions when you are even more desperate to be successful for them and that makes it even more disappointing when you cannot give them what they want. One of the best examples was when we played Chelsea at Stamford Bridge in the quarter-finals of the Champions League in 2009. The year, the opponents and the venue were not the most important thing, but the date was. It was April 14, the day before the 20th anniversary of the Hillsborough disaster in which 96 Liverpool supporters were tragically killed.

We had nothing to lose. We had lost the first leg 3-1 so everyone was expecting Chelsea to complete the job without too many problems. We saw things differently and when we went in at half-time we were two goals up. Fabio Aurelio scored the first with a sensational free-kick that caught Petr Cech completely by surprise. When Xabi Alonso added a penalty, the great escape was on. One more goal was all we needed.

The atmosphere in the dressing room at half-time was incredible, we were so pumped up it was unreal. We could not wait to get out there and complete the job. We really did believe that the impossible was within our grasp. Sadly, though, I made a mistake and allowed Didier Drogba to get a goal back and that meant we needed two more goals. I could do nothing about their second. Alex's free-kick was one of the most powerful I have ever faced and I didn't have a chance. Things got even worse when Frank Lampard scored a third in the 76th minute and it looked like we were finished.

We were on the ropes just waiting for the knockout blow to be delivered, but that was often when we were at our most dangerous that season and from somewhere within ourselves we summoned up the courage to fight back with two goals in the space of three minutes. The Chelsea players could not believe it because they had thought we were done for and understandably so, because by rights our spirits should have been broken by what had happened. Lucas scored an equaliser with a deflected shot that wrongfooted Cech with nine minutes to go and when Dirk grabbed a near post header from Riera's cross to take us back in front we were back in the position that we'd been in at half-time, needing just one more goal to take us through to the semi-finals.

Had we got it then everyone in football would have been stunned. To come back once is a great achievement, but to do it twice in the same game is something truly special. Frustratingly, Lampard ended our dream when he made the score 4-4 towards the end of the game. We were proud of what we had done and we were able to walk away from the stadium with our heads held high because we had given everything. But we were still disappointed for the supporters because we knew how important the game was for them coming, as it did, on the eve of the 20th anniversary.

The following day we attended the memorial service at Anfield, as we do every year, and as usual it was a humbling experience. If there is one thing more than any other that makes me feel proud to be a Liverpool player it is the way that the club and the supporters commemorate the 15th of April.

On the 20th anniversary there were more than 35,000 people in the stadium. I can remember travelling on the team bus from Melwood and passing car after car that was on the way to the ground. It was like a match day. As we got closer to Anfield the number of people was unbelievable and it wasn't just Liverpool supporters either, I saw a lot of Everton fans. This sums up the bond that still exists in the city even though the rivalry is so intense.

I kept on saying to myself "this is a memorial for a tragedy that happened 20 years ago and yet still there are tens of thousands of people coming to pay their respects". Would it happen anywhere else, in any other part of the world? I don't think so. Watching it with my own eyes I was moved and I was also humbled. I was talking to Fernando afterwards and I said to him, "for this alone it is worth being here." That is how special it is. The commitment, the passion and the loyalty that the people have for the fight for justice and also to the club is phenomenal. Because of that the very least you can do as long as you play for Liverpool is to give everything you possibly can because that is what the supporters do.

I have to admit that before I came to Liverpool I knew very little about what had happened at Hillsborough. I knew there had been a disaster and that 96 people had lost their lives, but I did not know what the causes were or how it had happened. The club educated me from the moment I arrived and now I understand about the fight for justice and what it means. It is something that once you have experienced it, it can never leave you.

Look at Rafa, he still came to the memorial service even after he had left the club because it had become so important to him during his time as manager.

He is someone from Spain who, like me, came to this country not really knowing a great deal about Hillsborough. But from getting to know about it and also by experiencing the memorial service he is now one of the biggest supporters of the campaign for justice. That says a lot about him. But it also says even more about the people who are leading the campaign, the families and friends who have never given up and who keep the search for truth in the limelight. When people show courage and spirit like this then you have to find a place in your heart for them.

It is hard to make comparisons because every situation is different, but my only other experience of this kind of movement comes from my own country where people hold vigils and protests whenever there is a terrorist attack by ETA. Tens of thousands of people come on to the streets and show solidarity with one another and it can last for a week or two or maybe even for a year. The Hillsborough families have been fighting for more than 20 years. That is unbelievable and I can only admire them for that.

It is because of my respect and my admiration for the supporters that I was so disappointed that for a couple of years they were forced into becoming protestors, marchers, politicians and activists. This was one of the biggest crimes committed by Tom Hicks and George Gillett – their actions took so much of the fun away from being a Liverpool fan. On the day of games, supporters would look at the business pages of newspapers instead of the sports pages to see the state of the club's finances. They would march to the stadium with banners and placards when they should have been in the pub enjoying a pint, and they stayed behind after the match to protest against the owners. These are people who love the club, who will go to almost any lengths to support us and yet the joy of being a Liverpool supporter was being taken away from them by the actions of Hicks and Gillett. In my eyes that is unforgivable.

If they were still the owners of Liverpool, I would no longer be at the club. It is as simple as that. But it wouldn't only be me. There would have been plenty of others who would have walked through the Shankly Gates, never to return. That wouldn't be the biggest problem for Liverpool either because I honestly believe that had the American duo been in charge a year longer as owners then the club would have become a mid-table outfit or even worse. They created a nightmare that only began to end with their departure and if I ever see either of them again it will be too soon.

What Hicks and Gillett put Liverpool through was disgraceful, but I have to confess that when they first bought the club in February, 2007 like everyone else I thought they were the right people to command the board and to take us to a higher level. They were saying all the right things and they were making all kinds of promises – to build a new stadium on Stanley Park, to provide cash for new players, and so on and so on – but at the end of the day nothing was delivered. They put us in a really bad situation for a couple of years, one that we are still recovering from.

The damage they did is there for everyone to see and the sad thing is we are seeing this kind of situation more and more often in football as people who have no love or understanding of clubs buy them just to use them to try and make money. It is not right that clubs can be the playthings of rich men who could not care less about the players or the manager or the fans, but it is a sad reality of the modern game.

It is a problem that is not going away and football has to find a way of ensuring that when a club is put up for sale it gets sold to people who will run it for the good of the club itself and also for the supporters. If they make money along the way then great, good luck to them, because football is a business and if businessmen invest money then obviously they are going to expect a return. This should never be at the expense of the club itself or the supporters because they are so precious that they need to be protected, particularly when vultures like Hicks and Gillett are hovering. The best solution would be for prospective owners to have to prove themselves to the fans. I don't know how this could be done. But unless the needs of the supporters and their love for the club is given priority then the kind of terrible situation we had at Liverpool will be repeated again and again and again.

Like all of the players, I met Hicks and Gillett on a few occasions when they came to Melwood, and when they came to Anfield for games. I never had any big conversations with them, it would just be small talk about our kids or the weather, stuff that people talk about all the time. But I was told all about their grand plans by the people who were working with them and in the end it all turned out to be a lie. There was no new stadium, there was no spade in the ground within

60 days as Gillett had promised and they were not prepared to fund the signings of the players who would take us to the next level. They cheated us and that is why they were so hated by the supporters. The Liverpool fans are loyal, sometimes to a fault, but if you lie to them and you cheat them then they will turn on you and this is what happened to Hicks and Gillett.

I had only been at the club for 18 months when they bought it and at the time Rafa was talking about building something special at Liverpool. He had an ambition to make us champions of England and champions of Europe, but he was counting on the money from the owners to make his dreams a reality. Don't get me wrong, even during this time Rafa still spent some big money and a few of his signings did not work out. He has to take his own responsibility for that.

This happens to every manager. Now and again you will make mistakes during the transfer window, and if you look at the clubs who are most successful almost always they are the ones who have the most money to spend on players because this reduces the risk of making mistakes. Had they backed him like they said they were going to – after we lost the Champions League Final to Milan in 2007, Gillett said that if Rafa wanted "Snoogy Doogy" he would back him – then who knows what we could have achieved? As it was, Rafa ended up having to sell to buy during his last couple of seasons in charge and whatever anyone thinks about the mistakes he may or may not have made in the transfer market that is not good enough for a club like Liverpool. Nowhere near good enough.

I started to worry that something wasn't right about the owners during the 2008/09 season when we came second in the league. When a team is playing as well as we were and is as close to major success as we were then that is the time to really squeeze that extra bit of money to bring three or four top players to the squad. It isn't the only way to win trophies, but it is the quickest way to take the next step. If owners don't do that then you have to question their ambition or their finances. Had winning been the main motive of Hicks and Gillett, as they claimed when they bought the club, then this was the perfect time to prove it by speculating to accumulate – but they did nothing. All we did was sell Xabi and a couple of others and reinvest some of the money in the squad. When that happens then you know that the owners either aren't interested in success or don't have the money to make a difference. Whatever the reason, we found out the hard way that their promises were worth nothing.

The supporters probably realised before anyone. If you go back to the Porto game in the Champions League in 2007 they staged a protest against the owners because it emerged they had approached Jurgen Klinsmann to become manager behind Rafa's back. Sometimes when you are working at a club every single day you are not able to see the problems straight away, but the fans recognised them earliest of all and they ended up having marches and demonstrations against Hicks and Gillett when they would have preferred to have been enjoying going to the match as normal.

I know there were those who questioned the supporters for staging protests, and accused them of putting politics before the club. That is not the way that I see it. I totally understand their reasons and if I'd been a Liverpool supporter rather than a player I would have been demonstrating with them. They expected the owners to deliver and they did not. For a group of fans who are always behind their team, even during the bad times this must have felt like a massive kick in the guts. Their trust in the club and their optimism for the future was taken away and when they opened their eyes to what was going on it was inevitable that there would be a reaction.

Of course, I wish that it had not happened and as a player I could not afford to get too involved in what was going on because I had to be a professional. All I could do for the good of the club was try to deliver for the team and that meant I could not get distracted by what was going on, even though I was aware of it and worried by it.

For the supporters it was different, Liverpool was their club a long time before I got here and it will still be their club a long time after I have gone. They give everything to Liverpool and all they demand in return is that the club and the players treat them well by doing everything that we possibly can to be successful. So when this contract was broken they reacted against Hicks and Gillett out of a love for their club and a feeling that they had been cheated, nothing else.

Rafa was really disappointed by what was going on because he felt that they had been telling him lies. As a manager you always want to get the best players in the market, that is only natural, but you need money to do that. So if they promised big money to Rafa and then failed to deliver it then it was a big lie, like the stadium and everything else. That was a problem that he had to deal with because as players there was not much that we could do about it. All we could do was try to highlight what was going on in the media because it wasn't right.

When I look back at that time, I was probably one of the loudest objectors in the dressing room because I believed it was really important that the supporters knew that I was with them. All I wanted the owners to do was sell up to people who could take the club forward, so I said so. It wasn't always easy because at a club like Liverpool the best situation is that any problems are sorted out behind closed doors and away from the media, but it was getting worse every single day so I felt that I had to say something whenever I could.

For me it is about principles. I believed that what was happening was wrong so I could not just sit there and say nothing, particularly when the owners were doing so much damage to the club. If a situation is not right then I have to speak, it is as simple as that. Some of the supporters might have thought that I was wrong to speak out, seeing as the club was paying my wages and that all a player should do is play and keep his mouth shut. I respect that opinion and, in an ideal world, no player would ever have to say anything about Liverpool because the club is so well run and all the promises that are made are kept. But at that time, Liverpool was not like this so I felt that I had to try and do something about it, even if it was only a small thing like telling the media about the concerns from within the dressing room.

Not everyone saw it like this. I know Carra has admitted that I asked him why neither he nor Stevie spoke out at this time. I understand their reasons, that they felt that they had to be professional and not get dragged into a war, and I respect them. We might have disagreed on this subject but that did not mean we fell out with each other or anything like that. The club had enough problems without the senior players having problems with one another because of a difference of opinion. The way I saw it, Stevie and Carra are the two principle members of our squad, the ones who the people love and if they had said something maybe it would have put Hicks and Gillett under real pressure. But in their view, it was more important to try to keep things as normal as possible rather than risk rocking the boat even more. What was not in doubt was that we all just wanted the best for the club.

This was an extraordinary time and it should never come down to the supporters to decide whether or not they should protest, or to the senior players to decide if it is right to speak out against the owners. It just shouldn't happen. We were all being put in a bad position by Hicks and Gillett. Whatever choices we made at the time should be judged against the backdrop of how bad the situation had become, not against us as individuals. My respect for Stevie and Carra did not change one bit, even though we saw things differently. We all did what we thought was right, that is all anyone can ever do.

It is not for anyone to judge us, not when Hicks and Gillett were causing all of the problems. Not only did they fail to make good on their promises, they made the club's debt bigger and bigger and bigger. When it was £60million it was under control because Liverpool are such a big club with assets on and off the pitch, but before we knew it the debt was hundreds of millions and people were talking about the possibility of us going into administration. How could this even be possible? The stadium was not being built, the investment in players was coming mainly from the club itself rather than the owners and we were making lots of money on the pitch because we were doing well in the Champions League almost every single season. And yet the debt was doubling, trebling and then quadrupling until it got to such a stage that the banks had to get involved. This is Liverpool Football Club, one of the biggest and most famous sporting institutions in the entire world, and our future was being put at risk by a debt that had not even been built up by spending. We had the right to ask questions and to seek explanations because the club was being put into such a bad situation. It was not right, it is as simple as that.

I know that David Moores and Rick Parry made the decision to sell to Hicks and Gillett and this had turned out to be a big mistake, but they cannot feel guilty about this because like all of us they believed that they were selling to the right people. In their eyes, they were selling to a pair of businessmen who made big promises about the stadium and the club that appeared to give us such an exciting future. The problem was that they did not keep their promises and we all suffered.

There was no future for Liverpool as long as Hicks and Gillett were in charge. That is why I know that I would not still be here if they were.

When I was having my doubts about my own situation at the start of the 2010/11 season it was because I saw no future for the club with them still in control. I was promised by members of the club that Liverpool would deliver that season and this did not happen. That is why it is so important that promises of this kind are kept so that players are able to believe in the club and its future.

We are doing better now and we are definitely going in the right direction. This does not guarantee success. On the pitch, our fortunes could turn out to be good, or they could turn out to be bad, but at least the organisation of the club now seems to be so much better.

It doesn't bear thinking about what would have happened to the club had Hicks and Gillett stayed in charge. They were the wrong people for Liverpool and when you have the wrong people it is almost impossible for good things to happen. I have admitted that my own future would have been in serious doubt, but the same thing would have applied to a few of the other top players. Once that starts happening, the team is weakened and the atmosphere becomes negative. Then it is only ever going to result in you becoming an ordinary club.

People might think that this is far-fetched that Liverpool, with all the trophies they have won in the past and with their wonderful history, could survive anything. But even the greatest clubs can be brought to their knees by bad owners and in Hicks and Gillett Liverpool had two of the worst.

Liverpool should never, ever be in this kind of situation. It is not where they belong. Because of the supporters that we have, because of their backing for us and their passion for the club, we have to be fighting for titles every single year. Everything that Liverpool stands for, everything that it is about means that, at the very least, we have to be competing to be successful.

We cannot be just another club that goes from one season to the next hoping for a decent cup run or to maybe qualify for the Europa League. Our history and our supporters demand that we are in the running for the biggest prizes and the longer Hicks and Gillett were running the show the less likely it was that we were going to be able to live up to our own expectations, never mind anyone else's.

When you go around the world and you see the fanbase that we have and the potential that this club has then it makes me wonder why mega-rich owners like the ones who bought Manchester City or Malaga did not buy Liverpool at that time because I believe that they would love to own one of the biggest clubs in the world. Because this club is so special it surely can't have been hard to find the perfect people and the only positive to come from this situation is that it now looks like we have found the people to take us forward.

I do not think for a minute that Hicks and Gillett had any affection for Liverpool. Hicks said something about buying Liverpool being the same as buying Weetabix, it was just a business deal to try and make money from. That pretty much sums the two of them up because they did not care about the manager, the players or the supporters. Their actions prove this. All they were bothered about was their own self-interest and the benefits to their own business.

The fans, more than anyone else, deserved better than this and hopefully they will never, ever be in this kind of situation again.

Red Rafalution

Liverpool was never Spanish Liverpool. To say that it was would be an insult to a great club and the unique blend of tradition, history and identity that make it what it is. There was a time when the Spanish influence was strong as Rafa Benitez used his extensive knowledge of La Liga and his contacts at home to recruit players and backroom staff, but this did not stop Liverpool from being the English club that it always has been and always will be.

It was exciting for me to be part of the Rafalution and the interest in our results in my homeland was incredible at times with people supporting us from Madrid to Malaga and Barcelona to Bilbao. There was even a time when players like Xabi Alonso, Fernando Torres, Alvaro Arbeloa and myself became known as 'El Benitels' in the Spanish media. But by the start of the 2011/12 season my compatriots had either left of their own accord or were sold to make way for new players and even Rafa's reign had come to an end, signalling the start of a new era at Anfield. Until Jose Enrique was signed from Newcastle United, I was the last remaining Spaniard in the first-team, although that didn't bother me, not in the slightest.

I do not need to be in a dressing room that is populated by lots of people from Spain. Of course I am Spanish, but that is only part of what I am. I try to be a positive person in whatever environment I am in. This means that my team-mates can be English, Irish, Chinese, Italian, African, whatever. The nationalities do not matter. They might not all understand my jokes, but I will keep on delivering them. It was easier for me to adapt to Liverpool in particular and English football in general because there were people from my own country here when I first arrived, but from that point on I had to become a Liverpool player. There is no question that in the years that have passed since then I have entered into the spirit of the Liverpool way of things and the club's philosophy.

Liverpool needs an English mentality, but what it has always done well is take influences from other countries and other leagues and use them to their advantage, going right back to the team of Macs at the very start of its history. The great AC Milan side which had Marco van Basten, Frank Rijkaard and Ruud Gullit, might have had a Dutch outlook, but they still managed to retain their Italian mentality. That is the way it was at Liverpool. The Spanish influence was strong, but we were not separate and we did not even try to alter the club's mentality in any way.

This was one of the reasons why Rafa thought it was so important that we all learned to speak English because if we hadn't done so, that is when you can get splits and different groups in the dressing room. His idea was that we were in Liverpool, playing for an English team and we had to adapt to them, not the other way around.

Rafa was the man responsible for this period in Liverpool's history. He created the team that went closer than any other since 1990 to winning the league title and he took the club to two Champions League finals in just three years. Without hesitation and with the greatest respect to all the other managers I have been fortunate enough to work under I can say that Rafa is the best manager that I have ever had. He is the one I learned the most from and I still regard him as the master when it comes to tactics. He also knew how to get the best out of me and I know that I will be forever in his debt for what he has done for my football career.

Having said that, when Rafa left Liverpool at the end of the 2009/10 season, I knew that it was the right time for him to go. It hurts me to say that, but the wheels had come off by then and there was no guarantee that he was going to be able to put them back on.

It is never nice when a manager leaves or loses his job, especially when it is one who has been as successful and popular as Rafa had been. He had been a massive part of the club and because of that, his departure was always going to come as a shock even though I had been expecting it to happen after such a disappointing campaign. People argue about the reasons why he went, but sometimes it is not as complicated as they try to make it appear.

There are times when, for whatever reason, the methods that have been bringing a manager so much success just stop working. There doesn't have to be an explanation or a clever reason, it just happens this way in football now and again and that year Rafa was unable to achieve the same results that he had done previously. When this happens, the club has to make a decision about whether you will be able to get back to winning ways again in the future, or if it is time to look for a new manager who might be able to freshen things up, just by having a different approach.

Liverpool wanted to go down the latter route and it was probably the right decision. But no-one should make the mistake of thinking that Rafa went from being a double La Liga-winning manager with Valencia, a European Cup-winning and title-challenging manager with Liverpool to a bad one overnight. He is still one of the best in the business and it was just the case at the time that a change was in the best interests of the club, of the team and of Rafa himself.

Had someone said to me at the end of the 2008/09 season, when we came so close to winning the league, that just 12 months later the manager would be gone then I wouldn't have believed them. That is football. It is not about what you might have done in the past, it can never be about that. It is about what you are doing in the here and now and what you are going to do in the future.

It is the same for managers as it is for players. None of us can live on past glories and the moment any of us think that we can is the moment that decisions about our future are taken out of our hands. If I have a really poor season in goal then the chances are that Liverpool will start looking at the possibility of replacing me. No-one will say: "Hang on, what about all those Golden Glove awards Pepe won a few years ago?" They will look at what I am doing at the time and make their choices on that basis. Unfortunately, for managers there are so many things that they can't control which will help determine the results they get.

Sadly for Rafa we went from second place in the Premier League one season to seventh place the next and that was always going to result in him coming under pressure. There were other problems as well, ones that were going to be really difficult to solve. They existed both in the boardroom and the dressing room so in the end that made a parting of the ways inevitable. Sad, but inevitable.

One of the problems we had was that we had lost some good players – the likes of Xabi Alonso, Peter Crouch and Jermaine Pennant – but never really replaced them. Signings were made with the idea of making improvements to the team, but the reality was that the ones who came in were not of the same standard as the ones who had left. In some respects you can look at the players who came in and ask why they didn't deliver because no footballer can ever be free of responsibility. But in football the buck always stops with the manager and if he makes signings that don't work out then it won't be long before the people who run the club are going to ask questions of him.

I first began to realise we were in trouble when we played against Espanyol in a pre-season friendly at the start of August, 2009, to open the new Cornella-Prat Stadium on the outskirts of Barcelona. It was a magnificent night for them because they beat us 3-0 and could even have scored more. I came off the pitch thinking Espanyol could become champions of Spain because they absolutely blew us away. There was also a part of me that thought, 'if we carry on like this, we are going to get relegated.' It was as if someone had flicked a switch at the end of the previous season and we had gone from being a really strong team to a really weak one.

The situation with Xabi was part of the problem because although he made a brief appearance against Espanyol, his move to Real Madrid was about to happen and we never really replaced him in midfield. The defeat gave me a really bad feeling and it did worry me, but I tried to convince myself that everything would be okay when the season began and that I should not get too concerned about a defeat in a pre-season friendly.

The alarm bells rang even louder when we lost at Tottenham on the opening day of the season. We lost 2-1, but we deserved to lose by more than that. The mood wasn't right and the way we played was simply not good enough. There was a definite feeling that we were going nowhere and when that happens in the first game of the season you should know that there is going to be big trouble ahead.

Again though, I tried to reassure myself that things could still turn around, particularly as Spurs are one of those teams who are always capable of getting victories against anyone if they are on form, especially at White Hart Lane.

Despite that, it would not be too much longer before the penny dropped with me and I realised the harsh truth. Not only were we not good enough to challenge for the title as we had done the season before, we were also going to struggle to get into the top four.

We had some good results after losing at Spurs, including a good win over Man United at home, but it was clear that we were nowhere near the level that we wanted to be at. When there are problems at a big club and the atmosphere turns, one of the first comments to be made is always that the manager has lost the dressing room. In this case that might be exaggerating the situation a little bit because there were still players who supported the manager, but obviously there were others who were not too happy with him for different reasons. My own opinion was clear. I liked Rafa and continued to support him – but I cannot speak for everyone.

It was a really tough time at the club because none of the players, none of the staff and especially none of the supporters deserved that kind of horrible season. If it felt like 2009/10 was all doom and gloom then that's because it was. There was nothing to smile about, nothing to bring us any pleasure and when playing stops becoming enjoyable then it has to be one of the most difficult times in your career. It was the same during the first six months of the following season when, if anything, things got even worse. It is not a period of my life that I will remember fondly and the whole period was summed up by that beach ball incident at Sunderland.

When I look back on it now I can afford to laugh because it is in the past and, to be honest, it is funny anyway. At the time, I was the victim and I could not smile about it, no matter how hard I tried. It was a goal that never should have happened, it was a goal that never should have stood and it was a goal that symbolised the way everything that could go wrong for us was going wrong. Even now when I see replays of it on television I cannot believe that it happened, even though I can't help laughing at the stupid, funny face I pulled after the ball went in.

Don't get me wrong, we were poor that day and we deserved nothing from the game. But when you lose to a goal like that one it is always going to leave a bad taste in your mouth. I have been asked so many times why I didn't just kick the beach ball off the pitch as soon as it was thrown on, but I only realised it was right in front of me when Andy Reid crossed the proper football into the box and there it was. If I'd seen it earlier then I would have booted it as far away from my goal as I possibly could, but even after spotting it I didn't think it was about to play a part in one of the craziest goals in English football history.

Darren Bent had a shot, it was pretty powerful, but I knew I had it covered until the ball collided with the beach ball and flew past me into the back of the net. My first instinct was to chase the linesman because I knew that something wasn't right. I have to be honest though and admit that I didn't know exactly what the rule was at that point.

I was shouting at the linesman. "You have to have seen that," I screamed at him. "The goal was not possible. I cannot control the deflection of the ball off the beach ball. That's not right." But he told me the ball hadn't been deflected off the other one.

"You're fucking joking," I said. "It was impossible not to see that. Either you are lying to my face or you think I am stupid."

He was adamant. "No, no, no. Pepe. I am sure."

"Are you sure you are sure?" I replied. "I was stood five yards away. You have got to be taking the piss. It's impossible for you not to see what happened. Are you telling me that the ball was not deflected by the other one?"

He was certain. "Then you really are taking the piss then," I replied.

It made no difference. The goal stood. The beach ball became the symbol of our season, but no matter how crazy that incident was, it should not cover the fact that we were not good enough on that day when Sunderland defeated us. Nor were we good enough during the season as a whole.

Despite everything, we still could have ended the campaign with a trophy because after being dumped out of the Champions League following the group stages we went into the Europa League. Although that competition was not our priority we still gave ourselves a really good chance of winning it. We were favourites after knocking Benfica out in the quarter-finals and when we were drawn against Atletico Madrid in the last four a lot of people fancied us to make it through to the final to meet either Roy Hodgson's Fulham or Hamburg.

In keeping with the rest of the season, we had nothing but problems in the build-up to that tie. First, we could not use Fernando against his former club because he had to have an operation to fix a knee injury that had been a problem for some time. Then, in March, a volcano erupted in Iceland and the resulting ash cloud meant we could not fly to Madrid for the first leg in April. UEFA insisted that the game went ahead, which meant that we had a 1,200-mile road trip just to get to the Vicente Calderon.

I always love the journey back to the city where I grew up. Madrid is a magical place for me, the place where I spent my childhood, where my father played football for Atletico and where I celebrated Spain's triumphs with my fellow countrymen.

But this time it was different. There was to be no direct flight from John Lennon Airport to Barajas. The volcanic ash cloud meant that we could not fly out of the UK, and the only way we could get there was by train.

I wouldn't like to do that kind of trip again before a big game because it is far from ideal, but when I look back at it now, the journey was funny and it gave all of us the chance to spend time together that we would not normally get.

We started off at Runcorn station and someone had the idea of having our picture taken in front of the sign. We then did the same thing when we got off the train at Euston, before we boarded the Eurostar at St Pancras, when we arrived in Paris and when we finally boarded a plane to the Spanish capital in Bordeaux the following day. It was good fun and an experience that none of us will ever forget. I will be happy if I never have to do it again though.

All in all, the journey took us more than 24 hours. Usually the trip only takes two-and-a-half hours in total so our preparation was anything but ideal. Probably because of the circumstances, we were not too disappointed by the 1-0 defeat we suffered due to a scrappy Diego Forlan goal. It was not a perfect result, far from it, but we were still in the tie and with the second leg at Anfield still to come we were confident that we could turn it in our favour, even though we knew our failure to get an away goal could be a problem.

When Alberto Aquilani brought the scores level on aggregate with a good finish I just presumed that we would go on to complete the job. That was what we had done really well in Europe in previous years. If we gave ourselves an advantage, more often than not we would go on to make the most of it. But this was a different Liverpool side and even when Yossi put us ahead in extra-time and took us to the brink of another final, we still could not complete the job with Diego Forlan's goal costing us.

We only went out on away goals. It was not as if we had been battered, but it was really sad for all of us because this was our last chance of salvaging something from a horrible season. That was the final bullet in the gun for Rafa and when the game was over and our trophy hopes had ended I think everyone knew that it was all over for him.

It was another month before Rafa lost his job, but the reality is that the beginning of the end of his time as Liverpool manager probably came that night. Had we gone on to win a trophy and the fans had enjoyed a day out in Hamburg then who knows what would have happened? But we didn't. I was not really that surprised when he called me at the start of June to tell me that he was leaving. I was actually with the Spain squad preparing for the World Cup when the call came and he told me he had an agreement with the club to leave.

I was upset, obviously, because it is always sad when a manager loses their job, but even more so when he has been as important to your career as Rafa has been to mine. But I also thought that it was probably for the best. The situation could not continue as it had been. There had been fights between the owners and Rafa; fights between Purslow and Rafa; half of the dressing room was not happy and so maybe for the club, if not for me personally, it was the best outcome for everyone. It was going to be either the manager or the board and in situations like that the board is not going to change.

I don't think that Rafa became distracted by all of the in-fighting because he is much too professional for that. The ownership situation affected his ability to buy players but that's it. As I say, he did still buy his fair share of players and he did spend some money. Some of the time he didn't get it right when he made a signing, that is clear.

But at the same time, maybe if Rafa had worked under better owners than the ones we had at the time – more like the ones we have now – then it would have been easier for him because they certainly didn't help, that's for sure.

By the end, he must have been tired because we all were. It had been a hard, hard season and he had been in the middle of so much that was going on. That's why I thought it was a good idea for him to have a break when he left Inter Milan, but I also know that he is the kind of manager who needs to be working every day.

Logic suggests that he must have been a happier, funnier, more content manager when he first came to Liverpool in 2004 than when he left because the process he went through, particularly at the end, was such a difficult one.

Because it went wrong for Rafa at the end, the temptation is always to look for the reasons why. One of the comments I have heard most is that Pako Ayestaran leaving in October 2007 was a turning point. But I don't see it this way. As a fitness expert and a physical coach, Pako was one of the best I have worked with and while he was at Liverpool he wanted to develop his role, which is totally understandable because everyone wants to improve and get better.

He is such a good character and he was important for us, but at some point he had some disagreement with Rafa and they broke apart.

This kind of fall-out happens in football all the time. It would be unfair to claim that this was the beginning of the end for Rafa because in the season that Pako left we got to the semi-finals of the Champions League and the following year we came as close to winning the Premier League title as any Liverpool team has since 1990.

Maybe our physical condition was at its highest when Pako was here, but when Paco de Miguel came in as fitness coach and then Darren Burgess, we still continued to be up there with the best when it came to our fitness stats. We were still a good team physically.

I have had my own arguments with Rafa because there are times when he can be annoying. He is so insistent that players should watch video tapes of games and learn from the mistakes that we have made that there were times when he could be a pain in the arse. But what I do know is that by being like this, he was giving me the best chance of making the best of myself.

It is like when you are a kid and your dad is telling you that you have to do your homework. You don't want to do it and because he is making you do it you get a bit pissed off but in your heart you know it is the best thing for you. Footballers can be a little bit selfish and not able to see our own mistakes so you don't like it that much when a manager points out your failings. It annoys you, it is as simple as that. You think you are doing everything perfectly and there are even times when you make mistakes that you look to blame someone else for them. You never want the manager to be telling you where you are going wrong, you just want him to pat you on the back and say, "Well done, you are going great" – but Rafa wasn't really like that.

His way of operating was to let you know that you were doing okay but there were always areas in which you could still improve. I would see him at Melwood and he would have another tape for me to watch that showed some detail or other that he wanted me to look at and correct. My first thought would be, 'not another one', but once I watched it I would recognise what he was talking about and try to make the corrections that were needed.

It can be annoying, there is no question about that, and once he is on to something he is like a dog with a bone. But I realise that by being like that he helped me improve and I also know that he made a bigger difference to me than any other manager I have worked with.

The biggest argument I ever had with him was about a beer. Not him having one obviously, he never touches a drop. Sometimes I like to unwind by having just one drink. Not going crazy or anything like that, just a beer to take the edge off.

On this occasion, in October, 2007, we had played Besiktas away in the Champions League and because Turkey is a four-hour flight away it was decided that we would stay in Istanbul after the game rather than return to Merseyside straight away. We were all disappointed because we had lost the game 2-1 and not played too well. Worst of all, it looked like we would be eliminated from the Champions League at the group stage because the defeat left us knowing that we would probably need to take the maximum nine points from our final three games. So the mood wasn't good and when we got back to the hotel I decided to have a beer. I don't see a problem with that because for me it is healthier to do that than it is to have a glass of Coca-Cola or a drink like that.

I sat down to have my dinner with the rest of the team and ordered the beer. I didn't think anything of it but I was waiting and waiting and my drink did not arrive. Suddenly, the bartender turned up and told me I was not allowed to have one. I was stunned.

"What do you mean I can't have one?" I asked. "The club doctor, the medical staff and the manager have made it clear to me that they do not want you to have one," he replied.

I asked Rafa what was going on and he said I was forbidden from having a beer. I still don't know why this was the case but whatever the reason I was fuming. I grabbed my bags and stormed off to my room without even having my dinner. That is how upset I was.

For me, Rafa was in the wrong on that occasion. It wasn't a major issue but it is one of those little incidents that can niggle at you because it suggests the manager does not trust you to look after yourself in the right way. As a player, you have to know when the time is right to relax and when it isn't and I like to think that I have that balance. We had lost a game, I was not happy and we were not flying back until the following day so I could not see what the problem was.

He saw it differently and maybe if he has a small weakness as a manager it is that he did not have a massive career as a player before he moved into management. I used to wind him up about this all the time and he would get angry when I reminded him that he had not played at the top level. He would list all the teams he has played for and they were like third division and university teams! I would say to him: "That's not football. Tell me where you got the experience that comes with being in the dressing room at the top clubs."

I was joking and I did it with the greatest respect because I knew how hard he had worked to get to the kind of status he had in football. I also knew that his achievements demanded my respect. But maybe it is a truth as well because by spending time in dressing rooms as a player and getting close enough to the players to understand their moods and the way they are I think it can make you a better manager. I'm not saying this is the only way because you only have to look at what Rafa, Jose Mourinho, Andre Villas-Boas and Louis van Gaal have achieved in football and the trophies they have won to realise that you don't have to have had a great career as a player to be a great manager. But in my opinion the most complete managers are always likely to be the ones who had a great career as players for many years as well.

I have always appreciated what a great manager Rafa is and that is something that will never change. He already had a really good reputation in Spain before he moved to Liverpool. The reason was simple – the Valencia team he managed had enjoyed fantastic success, winning La Liga twice in three seasons and the UEFA Cup. Winning any domestic title is an incredible achievement and at Liverpool we know just how hard it is to do that. In Spain, it is even more difficult for clubs like Valencia to become champions because of the domination of Real Madrid and Barcelona. By breaking their stranglehold, Rafa showed what a top manager he is and his Valencia side remains the only team, other than Deportivo La Coruna in 2000 to win the title ahead of Real and Barca in the last 15 years. They didn't just do it once either, they did it twice. That is probably why Liverpool were so keen to take him to Anfield, because they hoped he could help topple Manchester United, Chelsea and Arsenal in similar fashion. He could not manage that in the Premier League, although he came really close in 2009, but his work in the Champions League proved once again that he is a manager who is capable of being successful, even when the odds are stacked against him and his team.

The Valencia side he managed was not a special one in the sense that it was not full of players with incredible individual talent, but somehow Rafa was able to squeeze everything out of every single one of them on a weekly basis and this meant they played at their highest level in almost every game. By doing that he broke the monopoly of Barca and Real, an accomplishment which proves just how good he is.

He always had so much confidence in us as well. He would go to unbelievable lengths to prepare us for games and this meant we were all clear about exactly what we needed to do once we got out onto the pitch. It wasn't like we needed incredible, passionate team talks or anything, it was much more methodical than that, about us understanding our role as individuals and within the team.

Some people have claimed that Rafa actually helped stop us from winning the title in 2009 when he came out with his list of facts about Alex Ferguson and Man United at a pre-match press conference.

They say it was a little bit like Kevin Keegan's famous "I would love it" outburst. I can see that up to a point because it was a manager making a big statement to his rival, but it was different as well because Rafa was a lot calmer than Keegan had been. It certainly didn't cost us the league title.

It was a really memorable moment and I can even recall the date when it happened – it was the 9th of January and we were playing Stoke away the following day. If we had won that game then maybe what Rafa did would be looked upon differently today but we could only draw. After that we had another three draws in a row so results helped dictate how it would be remembered. Now, I look back at it as something that was funny. But it should not be forgotten that he was fighting for what he thought was right. He was defending the club and good on him for that.

If he was going to do it at any time it had to be then because we were top of the table and if he was ever going to take Alex Ferguson on it had to be when we were competing with them as equals, not when we were seven points behind. Everyone says Ferguson is the master of mind games and Rafa wanted to show that he would not just sit there and let him win. Whether he was right or wrong to do so everyone has their own opinion but for me a Liverpool manager must always stand up to Ferguson. He tries to play mind games all the time so we have to do the same and we have to stand up for ourselves and our club or else we just look weak. He has been there for 25 years and he is one of the greatest managers this country has ever seen but if he can defend his club then we have the right to defend ours. Me? I don't give a shit about what he says but I will always defend my club.

I still talk to Rafa now. Not for advice, just to see how he is and for him to see how I am. I have a really good relationship with him and I would happily work with him again in the future. This is not the same as saying I want him back at Liverpool. I love working with Kenny and Steve Clarke, who have done a brilliant job in a very short space of time and our future looks bright with them in charge. But at some point I would like to work with Rafa again because he is the best manager I have ever worked with. Maybe our paths will cross again at international level, who knows?

Absent Friends

After winning the World Cup, the Spain players returned to the dressing room at the Soccer City Stadium in Johannesburg and our private celebrations began. We all started answering the text messages that we had received on our phones from family and friends congratulating us on our success, and then we took pictures of one another with the trophy. After coming on as a substitute in the second half of the final, Fernando Torres, my close friend and team-mate for club and country, had come off injured towards the end of the game and he was obviously worried about the problem. But that didn't stop him from joining in with us as we celebrated our success and toasted our nation's first ever World Cup win.

When it came to his turn to have his photograph taken with the most famous trophy in football, Fernando put a Liverpool scarf around his neck to show that his achievement was one that he wanted to share with everyone at Anfield, and also to pay tribute to the Liverpool fans for what they had given him. He was basically saying that this was a victory for all of us, not just for him or for Spain.

There was a rumour that I had put the scarf on Fernando, but it had absolutely nothing to do with me. It was Fernando's own gesture, one that he came up with without prompting from anyone else and that says a lot about him because I don't think any other player has ever worn a Liverpool scarf to celebrate lifting the World Cup. But just six months after this photograph was taken Fernando was walking out on the club and as much as it hurt the supporters to see him go, I can understand his reasons for leaving.

The only thing that surprised me about his departure was the timing of it. Not because it was late in the transfer window, that had nothing to do with it. I had actually thought that he would leave in the summer straight after we had returned from the World Cup.

From the conversations I had with him and from what I was hearing I did not believe that he would start the season with us – but he did. The reason for this was the same as the one I was given. He was told he had to stay. The club made it clear that they would not allow any of the big names to go – although that did not prevent a deal being done that allowed Javier Mascherano, another top player, to join Barcelona – and this meant he had no alternative but to remain at Liverpool, even though it was an open secret by then that he was not happy at the direction the club was heading in.

Fernando spoke to Christian Purslow and he also spoke to Roy Hodgson. The message he received was that he would not be going anywhere. As a player all you can do is accept it when the club makes it clear that you cannot leave, but in return you want the club to prove to you that you should want to stay. Not because you have to, but because things have improved so much that you want to. Fernando never felt that this happened.

The reality was that all they did by making him stay was to delay the inevitable. It was sad for many reasons when he finally left and joined Chelsea, but the main disappointment for me was that Fernando had seemed to be made for Liverpool and Liverpool had seemed to be made for him.

Even now I think back to the Kop singing his song, "Fernando Torres Liverpool's number nine", and the hairs stand up on the back of my neck. One of the most incredible sights I have ever seen in any stadium was the whole ground bouncing – not just the Kop, but the Main Stand, Centenary Stand and Anfield Road – after he scored an unbelievable goal against Arsenal in the Champions League in 2008. The whole move must have passed in a blur to their defenders. Fernando latched on to a ball in the penalty area, controlled it with his chest and took two quick touches before turning and firing into the corner of the net. Anfield erupted as he clenched his fists and slid into the corner of the pitch on his knees in front of the Kop.

The supporters had such a special relationship with Fernando from the moment he arrived, and to see him leave feeling that he had been let down by the club and with their bond broken was really sad. This is football. Players come and players go but the club will always remain.

One of the most important points to realise about Fernando is that he is a really competitive guy. He wants to win. When he left Atletico Madrid to sign for Liverpool he said it was because he wanted to be successful. Atletico are one of Spain's greatest and most historic clubs, but for years they have struggled to turn their glorious past into an equally glorious future. Fernando joined us because he believed, like we all did, that Liverpool's success was not in the past, it was ahead of us and that anything was possible.

So when we were not up there challenging he got frustrated about that, again like we all did, but because he is one of the best forwards in the world it meant he had so many options available to him. That is what happens when you are a world and European champion and one of the best players in your position, clubs are always going to be interested in you and keen to sign you. Fernando may not have been at his best during his final year at Liverpool, but he was still one of the most highly-rated forwards in world football. Rival clubs and managers only needed to go back to his first season in the Premier League to realise just how good he can be.

You would have to search hard to find a manager who would not be glad to have him on their team. Usually, being sought after would not be a problem because top players are always in demand. But when Fernando started to feel that Liverpool were never going to be competitive again, it quickly became inevitable that he would accept the offer from Chelsea, who had also been interested in him the previous summer. It wasn't money. Fernando is not like that. He actually took a pay cut when he joined Liverpool from Atletico. He is just desperate to compete and he believed Chelsea would give him the best chance of achieving his ambitions.

Fernando is one of my best friends in football and he was also my neighbour – we lived in the same street in Woolton, and when he left to join Chelsea Luis Suarez moved into his old house – but I didn't speak to him that much about his feelings or his concerns about what was happening at Liverpool because he is naturally reserved. He would stick to his usual routine and take his dogs out early in the morning on a piece of grass close to our home. But I did know that he was really angry because he felt that he had been betrayed by Liverpool before he left. I know this because I had similar feelings.

There had been plenty of lies, plenty of promises which had not been kept and in the two years before Fernando left it became clear that the Liverpool we were at was not the Liverpool that either of us had joined. To put it in perspective, when Fernando signed for Liverpool we had just been to our second Champions League final in just three years and in the month that he left the only 'double' we did was losing our second game to Blackpool in a matter of months.

One of the crucial differences between Fernando and myself was that whereas we were both unhappy, he was the one who was always going to be in the most demand, so much so that Chelsea were willing to pay £50 million, an absolutely incredible amount of money, to sign him. As soon as he became aware of how strong the interest from Chelsea was he was placed in a very difficult position because he basically had the choice of going to a Champions League club or staying somewhere where he felt that he had been let down. In the end, he decided that he had to play at the highest level he could and that he could not wait for it to happen at Liverpool. Unfortunately for us, this meant that he left.

It was not until January 31, the final day of the transfer window, that I knew for definite that Fernando would be leaving. I knew what was going on six days earlier or so, but nothing was concrete until the morning of the last day.

Fernando came to the dressing room and said to me: "Chelsea have made an offer for me and the deal is almost done. There are just some issues still to be sorted out." I wasn't shocked because I knew that it was a possibility, but I was sad for him in the way that it all happened. He did not like the way it all ended.

He never got the goodbye that he deserved and the Liverpool fans never got the goodbye that they deserved from him. I'm not blaming anyone for that, it's just sad that it ended this way.

I understood his reasons for leaving but it was also understandable in some ways that the Liverpool fans did not because part of being a supporter is sometimes being blind to the problems at your club and seeing only a positive future. They want the players to stay no matter what, but the reality is that it is not an option to stay if you want to make the most of your career, even if it hurts you to leave.

I always say the same thing. When you are in a team you have to give everything you have to them in every single game you play and for me, the only cause for regret that Fernando can have is that during the last three or four months at Liverpool he wasn't himself. It wasn't the Fernando that we knew from his first couple of seasons in English football, when he put the fear of God into defenders and seemed to score a goal in every game he played. The supporters were probably angry about that, but this was a tighter Fernando, a sad Fernando, a betrayed Fernando. It wasn't Fernando himself and this made the supporters upset with him when he decided to leave. But what we all have to remember is what he gave to Liverpool in the time that he was with us.

He joined for a big fee but left for an even bigger one, more than twice as much as Liverpool paid for him. He scored an unbelievable amount of goals and had things turned out differently in 2008/09 he could have been the forward whose goals brought the league title back to Anfield. He was a special, special player for us and he gave an awful lot to Liverpool, to his team-mates and to the supporters. If the fans do not recognise this then I accept that, but I don't agree with them.

What I would also say is that Fernando had no chance of enjoying his football in his final months with us and he had no chance of being at his brilliant best at that time because we were so bad. You could have put any forward in our team in the first five months of the season and they would have struggled. It could have been Cristiano Ronaldo, Lionel Messi, anyone. We were playing without the kind of identity you would associate with such a big club.

The manager cannot take all of the responsibility for this either. He had a big part to play, of course, and things obviously did not work out for him, but the players also have to take personal responsibility for how bad things became on the pitch.

I consider those months to be the worst of my Liverpool career, apart from the first few months of the 2006/07 season which were so unhappy that I ended up thinking of leaving myself, because I was so far from my usual standards. The lack of form and crisis in confidence swept through the dressing room like a plague and it affected all of us in one way or another. Our performance levels dropped and the tactics were not working so the team struggled badly. When this happens, one of the worst positions to play is as a forward because it does not matter how good you are, you still need the service of others to be at your best. If our performance levels had been 20 per cent higher then everything would have been so much better for Fernando and for the team but it wasn't like that.

When circumstances are not right at the club you take that into your own personal life. I know that from my own personal experience and there are so many other players who can say the same thing. You try not to let it affect you, but it does and when that happens it affects your family as well. It happened to me and it happened to Fernando. I consider myself to be a happy guy who always tries to be positive but sometimes you cannot be like that when the situation is really bad – and the first five months of the 2010/11 season were bad.

It was a really, really difficult period and there were times when I was desperate. There was a feeling that no matter what happened the situation would still be shit and when it is like that, you are coming home from training and not being the same with your family as you would do normally. You have no energy for anything because it is all being sapped by the negativity that is all around you. The only respite you have is when you are with your family because even though you may not be the same and your mood might not be the best, they are there for you and this is something that you never forget. It is why you must always put them first.

The supporters don't see this part of your life. They see you coming and going from training and they see you on a match day but that is only one part of what I am. It is difficult for the fans to understand that we are also normal people who have a lot of the problems that everyone else has because they only see what we do on the pitch and judge us by that.

But we all have happiness and sadness, good days and bad days and often you only ever share that with your family. When things went bad for Fernando at Liverpool it will have affected his personal life and that will have played a part in his decision to leave.

After leaving, Fernando said that he had been in a dark place and I know what he means but it is not the way I could see Liverpool. There were times when it got bleak for me but even when we were getting beat by Blackpool, Northampton and so many other teams, I could not see Liverpool as a dark place. It was a bad team and a bad time, there is no question about that, but Liverpool is bigger than those moments.

At the end of the day, it was better for Fernando and it was also better for the club that they parted ways. It was a transfer that was in the best interests of everyone in the end. Fernando got the move that he felt he needed at that stage of his career and Liverpool got an unbelievable fee that they were able to reinvest in two new signings, Andy Carroll and Luis Suarez.

Luis showed how good he can be from the very first game he played for us when he came on as a substitute and scored in front of the Kop to make it 2-0 against Stoke. If anyone is in any doubt about that they should ask Fulham's big central defender, Brede Hangeland, what he thinks of him after the way he tormented him in our 5-2 win at Craven Cottage towards the end of the 2010/11 season.

He has shown already that he can be one of the best forwards in the world. He has so much talent and so much potential that there is no reason why he cannot become a truly great player, someone who gets supporters on the edge of their seats and has people talking about him all the time because he is so good.

Sooner or later he will be up there with the greats of the game but how quick he gets there will depend on the team because he cannot do it on his own. The better we do as a group, the better he will do as an individual. But it is clear that Luis is a very special player and I am just happy that we have him in our team because he must be horrible to play against, a defender's nightmare.

His arrival also proved that Liverpool can still attract the kind of players who every other club would want. Andy had his injury problems when he first arrived so he will need a little bit more time before he can show the kind of form that made him almost unstoppable for Newcastle United, but it is important to remember that it is about the team rather than just one or two players. If they can help us to become a proper team with a really good starting eleven and a strong bench then that will be great.

For me, that is how Fernando should be remembered at Liverpool – as someone who was an incredible player and who, when he left, allowed the club to bring in two more really good players through his transfer fee that will help the club in the future. If every signing was like Fernando then Liverpool would never have any problems.

Of course, the other problem for us going forward now is that Fernando will be an opponent rather than a team-mate. We have already experienced this once when we beat Chelsea 1-0 at Stamford Bridge shortly after he joined them, and it was a strange experience for us.

That is football, though, and our friendship would still be the same whether he plays for Liverpool, for Chelsea or even for Manchester United. I want to beat his team whenever we play against them but that is where our rivalry begins and ends. It is a sporting rivalry, no more and no less. Our friendship will always be bigger than that.

From a personal point of view, it is never nice to lose a friend from the dressing room but all you can do is wish them well and hope that their replacement will be just as good or, if you are really lucky, maybe even better than what they were. Your own feelings as an individual cannot come into it.

I was gutted when Fernando Morientes left in 2006 because we were really close and he had been so important to me and my family as we tried to settle into a new life in Liverpool, but I had to get on with it. It wasn't easy as his departure coincided with the worst run of form in my career but I could not complain about the club selling him just because he was my friend. The club had to make the best decision for the club, not for me, for Morientes or for anyone else. Their job is to buy and sell players so that we have a squad capable of challenging for honours, not so I have good neighbours or my closest friend around.

As a player you just have to accept that team-mates will leave from time to time because transfers have become part and parcel of football, particularly at a big club like Liverpool. I have to say, though, that losing Xabi Alonso was a big blow, partly because he is such a good person, but more importantly because he is such a great player, one who is almost impossible to replace.

I knew that there had been problems between Rafa and Xabi, everyone in the dressing room did, because Rafa had been the one who decided Xabi was for sale in the summer of 2008. For a time it looked like Xabi would be leaving then but a move didn't happen and he stayed with us for the following season – but it was clear that it was no longer the same between him and the manager. Again, that is football.

When the manager likes you everything is fine, but if the manager doesn't obviously there are going to be periods when you have rough times with him.

This is normal. I have been in this situation myself and I have no problem with it. I left Barcelona because the manager did not want me so I went to another club where the manager did and moved on.

At the time it was difficult to understand why Rafa did not want Xabi because he was such an important player for us, but the manager must have had his own reasons. But the moment Xabi felt that he was no longer wanted – or that he wasn't valued as much as he thought he should be – then he was within his rights to go, especially as he had an opportunity to join Real Madrid, who were building a team to take on Barcelona. They saw him as a crucial part of their plans.

Like Morientes, he had given really good service to the club, playing a key role in the Champions League-winning team of 2005 and becoming one of the best players in the world in his position. Liverpool ended up selling him for a massive profit when he felt that he could stay at the club no longer.

We missed Xabi as a player and I missed him as a friend. The intelligence he shows on the pitch is influential. He is one of the cleverest people I have come across in football. He is quiet and gentle but he has his culture and whenever I see him he always has a book with him.

He is far more intelligent than the average footballer, taking in the news from around the world, making the most of technology and studying lots of different things. Tactically he is very aware and this makes me think that he can be a top manager one day if that is what he wants to be. He understands the game and what he does not know he tries to find out so there is no question that he has what it takes to be a manager in the future.

I have heard many people say that the reason we went from title challengers in 2009 to strugglers in 2010 was down to Xabi leaving. I don't see it quite like that because success or failure can never come down to just a single player.

Xabi was a really important player for us but we had won games when he was injured or suspended and one of our greatest victories, the 4-1 win over Man United at Old Trafford, came when he was unavailable. But he is such a good player and he was so important to us that losing him was only ever going to be a major blow. It was a turning point for us and it was a big loss.

We were all actually expecting Xabi to leave the year before when Rafa was looking to sell him and Arsenal and Juventus were both interested in signing him. At the time we were looking at signing Gareth Barry as a replacement but that did not make much sense to me because – and I say this with the greatest respect to Barry – he is not in the same class as Xabi, nowhere near.

But that deal did not happen and we got one more season from Xabi, which was brilliant for him and even better for us. Then he was sold and everything changed. We missed him badly.

The sadness for me, though, wasn't caused by any single individual going to play for another club. It was because so many of the people who were at Liverpool when I first joined and who helped me on and off the field ended up leaving in such a short space of time.

When I first arrived on Merseyside, there were four of us Spaniards – Xabi, Luis Garcia, Josemi and myself – plus the coaching staff and some of the physios. I would have liked a lot of them to stay and when I became the only one left it did leave me feeling nostalgic for my friends and for an era that had passed into history.

There was no point in allowing my disappointment to become anything more than that though. I still had more than 20 other teammates after all.

New Leaders

After the pain caused by Hicks and Gillett, Liverpool needed a fresh start to give everyone hope for the future. We got one when Fenway Sports Group bought the club in October 2010. At the time, the take-over gave everyone a mixture of emotions because although we were all so relieved to see the back of the previous owners, we were going into the unknown with the new ones. We all wanted to know what the future held and whether we would have money to spend on the players we desperately needed to become competitive again.

It wasn't long before the senior players were given an opportunity to get the answers that we were looking for, although it didn't turn out quite as planned. When I was called into a meeting with John W Henry, the principal owner, I thought I would end up quizzing him. But it was the other way around. He wanted to know what my views were about how Liverpool could improve and by doing that he earned my respect straight away.

The meeting took place in a room at Melwood which is now Damien Comolli's office. Stevie, Carra, Fernando and myself were all invited in and introduced to Mr Henry. We all shook hands with him and sat down, expecting to interrogate him about his plans for the club he had just paid a fortune for. But, as I say, he had other ideas. He was going to be the one asking the questions. It was as if he had realised that he was new to a sport and to a club that we had been part of for a number of years, and wanted to learn from us.

I thought straight away that he was a good guy. It was obvious that he was looking to improve our club and increase our chances of being successful. By making his starting point a meeting with the senior players to listen to our views he immediately made a positive impression on all of us. Most others would have come, told us what they were going to do and then disappeared. It is rare to find one who actually cares about the players' opinions and our ambitions. It was a good start. It's always nice to be listened to and be heard.

I know some people had fears because Fenway are also Americans, but you cannot look at things this way. You can only judge people as you find them, not on where they come from. From the little bit of knowledge I already had about the Boston Red Sox and the work that they had done there I was able to have some optimism about them, even if I was a bit cautious because of what we had been through. I trusted them a bit more from the beginning and from my first meeting with John Henry I got the impression that he was telling me the truth.

He spoke to me about my situation and how I thought the club could make progress, but because it was still a feeling-out period and we had as many questions for him as he had for us I answered him with some queries of my own. The trust between the dressing room and the owners had been broken by Hicks and Gillett. This was the starting point for the restoration of that bond and it was crucial that it happened so early because it gave everyone an opportunity to start again.

For me, the most important point to make was that Liverpool needed to start realising its potential. We were not making the most of ourselves. So I told John Henry that with our massive fanbase around the world, we had to start exploiting the club to the full instead of just doing bits and pieces that don't make a massive difference.

I am not an expert on marketing, but it had been obvious to everyone in football for a long time that the club had not been making the most of itself in terms of our shirt sponsorship deal, the stadium situation and so on. It doesn't take a genius to realise that if we only have enough capacity for 45,000 people to come to our home games then, given our massive fanbase, that leaves thousands more who cannot come because they can't get tickets which, in turn, means we will not make as much money. That problem has been going on for far too long and it was made worse by Hicks and Gillett because they promised the stadium that could have made a massive difference and then failed to deliver it. This is one of the main reasons why we are lagging behind Manchester United as a club. They have exploited their brand much more effectively than we have for a long time and it shows on and off the pitch. In terms of supporters we are probably as big as United are and hopefully now we will start to realise our potential because we have drifted for too many years.

In some ways we are quite lucky to have so many people who still support us around the world because we have not had the level of recent success that the likes of United and Barcelona have enjoyed. But people see something special in our club. They see our wonderful history and they see that we are a humble club with principles and ideals and they like that. They see also that the people of Liverpool are humble, working-class people and that gives us a special identity. This is why 80,000 people came to see us when we played in a pre-season friendly in Malaysia and why 38,000 others turned up to watch us train. When it is said about Chelsea and Manchester City that they cannot buy history it is true. You can buy a league title and you may even be able to buy a European Cup, but you cannot buy history. Together with our identity, our past makes us a special club that people are able to identify with no matter where they are from.

It is a mystique that was created when Bill Shankly first arrived at Anfield in 1959 and it has fuelled us ever since. It is similar in some respects to Atletico Madrid in Spain.

But that cannot fuel us forever. Giants can go to sleep, but they cannot afford to sleep for too long and Atletico have discovered how difficult it is to bring back the glories of the past. We have to make sure that we do not make the same mistakes.

We have to earn our position amongst the elite once again because if we don't do that we run the risk of losing some of our aura and putting ourselves in a position where the people around the world do not feel the need to support us as much any more. We have to be realistic about where we are now. Where we've been in the past is another matter entirely and we can't feel any pressure from that. Some time soon we need to start punching our weight.

Only time will tell how well the new owners can restore Liverpool to former glories. In their first year at the club they have done all that could have been asked of them and more. Up to now they have kept every promise that Mr Henry made to us in that meeting.

They have had to make some tough decisions, but that is what owning a football club is all about. Comolli has been brought in to take charge of buying and selling players and we have to give him time in this role because you cannot build a team in six months. He will continually take stock of what is required and speak to the manager about what he needs, but there is no question that Comolli and the owners are working really hard to improve things.

From the moment Damien first got here he has been speaking to players about joining Liverpool and even though we did not qualify for Europe in the season that Fenway took over – which makes it more difficult to attract big names – we still have the advantage of knowing that a lot of top players want to play for Liverpool. Stewart Downing, Charlie Adam, Jordan Henderson, Doni, Jose Enrique, Sebastian Coates and Craig Bellamy were all signed in one summer. That shows that the club now has its ambition back and that the owners are willing to give the backing needed.

From the moment they first arrived the owners have been talking about winning things, not just as a one-off but over and over again. They say being successful is what they want to be remembered for. If their mentality is like that then it can only be positive for us. I certainly didn't ever hear the former owners say anything like that. We have a period of one or two years in which we can build the club up and then we have to deliver.

If the new owners' arrival brought a golden sky, then the months that led up to the takeover were undoubtedly the storm. That period was probably the most turbulent in the club's history and it even featured a High Court case which made headlines all around the world, but for the wrong reasons.

When Liverpool ended up in the High Court, I watched the news on the television and read the newspapers to keep up with what was going on. It is almost surreal to think back to the scenes outside the court now. That there was even a need for Liverpool to go to one of the highest courts in the land to break free from bad owners illustrates just how disastrous the situation had got. With the rest of the world looking on I couldn't help but feel sad that it had come to this.

When I first came to the club we were the European champions and we were in the press for all the right reasons and yet here we were, just five years later, captivating people for the wrong reasons. If someone had written the story of how Liverpool had gone from being kings of Europe to the brink of administration in just five years then nobody would have believed it. Even now, it feels like it was just a bad dream but it really did happen and that brings shame to those who caused it.

Just to hear the word administration was unthinkable and it was a very difficult time for everyone associated with the club. We always said that the problems in the boardroom did not affect us in the dressing room, but they did. Of course they did. It was like the whole club was unable to escape this cloud that followed us everywhere we went. You would not be human if it did not make at least a little bit of an impact on you. We were not looking for excuses, but the reality was that our performances did suffer during this time.

If you look back on the era when Liverpool was the most successful club in Europe, one of the main reasons for this was that it was so well run off the pitch. So when the boardroom went into civil war, when the owners caused so much damage and when the possibility of going into administration was genuine, it was no surprise that results on the pitch suffered too.

The only way I can compare the seriousness of what was happening to Liverpool at that time is with the recent situation with River Plate in Argentina. They were relegated and that was a massive shock, not just in Argentina but also in world football because the biggest clubs just do not have these problems. If it is almost impossible to imagine the top division of Argentinian football without River Plate then seeing Liverpool fighting for their future, not on the pitch but in the courtroom, is an even bigger shock. It doesn't make sense.

My family and friends back in Spain were keeping an eye on events and they were worried for me and for the club because they could not believe what they were seeing. We were trying to build a team with owners who didn't care and we were having big problems so it was only natural that they should have concerns for me and for my future. Our problems were all over the press all the time so it was a very difficult period for everyone, not just for me.

The only consolation for me was that I knew that no matter how bad things got for us there were still other clubs in a worse position. It might not have felt like it at times, but it is true. There were players in Spain who were not even getting paid because their clubs had got into financial troubles that were much worse than ours. Rayo Vallecano, for example, recently won promotion to La Liga with a team that had not been paid and the players ended up going on strike. That is an incredible situation and things never got quite that bad for us because we were still getting our wages on time every single payday.

I'm not saying that the money made things okay for us because it didn't, but it at least showed that the club was still functioning on at least some basic levels. We were still worried. Very worried. So it wasn't very easy to be focused on matches, even though that was our job. Whether or not we were focused enough is another question, but we tried our best.

For all of these reasons all I wanted was to ensure that Hicks and Gillett had gone from the club for good. I was as happy as every single Liverpool supporter when the club was sold. It was like a massive weight had been lifted from the shoulders of everyone.

It can't have been easy for the new owners at the start because they walked into a club that was broken. The mood was not good, spirits were low, we did not have anything like enough good players to challenge for trophies and we had a manager in Roy Hodgson whom the supporters had made it clear they did not want.

If I am honest, Roy was not the manager who I wanted to replace

Rafa Benitez either. Had it been down to me I would have given the job to Manuel Pellegrini, who I had worked with at Villarreal. Pellegrini had just lost his job at Real Madrid despite doing a really good job there and giving Barcelona a great run for their money in the race for the La Liga title.

He was available and we needed a manager. For me it made perfect sense. I said so, telling Purslow that Pellegrini was the right man for us. It wasn't just because I knew him. It was more about the style of football that he plays, getting his teams to attack all the time. He would never sit deep and just accept being put under pressure by opponents. For me, that style is Liverpool's style and it seemed a perfect fit. I know that the club spoke to Pellegrini a couple of times when they were looking for a new manager because he told me. He called me and asked what the mood was like in the dressing room, what the players were thinking and so on. I really hoped that he would get the job, but in the end the club went for Hodgson and he missed out.

Pellegrini has an attacking mentality and when Purslow asked me about him I said: "He is a great manager and he is a great man in the dressing room." The only slight concern I had was that he didn't have any experience in English football and I knew this could go against him. I told Purslow that I realised this could be a problem, but my argument was that he would not be afraid to lead us despite that weakness and with time he would have the experience to go with his other qualities. He didn't see it that way though.

That decision may not have worked out, but part of me can still understand it, even though he would not have been my first choice. Hodgson had done a great job with Fulham, he had taken them to the Europa League final in the season before he joined us and he had a lot of experience in England and in Europe. His Fulham team was well organised and difficult to beat and Liverpool decided that he was the right man for us at that time. Kenny Dalglish was also in the frame but the club felt that he had not been involved in management for too long.

I found out Hodgson would be manager after the World Cup when Christian Purslow called me to tell me he was the man that the club wanted. I met him for the first time after coming back from my holidays following the tournament. We had a short chat, I offered to help him in any way I could and he came across as a really nice man. I might have preferred Pellegrini but that didn't matter any more. I knew that I had to work with the new manager as well as I had worked with Rafa.

We were all confident at the time. It has to be this way when you have a new manager and you are about to start a season. But our sense of optimism was to be short-lived. When we did not sign too many good players and it became clear that we were going to be relying on how Stevie and Fernando were going to be physically, it was always going to be only a matter of time before the mood changed as we looked ahead to another difficult season.

The problem was, only two months into the 2010/11 campaign, we realised that things were even worse than we had feared. We struggled badly, getting knocked out of the Carling Cup by Northampton Town in September and slipping to the wrong end of the table in the league.

It is always easy to point fingers at the manager when things don't work out, especially when he is new, but it is important to remember that the club was in absolute chaos when Hodgson took the job. It was not as if he had taken over Liverpool when we had good owners and we had money to spend. He was coming to a club that had gone off the rails badly. He knew that things were bad when he came to us and he took the job with his eyes wide open.

His belief, like many of ours, was that to have the opportunity to work for Liverpool is always great, especially when you come from a smaller club, and he could not let the chance pass him by just because of the problems in the boardroom. He would have stood a better chance of being successful had his appointment been confirmed as soon as Rafa's departure was announced, but a month passed before his arrival and this was wasted time. The club was moving too slowly and it limited the new manager's ability to make a positive and immediate impact.

Hodgson is one of the nicest people I have ever come across in any-dressing room. He is so humble, so correct and he was fair to all of us. But things just didn't work out for him at Liverpool. That happens in football sometimes when the methods that have served a manager well at some clubs don't work as well at others. This doesn't mean that Hodgson is a bad manager. His tactics did not suit us though and that showed in our performances. We were just sitting back and waiting for our opponents to come at us.

In my view, Liverpool always has to be the kind of team that closes our opponents down, presses high up the pitch and tries to make the play. Hodgson liked to do things differently to that by using two banks of four in midfield and defence to try and keep things organised. The problem was that when teams got in between those lines and created chances we would find it hard to get up to the opposite end of the pitch when we had the ball because we were so deep.

Training changed as well – and not for the better. It was the same every single day and I was probably unhappier about this than most. As far as I was concerned, things started badly and then got even worse.

After Rafa took the manager's job at Inter Milan, Xavi Valero, the goalkeeping coach who I had been working with and enjoyed a good relationship with, went to join him in Italy. Xavi was brilliant for me. He continued with the same kind of philosophy as Jose Ochotorena, who I worked with when I first came to Liverpool, and this meant there was no period of transition or anything like that. We just got down to work as if there hadn't been a change after Ocho went to work for Valencia. The two of them had worked together previously and came from more or less the same school so I was more than happy to work with Xavi for a few years as well.

The problems started when Xavi left and I was told by Purslow that I could pick my next coach. That was one of the things that he offered to me to make me stay after Arsenal made the offer for me. I identified Xabi Mancisidor, who worked with Manuel Pellegrini at Real Madrid as the man I wanted to work with. Xabi even came to Melwood to see the training facilities and he was about to come, but it never happened because when Hodgson came he brought Mike Kelly with him.

Roy told me Mike was good enough because he was an eminent goalkeeping coach, but he turned out not to be the right one for me. The problem was that the system he used and the type of training he did with me meant I never felt comfortable with his way of doing things. My discomfort even extended to the way we were playing in games because we were sitting deep and that isn't good for me. I'm not a goalkeeper who likes to sit deep. I'm the exact opposite because I know this is the best way to make the most of the skills that I have. So there was never a moment when I found myself totally happy with what we were doing in games or on the training pitch. I had a couple of really difficult months but as the games came thick and fast, we trained less. As a result things got a little bit better, but it was difficult for a while because it was a new system and I had been used to working with different methods for the whole of my career. That was hard.

There were so many games at Anfield where we just were not good enough and we were allowing our opponents, quite often teams that Liverpool should be expecting to beat and dominating, to set the tempo and dictate the play. That wasn't right. The way we played just wasn't good enough. It cannot all be pinned on the manager. None of us were playing well so it wasn't just Hodgson's fault. The players also have to take responsibility for what went wrong. In his final game as Liverpool manager away to Blackburn on January 5, 2011, none of us could walk off that pitch and say that we had given our best. I know I had a really poor game by my own standards. The mood in the team was not right and Blackburn were better than us throughout. We did not know that this would be Hodgson's last game because the rumours had been going around for some time without any changes being made, but it was one of those bad days when it felt like something was going to have to change. The mood in the dressing room afterwards was really pessimistic. There was a complete lack of belief and ambition. It was as bad as it's ever been, a really low moment. I was not happy with myself more than anything. I had conceded three goals and it felt like I could not stop a cab in the Gran Via in central Madrid.

I was sad when Hodgson lost his job. It is the same when any manager loses his job because you know that they have been doing their best, trying everything to be a success, and it just hasn't worked out. I felt guilty as well. I knew that if I had done better then maybe I could have helped him to save his job.

Kenny was being mentioned as a possible candidate to take over from Hodgson much more than any other manager, so I knew that there was a chance that it could be him. When you look at the decision that the owners made it is clear that it was the right one because we improved so much after Kenny was appointed. He came in and just told us that we had to trust in ourselves and that we were not as bad as we had been showing in the first half of the season. He was really confident that with a bit of work and some adjustments we could come back strong. It did not take long for the style of football to improve and it is now back to the way it should be at a big club – attacking, closing down and playing high up the pitch. Of course there will still be times when we have to defend deep, but on a regular basis we have to take the initiative in games.

The beauty of Kenny's appointment was that it brought a calmness to the situation that no other manager could have brought. When you are a club legend and a hero to the fans and the players then you are going to be given time to get things right and you are even going to get some understanding when things don't work out. That was really important at the time because obviously under Hodgson we had been playing under a manager who had been under a lot of pressure. We went from that to Kenny, someone who was going to be given time to get things right because of what he has achieved for the club.

The owners were right to bring him back, not just because results got better, but because Kenny is Kenny and he means a lot to everyone at the club. His presence created a calmness that we really needed because it had not been there for some time. In some ways it was a no-brainer because even if things hadn't gone well under Kenny everyone would have said thanks very much to him for trying to help. Football is like that, it can be fickle sometimes and if you are a legend at a club then you are always going to be given more understanding, no matter what. The owners probably knew this when they made their decision.

I did not see anything of Kenny as a player. He retired not long after I was born, and even though I have only seen the odd video of him on LFC TV I did not need to sit down and watch tape after tape of him in action to know what he means to Liverpool. He stopped playing more than 20 years ago and yet still the fans sing about him every week, calling him King Kenny. So when I first came to the club and got involved in its history it did not take me long to realise that he had been Liverpool's greatest player of all.

Before he came back as manager I used to bump into him at Melwood every now and again and we would have a little chat, usually about golf because we are both crazy about it. That was special for me because Kenny has an aura about him that not many people in football have. When I was at Barcelona, Johan Cruyff had something similar about him, he was the main man at the club and it is the same for Dalglish at Liverpool.

It is not just about him, though, and I know Kenny is the first to admit this because he also has some really important people working with him. I cannot overstate the value of the work that Steve Clarke has done since he came to us as a coach. His appointment was a masterstroke and it was one of the keys to our recovery. He is really clever because he completely understands the qualities of his own team. When this is applied to our tactical approach to games it can make a big difference to how we play.

Probably the most important thing he does for us is prepare us, not so that we are in a routine, but so we are able to react in the right way when faced with all kinds of different situations. He reads the game very well and his winning mentality was obvious from his time at Chelsea so it is really good to have him with us because he and Kenny have such a good balance.

In football nowadays it is massively important to have specialist coaches and top-class backroom staff because there is no point paying £25-30 million for a player and then not having the physical and technical experts who can help them to be at their very best on the pitch as often as possible.

For me, a good coach is as important as a good player because that is how important their influence can be. If you have the right people around the team then the side has a much better chance of being successful. Go back to the days of Shankly when he was helped by people like Bob Paisley, Joe Fagan, Ronnie Moran, Roy Evans and Reuben Bennett and this shows how important it is for even the greatest managers and the greatest teams to have the right people around them.

Fortunately, Liverpool continue to be a club where we try to make sure that this happens and even though it does not work out every time at least the desire is always there to have the right people in place in important roles. It is maybe even more important for a goalkeeper to have a top coach to work with because it is a one-on-one relationship. Following Hodgson's departure, Mike Kelly was replaced by John Achterberg, who is a really good guy. I work really hard with him, get on well with him and can have no complaints about his coaching.

I have been lucky in my career because I have worked with some great coaches but the one who stands out, the one who is the absolute master is Ochotorena. I worked with Ocho when I first came to Liverpool and then with the Spanish national team and he is different class. He knows me better than anyone else, understands everything about my strengths and weaknesses, and working with him has been one of the greatest experiences of my career.

Being taught by him is perfect because he only has to look in my eyes to know how I am feeling and whether he needs to give me some advice, give me a hug or if I need pushing, squeeze my balls – so to speak! Because he recognises my mood so quickly he is able to guide me in a way that no-one else can and this is not an insult to any of the other coaches I have worked with, it is an indication of how special Ocho is. Just being in his presence gives me confidence and when you have that kind of influence as a goalkeeper you really cannot ask for anything more. It isn't just about watching videos and being told what to do, it is about the relationship you have with a coach. That is what makes the difference.

At the end of the 2010/11 season there was a chance that we could get Ocho back and I wanted to make it happen. This does not mean I didn't want John Achterberg or I thought he was not helping me or anything like that because the opposite is true. But Ocho is the one who knows me better than anyone else and the one who can bring the very best out of me. If there is any chance of working with him again I am always going to look to make it happen. The club were unable to agree a deal with Valencia that would have allowed him to come and as soon as I realised it was not going to happen I said to the club that it was fine because we had John. I'd rather have him than someone I don't know. It was not out of any disrespect for him that I even thought of bringing Ocho back. It was because he is the best goalkeeping coach on the planet.

I was disappointed that we could not bring Ocho back because of what he means to me as a friend and as a coach, but after the positive changes the club have made since Hicks and Gillett were forced out it was only a relatively minor setback. We have new owners who aren't afraid to spend money, a new manager who wants us to play the Liverpool way and new players who are giving us hope for the future.

This is a new Liverpool, one where we can be positive and where we can believe in ourselves and in the club. These changes may not guarantee that we will win trophies, but they do give us a chance of being successful. After everything this club has been through in the last few years, that is all we can ask for.

End Game

As the final whistle blows I turn to collect my towel from inside the goal before saying goodbye to Anfield. I return to the dressing room, check the results of our rivals to see how they have affected us in the table and then sit down to have a can of Red Bull to try and get my energy levels back up.

If we have won I make sure the music is played nice and loud so that we can enjoy the moment, but if we have dropped points the atmosphere is always much more low-key. I head out for the warm-down with the rest of my team-mates and then come back in for a shower.

I take off the shirt bearing the number that has become part of my identity. The great goalkeepers in Liverpool's history have traditionally worn the number 1. Not me. I am 25. Always will be.

I first took the number 25 shirt when I was at Villarreal. It wasn't a number that meant anything to me at the time, but it has come to be really important in more ways than one. At first, all I wanted was a shirt that wasn't number 13. I wasn't superstitious, but I had worn 13 during my final season at Barcelona and it hadn't been a particularly good year for me. From the moment I left Barca I promised that I would never wear that shirt again. So even though 13 was available to me when I signed for Villarreal, I rejected it straight away and went with a different number instead.

It was only a gut feeling that made me choose 25, there was no significance about it. But maybe it was an omen because my first child, Grecia, was born on February 25 and that meant it quickly became very important to me.

There is no-one who will take that number off me now. I will wear it until I retire. Stevie has said to me a few times that I should take the number one shirt because there is something really special about being Liverpool's number one. I agree with him about that and I appreciate the honour that goes with taking that number at this club, but 25 has become my number and I want it to stay that way.

No matter what has happened, I am always the last one to leave the changing rooms after a match. I always take my time getting changed. Then I go to my executive box overlooking the pitch to see my family and talk about the game that has taken place.

My Anfield ritual only comes to an end when I go back to parking bay number 39, the place where it all began a few hours earlier, to get my car and return home.

I am so lucky to be at a club that you don't just play for. You live and breathe it from the minute you get up in the morning to the minute you go to bed at night.

I am even more fortunate to have worn the captain's armband when Stevie and Carra, the two leaders of the team, have not been available. That is one of the greatest honours I have ever had. It is rare for a keeper to be a captain and it is even rarer for a keeper from abroad to captain one of English football's biggest and most prestigious clubs.

Stevie and Carra are two of Liverpool's greatest servants. I would just be happy and proud, so very, very proud, to get to wear that armband whenever they can't. No matter what happens, I know that when I retire and look back I will be able to say, 'I was the captain of Liverpool.' Few people are given that honour. I am one of the lucky ones.

I have learned something from everyone who I have played alongside and from many of those who I have played against. My first captain at Barcelona was Guardiola – a leader who was as passionate about the club as Stevie or Carra here at Liverpool. Later, I played alongside Raul, who captained the national team as well as Madrid, again a man who led with brains and passion. Now, the captain of the national team is a goalkeeper in Iker and he too is a person who knows how to lead by example, despite being in goal.

I have been lucky to be around so many captains in my career and they have all influenced me in a positive way. They are the ones whose standards I have to live up to and even if I never get to wear the captain's armband for Liverpool again I hope I can still continue to be a leader for the club. To be considered one of our most senior players is a privilege in itself.

Of course, the greatest leader and personal inspiration to me has been my father. My grandfather, too. I have already followed in my father's footsteps by playing for Barcelona and appearing in a European Cup final. One dream I have for the future is to play for Atletico Madrid. I have said this many times because I really like the club and the supporters. I have a big admiration for them and my father played there, so it has an emotional pull for me. I would like to play for them, even if it was just once, to experience the Estadio Vicente Calderon as an Atletico player and to wear the goalkeeper kit that my father wore.

But I can't dictate my own future like that. Maybe in a few years time they won't want me anyway and the way I feel about Liverpool at the moment means it is hard to imagine ever playing for anyone else.

I know that the club might have to leave Anfield behind one day and build a new stadium elsewhere. It would be a terrible shame if that happened. You don't knock down cathedrals unless you absolutely have to. Whenever I speak to people in Spain they all want to know what it is like to play at Anfield Road in front of the world famous Kop.

I do not have too much knowledge of the legalities of the situation regarding the residents in the area around the stadium, but in an ideal world all of the players would prefer to stay at a redeveloped Anfield. The atmosphere there is unique. It doesn't matter how good the architecture is on a new ground or how many people it could hold, it would be impossible to recreate the atmosphere of Anfield at its very best. Every time I run out there before a game I get a tingle down my spine. I see the Kop and the people who go there every week as their fathers and grandfathers did before them and you can't help but be impressed by the history of the place and the emotion that goes with it.

The fans make the biggest difference, of course they do, and I say all the time that if we played at the Bernabeu and filled the seats with our people, 80,000 of them giving everything they have got to support us, then we would not lose a home game all season. They play a crucial part for us and always will, no matter where we end up playing our matches. When you put the combination of the Liverpool fans and Anfield together it can be unbeatable. There are more than enough examples to prove this.

At times it is hard to put into words what it is like playing at Anfield. I try, but inside I know that others cannot possibly understand what it means if they have not been fortunate enough to play there themselves. That is why I do not want to leave. Anfield is part of me now. It means something beyond words.

No matter what happens from this point on I know that I will always be involved in football. I just cannot imagine doing anything else. Whether it is as a coach or working in the media, I do not know. I have already started learning the ropes of both professions to keep my options open, but I am still to decide which avenue I want to go down.

I know there have been few goalkeepers who have gone on to become top managers, which is strange because we spend so much time trying to watch the game and concentrating on what is happening in front of us. Maybe it's because we dive too much during our playing careers and suffer too many knocks to our heads! By the time we hang up our gloves all we want to do is play golf and relax. But I am not like that. I like golf – I am a member of the Blundell's Hill Golf Club in Rainhill where I play quite often with Dirk Kuyt – but I like football more.

The media would be the easiest path for me to follow. I already do some bits. But I just want to focus on being a footballer as much as possible now. Almost everything I do revolves around the game and I have already started my own coaching academy in Cordoba.

Campus Pepe Reina opened its doors for the first time in the summer of 2011 as I was continuing my recovery from a hernia operation carried out at the end of the previous season. Friends of mine from Madrid had been running an academy, but it was more for fun than anything else. It was well organised but nothing compared to the way it is now. It was taking place in the north and my marketing people thought it would be better if it moved to Cordoba because it would be so well received there. The only problem we had was the weather because in July the sun is like a furnace. But they managed to organise it really well and our first year in Cordoba was a great success.

Hopefully now it will go from strength to strength. The course is just one week long and it's a chance for children to be in a good environment with other kids where they can learn about football, but also to give them a chance to share the kind of experience that I had when I was young. They get to live their dreams a little bit, learn to respect their team-mates and rivals and maybe even learn a few principles along the way. To have a place like this in my home town means so much to me and if it gives the children of Cordoba a chance to follow in my footsteps then that will make me even happier because I feel that I owe so much to the place that has given me a mother, a father, a wife and a sense of belonging.

I love coaching there, I really do. It is a great privilege to be able to pass on my experience and some advice to children who really appreciate it. But I am not sure that coaching would suit me, not with young people anyway. If I ever consider being a manager it will be at the very top level. Hopefully I will be able to go on for many more years before I even have to make a decision about what I will do once my playing career has come to an end.

If I am lucky and I steer clear of injuries I might still have another 10 years as a player at the highest level. It is a sobering thought to imagine that one day I will get out of bed in the morning and I won't have a training session or a game to go to.

I have always said that football will leave me, I will not leave football, but already I am preparing for the inevitability of my career coming to an end.

Time will not stand still so I have to be ready for that, even if the last thing I want to do is hang up my gloves for the final time. There is so much that I still want to achieve before then, trophies that I need to win, places I would like to play, personal targets I hope to accomplish.

I do not want to get to the end of my playing career and look back at my time with regrets and thoughts of what might have been. I have winners medals from the World Cup and the European Championships, two of the biggest competitions in sport, but they do not make me complete. There is only one prize which can do that – a Premier League winners' medal.

If I only win one more medal between now and the end of my career that will be fine, as long as it is for winning the title with Liverpool. If that makes it sound like I am obsessed then that is because I am.

As a Liverpool player, you have to be desperate to be part of the team that ends the wait for the league title to return to Anfield. If you are not, you should not be here. That is how strongly I feel about it. We have been stuck on number 18 for far too long and we have seen Manchester United pass our club's record with their own run of success. I cannot accept that and when I look around the people at the club now I know that they cannot accept it either.

There would be nothing worse than being at another club somewhere else when the league title finally returns to Anfield after all these years. If and when it does happen – and it will – we will have one of the biggest parties in its history and as a player you don't want to miss that. Anfield has witnessed 18 championships and after waiting so long, it deserves to host the party to celebrate the 19th.

I know it might seem a bit romantic – and you may wonder how I was even thinking this when we were edging closer and closer to the edge or even going into administration during 2010/11 – but it also shows how desperate I am to be part of something as special.

Liverpool's rightful place is at the very top, not amongst the also rans looking on helplessly as others pick up the trophies that used to be paraded at Anfield as a matter of course.

We can be successful again, there is no question about that. When the great teams of the 1970s and 1980s were winning big trophies almost every single year one of the main secrets of their success was that everyone at the club believed that they could win.

When you have this kind of attitude, a shared confidence in one another and in the club as a whole, then anything is possible.

It is all about having a winning mentality as a group. You only have to look at the difference in Spain once we won the European Championships in 2008 to understand this.

Before then, Spain had not won a major trophy since 1964 and it was like a hoodoo to us because in every big tournament we would be tipped as one of the favourites, but then nothing would happen.

Once we got that first big trophy under our belts we went on to win the World Cup, the biggest prize of all, two years later. That success was as much down to mentality as talent and now Spain are seen as a nation who can win tournaments at all levels.

Once Liverpool win that all important first league title since 1990 then there is no reason why we can't repeat that success.

It is all about getting over that mental barrier. Spain have done it and so can Liverpool. We just need to believe it.

I know it is now harder than ever to win it, but we can do it.

It is time for Liverpool to become champions again.

Career Stats

José Manuel 'Pepe' Reina Páez

Birthdate: August 31, 1982
Birthplace: Madrid, Spain
Height: 1.88m. **Weight:** 92kg
Other clubs: Barcelona (August 1, 1999 – July 1, 2002; 49 apps; 41 Barca 'B'). Villarreal (July 1, 2002 – July 4, 2005; 136 apps)
International debut: August 17, 2005 v Uruguay
Liverpool FC debut: July 13, 2005 v TNS
Liverpool FC Premier League games: 226
Total Liverpool FC appearances: 317
Liverpool FC honours: UEFA Super Cup (2005), FA Cup (2006)
Honours for Spain: UEFA Under-16 Championship (1999), European Championship winner (2008), World Cup winner (2010)

Up to and including September 24, 2011

Golden Glove

Premier League Golden Glove Award

Season	*Winner*	*Club*	*Clean sheets*
2004/05	Petr Cech	Chelsea	21
2005/06	Pepe Reina	Liverpool	20
2006/07	Pepe Reina	Liverpool	19
2007/08	Pepe Reina	Liverpool	18
2008/09	Edwin van der Sar	Man United	21
2009/10	Petr Cech	Chelsea	17*
2010/2011	Joe Hart	Man City	18

* Pepe Reina also recorded 17 clean sheets in 2009/10. Petr Cech was awarded The Golden Glove due to a superior clean sheets to games played ratio.

Spain Appearances

Appearances for the national team
Spain Under-16: 9
Spain Under-17: 2
Spain Under-18: 1
Spain Under-21: 20

International debut: August 17, 2005 v Uruguay
Spain senior appearances (2005-): 22

Up to September 24, 2011

LFC Appearances

Appearances for Liverpool FC, up to end of 2010/11

Season	*Lge*	*FAC*	*LC*	*Europe*	*Other*	*Total*
2005/06	33	5	0	13	2	53
2006/07	35	0	1	14	1	51
2007/08	38	0	0	14	0	52
2008/09	38	2	0	11	0	51
2009/10	38	1	0	13	0	52
2010/11	38	1	0	11	0	50

Milestone appearances for Liverpool FC

Games	*Date*	*Opposition*	*Venue*	*Result*
1	13/07/05	TNS	Anfield	3-0
50	16/04/06	Blackburn	Ewood Park	1-0
100	21/04/07	Wigan Ath	Anfield	2-0
150	13/04/08	Blackburn	Anfield	3-1
200	11/04/09	Blackburn	Anfield	4-0
250	01/04/10	Benfica	Estad da Luz	1-2
300	17/03/11	SC Braga	Anfield	0-0

Liverpool FC Records

Clean sheets and goals conceded by Liverpool goalkeepers in their first 50 (full) League games

Goalkeeper	*Clean sheets*	*Goals conceded*
Jose Reina	28	36
Ray Clemence	25	33
Bruce Grobbelaar	25	39
Jerzy Dudek	25	41
Harry Storer	18	57
Ted Doig	18	62
Sander Westerveld	17	50
Mike Hooper	17	59
Sam Hardy	15	56
Cyril Sidlow	15	58
David James	14	59
Tommy Lawrence	14	60
Bill Perkins	14	67
Elisha Scott	14	70
Charlie Ashcroft	13	69
Bert Slater	13	71
Tommy Younger	12	67
Doug Rudham	10	88
Kenny Campbell	10	91
Russell Crossley	8	87
Arthur Riley	8	95

(Criteria: Keepers have to play the full game for the clean sheet to be awarded. However, if injured, substituted or sent off having conceded during that game, the appearance counts.).

Stats compiled by Mark Platt and Ged Rea

Liverpool FC Records

Clean sheets in first 200 full League games

Goalkeeper	*Clean sheets*	*Date of 200th start*
Pepe Reina	100	December 29, 2010
Ray Clemence	93	December 7, 1974
Bruce Grobbelaar	86	March 8, 1986
Elisha Scott	75	December 6, 1924
David James	70	December 28, 1998
Tommy Lawrence	63	September 9, 1967
Sam Hardy	52	November 11, 1911
Arthur Riley	32	February 23, 1935

During 2005/06, Reina kept a record 11 successive clean sheets

Date	*Opposition*	*Competition*	*Venue*	*Result*
29/10/05	West Ham	Prem Lge	Anfield	2-0
1/11/05	Anderlecht	Champs Lge	Anfield	3-0
5/11/05	Aston Villa	Prem Lge	Villa Park	2-0
19/11/05	Portsmouth	Prem Lge	Anfield	3-0
23/11/05	Real Betis	Champs Lge	Anfield	0-0
26/11/05	Man City	Prem Lge	City of Manc	1-0
30/11/05	Sunderland	Prem Lge	Stad of Light	2-0
3/12/05	Wigan Ath	Prem Lge	Anfield	3-0
6/12/05	Chelsea	Champs Lge	Stamford Br	0-0
10/12/05	M'boro	Prem Lge	Anfield	2-0
15/12/05	Depor Sap	World CC	Yokohama	3-0*

* Liverpool 3, Deportivo Saprissa 0, World Club Championship semi-final, Yokohama International Stadium

LFC Clean Sheets

Opposition	*No.*	*Games*	*% Ratio*
Chelsea	9	22	41
Sunderland	8	10	80
Manchester City	8	12	67
Bolton Wanderers	7	12	58
Fulham	7	12	58
Newcastle United	6	10	60
Aston Villa	6	12	50
Tottenham Hotspur	6	12	50
West Ham United	6	12	50
West Bromwich Alb	5	6	83
Blackburn Rovers	5	12	42
Everton	5	14	36
PSV Eindhoven	4	5	80
Stoke City	4	6	67
Middlesbrough	4	8	50
Birmingham City	4	9	44
Portsmouth	4	9	44
Wigan Athletic	4	11	36
Wolverhampton W	3	4	75
Manchester United	3	14	21
Anderlecht	2	2	100
Bordeaux	2	2	100
Burnley	2	2	100
Charlton Athletic	2	2	100
Debrenci VSC	2	2	100
Inter Milan	2	2	100
Real Madrid	2	2	100
Sparta Prague	2	2	100
Standard Liege	2	2	100
TNS	2	2	100
Toulouse	2	2	100

Opposition	*No.*	*Games*	*% Ratio*
Watford	2	2	100
Marseille	2	4	50
Deportivo Saprissa	1	1	100
Utrecht	1	1	100
Besiktas	1	2	50
Derby County	1	2	50
Lille	1	2	50
Napoli	1	2	50
Real Betis	1	2	50
Sporting Braga	1	2	50
Trabzonspor	1	2	50
Unirea Urziceni	1	2	50
Hull City	1	4	25
Reading	1	6	17
AC Milan	0	1	0
CSKA Moscow	0	1	0
CSKA Sofia	0	1	0
FBK Kaunas	0	1	0
Fiorentina	0	1	0
Galatasaray	0	1	0
Sao Paulo	0	1	0
Sheffield United	0	1	0
Barcelona	0	2	0
Blackpool	0	2	0
Lyon	0	2	0
Maccabi Haifa	0	2	0
FC Porto	0	2	0
Steaua Bucharest	0	2	0
Atletico Madrid	0	4	0
Benfica	0	4	0
Arsenal	0	13	0
TOTAL	146	309	47

Stats up to end of 2010/11 season. Compiled by Ged Rea and Dave Ball

LFC Clean Sheets

Clean sheets in first 300 full games

Goalkeeper	*Clean sheets*	*Goals conceded*	*Date of 300th start*
Ray Clemence	146	225	March 8, 1975
Pepe Reina	142	238	March 17, 2011
Bruce Grobbelaar	135	241	March 5, 1986
Elisha Scott	107	335	December 25, 1926
Tommy Lawrence	97	329	May 4, 1968
Arthur Riley	61	552	April 18, 1938

Liverpool FC Total

Total Liverpool FC career stats, up to end of 2010/11

Goalkeeper	*Games played*	*Goals conceded*	*Goals per game*	*Clean sheets*	*% Clean sheets*
Ray Clemence	665	488	0.73	323	48.57
Pepe Reina	309	248	0.80	146	47.25
Bruce Grobbelaar	628	532	0.85	266	42.36
David James	275	273	0.99	102	37.09
Tommy Lawrence	390	404	1.04	133	34.10
Elisha Scott	468	647	1.38	137	29.27
Sam Hardy	239	340	1.42	63	26.36
Arthur Riley	338	608	1.80	69	20.41

Stats compiled by Ged Rea and Dave Ball

Index